Outfoxing
Fear

ALSO BY KATHLEEN RAGAN

Fearless Girls, Wise Women,
and Beloved Sisters:
Heroines in Folktales from Around the World

Outfoxing Fear

FOLKTALES
FROM AROUND THE
WORLD

EDITED BY

Kathleen Ragan

with an introduction by Jack Zipes

W. W. NORTON & COMPANY

NEW YORK   LONDON

For information about permission to reproduce selections from this book, write to
Permissions, W. W. Norton & Company, Inc., 500 Fifth Avenue, New York, NY 10110

Manufacturing by Maple-Vail Book Manufacturing Group
Book design by Chris Welch
Production manager: Julia Druskin

Library of Congress Cataloging-in-Publication Data

Outfoxing fear : folktales from around the world / edited by Kathleen Ragan ;
with an introduction by Jack Zipes. — 1st ed.
p. cm.
Includes bibliographical references and index.
ISBN 0-393-06036-5 (hardcover)
1. Tales. 2. Folklore. 3. Fear in literature. 4. Heroes—Folklore.
I. Ragan, Kathleen.
GR74.R34 2006
398'.27—dc22

2005024359

W. W. Norton & Company, Inc., 500 Fifth Avenue, New York, N.Y. 10110
www.wwnorton.com

W. W. Norton & Company Ltd., Castle House, 75/76 Wells Street, London W1T 3QT

1 2 3 4 5 6 7 8 9 0

FOR

Mary Irene Howley Ragan, my mom

AND

William Andrew Ragan, my dad

CONTENTS

On Death's Payroll   164

A Shared Destiny   179

Consider the Source   188

Unhistoric Acts   208

Sunrise Never Failed Us Yet   228

ACKNOWLEDGMENTS

I would like to thank everyone who has helped make this book possible. Thank you for the discussions, the babysitting, the comments on drafts, and the encouragement.

Specifically and very specially, I would like to thank Charley Lineweaver, my husband, for his love, support, discussions, and for reading the draft so many times I've lost count. I couldn't have done it without you. Thank you to my daughter Colleen, with whom I have learned so much and who gave excellent comments on the draft, and to my daughter Deirdre, for her staunch support and many loving hugs. Thank you to Irene Ragan, my mother, for her support and insightful comments on the draft, and to my other wonderful readers: Nicolette Bispham, Olivia Brincat, Maret Hensick, Rosanna and Rosetta Lee, Sally Lineweaver, Cole and Tom Paiement, Brydie Ragan, and Deborah Wild Smith. A special thank-you goes to Narelle Brincat and Catherine and Kelvin Watson for relieving me of parenting duties for days at a time when the crunch came. Thank you to Robin Straus, my agent, and Jill Bialosky, my editor. My admiration and thanks also go to reference librarians Sylvestra Praino and Peter McNiece and to all the people responsible for the libraries I used with open stacks and "unweeded" collections. I owe a great intellectual debt to such scholars as Jack Zipes, Sarah Hrdy, and Marcia Westcott, who taught me to describe with an eye for transformation. My thanks also to the women of the women's movement for their courage and determination to effect change.

———

Permission to reprint copyrighted material is very gratefully acknowledged to the following:

Thomas C. Blackburn, "The Old Woman and the Lame Devil," from *December's Child: A Book of Chumash Oral Narratives*. Copyright 1975 by the Regents of the University of California. Reprinted by permission of the University of California Press.

Mody C. Boatright, Wilson M. Hudson, and Allen Maxwell, eds., "Ole Sis Goose," from *The Best of Texas Folk and Folklore, 1916–1954*. Texas Folklore Society no. 26. Denton: University of North Texas Press, 1998. Reprinted by permission of North Texas Press.

Joseph Bruchac, "The Stone Coat Woman," reprinted by permission from *Heroes and Heroines, Monsters and Magic: Iroquois Stories* by Joseph Bruchac. Copyright 1985 by Joseph Bruchac. The Crossing Press, a division of Ten Speed Press, Berkeley, Calif. www.ten speed.com.

Alan Bruford, "The Milk and Butter Stones," based on the story of the same title recorded from Jamie Laurenson by Dr. Alan Bruford and included in *The Green Man of Knowledge*. Rewritten by Kathleen Ragan in standard English by permission of Dr. Margaret A. Mackay, director of the School of Scottish Studies Archives, University of Edinburgh.

Ella E. Clark, "Old Man and Old Woman" and "Bluejay Brings the Chinook Wind," from *Indian Legends from the North Rockies*. Copyright 1966 by the University of Oklahoma Press. Reprinted by permission of the publisher. All rights reserved.

Francis Mading Deng, "Ayak and Her Lost Bridegroom," in *Dinka Folktales: African Stories from the Sudan* (New York: Africana Publishing Co., a division of Holmes & Meier, 1974). Copyright 1974 by Francis Mading Deng. Reprinted by permission of the publisher.

Wolfram Eberhard, "The Tale of Nung-kua-ma," from *Folktales of China*. Copyright by the University of Chicago, 1965. Reprinted by permission of the University of Chicago Press.

Magnús Einarsson, story entitled "Girl Learns to Write by Practising on Frozen Pond," informant Mrs. Steinunn Inge, from *Icelandic-Canadian Oral Narratives* by Magnús Einarsson. Hull, Canadian

Museum of Civilization Copyright, Canadian Centre for Folk Culture Studies, Mercury Series Paper no. 63, 1991, pp. 169–70.

Bradford Haami, "Mereaira and Kape Tautini," from *Traditional Māori Love Stories*. Reprinted by permission of HarperCollins Publishers New Zealand.

Melville J. Herskovits and Frances S. Herskovits, "Magic to Overcome Anxiety: Turtledove Cannot Change Its Nature: What Turtledove Says," from *Dahomean Narrative: A Cross-Cultural Analysis*. Copyright 1958 by Northwestern University Press. Reprinted by permission of Northwestern University Press.

A. C. Hollis, "The Story of the Caterpillar and the Wild Animals" and "The Story of the Demon Who Ate People, and the Child," from *The Masai: Their Language and Folklore*. Reprinted by permission of Oxford University Press.

Zora Neale Hurston, "the snail" tale, p. 251, and "De White Man's Prayer," p. 109, from *Every Tongue Got to Confess: Negro Folk Tales from the Gulf States* by Zora Neale Hurston and edited by Carla Kaplan. Copyright © 2001 by Vivian Hurston Bowden, Clifford J. Hurston, Jr., Edgar Hurston, Sr., Winifred Hurston Clark, Lois Hurston Gaston, Lucy Anne Hurston, and Barbara Hurston Lewis. Foreword copyright © 2001 by John Edgar Wideman. Introduction copyright © 2001 by Carla Kaplan. Reprinted by permission of HarperCollins Publishers Inc.

Mary Harris Jones, "How the Women Sang Their Way Out of Jail," from *The Autobiography of Mother Jones*. Reprinted by permission of Charles H. Kerr Publishing.

Gunnar Landtman, "An Evil Being Appears at an Appointment Instead of the Right Person," from "The Folk-Tales of the Kiwai Papuans." Reprinted by permission of the delegation of the Finnish Academies of Science and Letters.

Robert Laughlin, collector and trans., Carol Karasik, ed., "The Revolution" and "Still Another Spook," from *Mayan Tales from Zinacantán: Dreams and Stories from the People of the Bat*. Copyright 1988 by Carol Karasik. Reprinted by permission of the Smithsonian Institution Press.

Shujiang Li and Karl W. Luckert, "Xueda and Yinlin," from

Mythology and Folklore of the Hui, a Muslim Chinese People. Copyright 1994 by the State University of New York. Reprinted by permission of the State University of New York Press.

Morag Loh, "The Moon Goddess," from *People and Stories from Indo-China*. Reprinted by permission of the author.

Emerson N. Matson, "Legend of Sway-Uock" and "The Maiden Who Lived with the Wolves," from *Legends of the Great Chiefs*. Copyright 1972 by Emerson N. Matson. Reprinted by permission of Mrs. JoAnne Matson.

Fanny Hagin Mayer, " 'What Are You the Most Scared Of?,' " from *Ancient Tales in Modern Japan*. Reprinted by permission of Indiana University Press.

Ursula McConnel, "The Oyster and the Shark" from *Myths of the Muŋkan*. Reprinted by permission of Stephen Kent-Biggs.

Ibrahim Muhawi and Sharif Kanaana, "Im 'Awwād and the Ghouleh," from *Speak, Bird, Speak Again: Palestinian Arab Folktales*. Copyright 1989 by the Regents of the University of California. Reprinted by permission of the University of California Press.

Dov Noy, ed., with the assistance of Dan Ben-Amos, trans. Gene Baharav, "The Landlord and His Son," from *Folktales of Israel*. Copyright 1963 by the University of Chicago. Reprinted by permission of the University of Chicago Press.

Jessie Alford Nunn, "Today Me, Tomorrow Thee," from *African Folk Tales* by Jessie Alford Nunn and illustrated by Ernest Chrichlow, pp. 21–25. Copyright 1969 by Jessie Alford Nunn. Reprinted by permission of HarperCollins Publishers Inc.

Séan Ó hEochaidh, Máire Ní Néill, Séamas Ó Catháin, *Síscéalta Ó Thír Chonaill / Fairy legends from Donegal*, Baile Átha Cliath / Dublin: Comhairle Bhéaloideas Éireann, 1977, pp. 336–43. Published with permission.

Sean O'Sullivan, "The Cakes of Oatmeal and Blood," from *Folktales of Ireland*. Copyright the University of Chicago, 1966. Reprinted by permission of the University of Chicago Press.

Douglas R. Parks, "The Woman with Red Leggings," from *Traditional Narratives of the Arikara Indians*, vol 4. Copyright 1991 by the University of Nebraska Press. Reprinted by permission of the University of Nebraska Press.

R. Sutherland Rattray, "There Is Nothing Anywhere (That We Fear)," from *Akan-Ashanti Folk-Tales*. Reprinted by permission of Oxford University Press.

R. Macdonald Robertson, "The Ghost of Farnell," from *Selected Highland Folk Tales & More Selected Highland Folk Tales*. Reprinted by permission of Pearson Education.

Eleanor Roosevelt, from her speech "The Great Question," given to the United Nations in 1958. Reprinted by permission of Nancy Ireland.

Dagobert C. Runes, "The Devil's Little Joke," from *Lost Legends of Israel*. Copyright 1961 by the Philosophical Library. Reprinted by permission of the Philosophical Library.

Arthur Scholey, "The Frightened Fox" and "The Good Lie," from *The Discontented Dervishes and Other Persian Tales*. Copyright 1977 by Arthur Scholey. Reprinted by permission of the Carlton Publishing Group.

Amina Shah, "The Meatballs' Leader," from *Tales of Afghanistan*. Copyright 1982 by Amina Shah. Reprinted by permission of the Octagon Press.

Jacqueline Simpson, "The Neckbone on the Knife," from *Icelandic Folktales and Legends*. Copyright Jacqueline Simpson, 1972. Reprinted by permission of the University of California Press.

Warren S. Walker and Ahmet Uysal, "Solomon and the Vulture," from *Tales Alive in Turkey*. Copyright 1966 by the President and Fellows of Harvard College. Reprinted by permission of Barbara K. Walker.

William Butler Yeats, "How Thomas Connolly Met the Banshee," from *Fairy and Folk Tales of the Irish Peasantry*. Copyright 1888. Reprinted by permission of A. P. Watt Ltd. on behalf of Michael B. Yeats.

Introduction: Recalling Scheherazade

In *Thousand and One Nights*, all the intriguing stories are framed by one major tale about Scheherazade, who cleverly tells numerous tales to cure a king's mania and to prevent him from committing even more atrocious acts than he has already done. Her tales are survival stories and compel the king to reflect upon brutality and barbarism. In fact, he is civilized through Scheherazade's marvelous tales about common people and moral dilemmas. Thanks to the wit and sagacity of Scheherazade, his humanity is restored, and many lives are saved. In the end, the tales blend into one story, the story of how she outsmarts a ruler turned tyrant, and this is her most significant tale of tales.

Kathleen Ragan is a contemporary Scheherazade, who, like her ancient predecessor, wants to outsmart tyranny. But this time it is the tyranny of fear that she wants to "outfox" with her collection of unusual folktales gathered essentially from around the world. Obviously, her situation is somewhat different from the fictitious Scheherazade, but her intent is just as admirable if not more daring: she seeks to cope with the insanity of our present-day world and with the fear that has arisen from horrific acts and conditions by recuperating old tales that stem from desperate situations in people's lives in our darkened world. She encourages us to turn to these tales to grasp who we are, where we are, and whether there are alternatives to our present dilemma after September 11, 2001. She wants us to "plunge" into her book and be guided by her frame tale, and there are two ways, if not more, that one can read her extraordinary collection of tales told to restore our sense of security, sanity, and sense of justice.

The reader can simply read through the entire book from beginning to end as we generally do and remark on how Ragan weaves her own life story as the frame for all the tales. Or, one can dip into the book and read selected tales and perhaps single out the episodes that constitute the real-life situation of Kathleen Ragan, worried about her children and husband, and concerned that the perilous events of the present will bring about the destruction of our world. I have done both kinds of reading, and what fascinates me most is the manner in which Ragan has woven herself passionately into every tale that she records and how she uses each tale to regain a sense of hope for the future with a smile on her face.

Nevertheless, despite the triumph of Scheherazade and Ragan, one must ask whether folktales can do this—whether they can provide remedies for sick kings and sick civilizations. Truthfully, I am not certain. That is, folktales are neither remedies nor antidotes. However, as Ragan makes clear, they can nurture us, offer counsel, and create a therapeutic effect. Bruno Bettelheim and other psychologists such as Jerome Bruner have written about the meaning of folk and fairy tales for children and how these narratives help them work through inner conflicts and develop cognitive capabilities to assess their place in the world. Yet, too much emphasis has been placed on children and how tales function for their well-being. Not all tales and storytelling are helpful and beneficial. Thousands if not millions of tales lead children astray—they distract them from dealing with real social problems, condition them to become consumers, con them into believing lies, drill them with fundamentalist religious lessons, and so forth. Moreover, folktales were never intended just for children. They are part and parcel of the fabric of every human being. They are exactly what Ragan emphasizes: tales that emanated from the folk of all social classes, lower and upper, and were created by human beings to communicate and share experiences that can enable all people to survive in a dangerous world.

This is the significance of Ragan's collection: the tales that she turned to in a moment of crisis—the tales that she has woven together to take a stand against fear—are tales that derive from the experience of common people throughout the world. What is stunning about many of these tales is that they are specific and universal at the same time. As every folklorist knows, there are tale types with almost the exact same motifs and themes that can be found in Korea, Tanzania, Germany, Mexico, and Australia. In each instance they reveal something particular about a culture while also reflecting upon common human attitudes, strategies, humor, and beliefs. These tales survive because they have been shaped by storytellers and writers to communicate relevant messages about survival. Each time a tale is retold, no matter how old it may be, it is retold to address the present, to provide advice, to illustrate an example, to amuse, or to assuage one's fears.

Ragan asserts that most stories, especially fairy tales, end on a happy note, and that they are essentially utopian and point to possibilities and transformations that might enable us to lead a better life. While this may be true, it is not necessarily the resolution that attracts us to folktales of all kinds but the task, the struggle, the dilemma, the crisis, and the crime. One of the first questions we all ask when hearing a folktale is: how will the protagonist overcome adversity? Whether it be a young man or young woman, or whether it be an animal, there is always a dilemma: the protagonist is inevitably faced with banishment, treason, rape, abuse, abandonment, exploitation, deception, torture, cannibalism, ambush, and disease. Either through cunning, the help of other people and animals, or magic, the protagonist learns survival skills or dies. The evil figures do not die because they are evil but because they do not know how to maintain their power and are unmasked. Folktales—and this includes fairy tales—are not moralistic but drastically realistic and relate what people must do to obtain power so that they can take control and narrate their lives. The moral justification for the actions of protagonists is minimal in most folktales, and if this is the case, one must wonder why Ragan has chosen these tales to deal with the fear and hysteria that are spreading like wildfire in this age of terrorism.

Clearly, it is because they do not mince their words and deceive us. They startle us with relative truths that remind us how flexible and tolerant we must be in all our quotidian encounters and struggles. Each day that we leave our homes to go off to school, work, shop, or meet a friend is the beginning of a new adventure, and most of the day, we shall be bombarded by messages and stories that want to determine our responses and behavior. In fact, even if we stay home and watch television, listen to the radio, or answer the phone, the outside world will invade our homes and confront us with stories and tasks that are unnecessary and deceptive. We can never be certain these days what is real, genuine, or authentic. We cannot trust politicians, religious leaders, or the media. The absolute truths that seem to be self-evident are constantly challenged and undermined by those very people who pretend that they are funnels for such truths. Although folktales tend to be metaphorical and filled with magic, they do not pretend to be absolute or to establish commandments and the utter truth. Their truths are almost always relative and can only be momentarily helpful. If anything, they demand that we act like their own triumphant protagonists—seize the opportunity, rectify an injustice, learn to distinguish between bad and good faith. In this regard, as Ragan at one point suggests, folktales are explorations—they explore options and variants, and it is because of the daring and subversive explorations in the tales that we tend to keep them alive.

Paradoxically, it is because folktales do not "teach" us to overcome fear that they help us deal with fear. It is the unknown that fundamentally scares us in life—not knowing what lies around the next corner, what might be in a box, what might happen during a trip, who might be our enemy, and so on. Folktales not only explore this unknown fear, they unmask it. When we hear or read folktales, the protagonists inevitably plunge ahead toward their destiny; they fear no fear. They don't offer us a lesson in overcoming fear; they simply recognize it for what it is, confront it, and tell us to get on with our lives as best we can. Shuddering and lamenting never help a protagonist. But faith in one's ability to solve a problem and unmask villains and enemies is crucial for survival.

There is something profoundly existentialist about folktales, whether it be a fairy tale, legend, anecdote, fable, or myth. They call upon both protagonist and listener to become divine artists of their own lives. There are rarely gods in folktales, and even in fairy tales, we hardly encounter fairies. In short, folktales depict godless realms. They portray very human realms and nature. It is sheer fate or chance that determines the destiny of a protagonist, and if the protagonist does not know how to collect the proper instruments, people, and animals and mold them in such a way that he or she can perceive how to act in his or her own best interests, there will be no meaning or pleasure in life. The protagonist must learn to create meaning and values through courageous conduct and action. There is no one answer to the protagonist's dilemma. Like an artist, he or she must work toward a resolution.

This is why there is no resolution at the end of Kathleen Ragan's frame tale. It is open-ended. It is a challenge. Unlike *Thousand and One Nights*, there is no final happy end in *Outfoxing Fear*, and there cannot be one in our world as it is taking shape and as we shape it today. Ragan responded to fear in her own unique way, and she wants to share her unique experience with us. Like the tales that she has collected, she takes us on a journey of exploration that, she hopes, will open our eyes to the causes of fear and trembling. It is a journey worth taking. It is not every day that one meets a contemporary Scheherazade.

Jack Zipes

ermany
Ukraine
Hungary
Turkey
Israel
Iraq
Iran
Persia
Afghanistan
Punjab
Palestine
Arab
India
Santal
Parganas
Sudan
Dinka
Kikuyu
Masai
Hui
China
Korea
Japan
Kwangtung
Philippines
Guam
New Guinea
Munkan
Australia
Maori

Pacific
Ocean

Indian
Ocean

Outfoxing Fear

Building Stories

September 11, 2001. "You better come see this. Something's happened." One look and I sank to the floor in front of the television. Far away from family and friends who might have been caught up in the tragedy, I watched the television. For hours, day after day, I watched the television. Even when I turned off the television, the planes kept crashing like a broken record and I couldn't turn off the fear.

A few days later, I watched with mixed horror and amazement as my daughters built two block towers and flew toy airplanes into them. I almost stopped them from doing it. Instead, I phoned another mother who told me her children had done the same thing. Off and on for several days, my daughters built block towers and destroyed them. Some things stayed the same: There were two towers of equal height. There were airplanes. Some things were variable: The people leapt to their deaths. The planes missed. The people had parachutes. Then one day my children played something else.[1] I still watched the news several times a day and fear still crept into everything I did.

After weeks of news reports, I felt powerless and afraid. My children got on with their lives. There was a difference between their stories and the ones I was being told.

I grew up in prosaic Williamsport, Ohio, but I lived in an enchanted mansion and the public library was my castle. I stood in the castle's dark, round turret. Its block stone walls reached to a ceiling so high it dissolved into the darkness. Sunlight slanted into the room through long, narrow windows. Mystery and magic hovered between the sunbeams and the shadows. I prowled the rows of shelves, trailing my fingers along the library books. At the corner of the row of fairy tales, I paused. I pulled a thick blue book off the shelf. It fell open to a page with a delicate ink drawing of Scheherazade reclining upon cushions. She told desperate and wonderful stories of screaming stones and glittering treasure caves and of tales within tales within tales. I've loved stories ever since.

Only when I had my own children did I begin to tell stories. When both girls were very young, our family moved to France. There, both my little girls were learning French the hard way, by total immersion. My eighteen-month-old daughter Deirdre simply stopped talking for a year. Then she burst into complete phrases of neatly segregated French and English. My older daughter Colleen had a harder time of it since the French school system required her to be in school daily at the age of three. Colleen was four. The first day, Colleen went to school eagerly and happily. The second day, she kicked and screamed in protest. For more than half her life she'd worked to give English words to her thoughts and feelings. Suddenly, it was gone. Gone was her ability to say, "Hi, my name is Colleen, what's your name?" or, "I have a tummy-ache." She had to start again from zero and this time she wasn't accompanied by a smiling mom and dad who praised her every new syllabic milestone. She was surrounded by children who didn't understand her inability and who teased her for being stupid.

At that time, I was editing an anthology of folktales with heroines.[2] So, after the girls went to bed at night, I would sift through stories. It served a dual purpose: I found tales for my anthology and I armed myself for the next morning's onslaught. I told Colleen stories as she got dressed. I told her stories as I brushed her hair. I told her stories as we rode our bikes to school. I told her stories up to the threshold of her classroom. There she steeled her shoulders and faced her day like a little soldier.

Seven years later, after September 11, 2001, I watched my children build stories. I watched them solve and not solve and resolve their fear, and I wondered with regret where my own stories had gone. When had I lost the protection of my castle's stone walls and the comfort of Scheherazade's wisdom on the shelf? Scheherazade knew fear. What did she say about fear? What do folktales say about fear?

I entered my study, my personal realm of make-believe. It seemed a safe retreat. I stood in a dark room, the wall of books behind me reminiscent of *that magic-filled medieval turret. The closet was stuffed with books and binders of tales I've collected from libraries all over the world. I pulled out a binder and began to thumb through folktales, reading the titles. After a few minutes, one title leapt out at me: "What Are You the Most Scared Of?" It sent shivers up my spine. My imagination cooked up horrific answers in shocking detail. I was almost afraid to read the story.*

"What Are You the Most Scared Of?"

JAPAN[3]

An old woman lived in a little hut made of firewood at a place back in the hills. She would warm herself at night by building a fire.

A *tengu** with a cross looking face called to her. It sounded so much like a human that the old woman opened her door. A scary looking *tengu* with a big nose came in. The old woman was frightened, but there was nothing she could say, so she let him come over to her fire.

The old woman asked the *tengu*, "What are you the most scared of?"

It replied, "I'm most scared of dense brush growing in a thicket. What are you the most scared of, Granny?"

The old woman said, "I'm the most scared of *botamochi*† and little gold coins."

Then nothing more happened and the *tengu* went out. The old woman decided to stack green boughs all around the walls of her hut so such a dreadful thing would not come again. She waited impatiently for morning when she could put up the branches.

The next night the *tengu* came again and found the brush stacked all around, but there was none on the roof. He said, "I'll get even with you, you hateful old thing."

He went to a certain house and had a lot of *botamochi* made for him and he got a lot of little gold coins. He brought them to the

tengu: a monster with a big nose
†*botamochi*: rice cakes

6

old woman's hut to get even with her. He called from above the roof, "I'll get even with you, Granny!" Then he threw in the *bota-mochi*.

The old woman cried, "Oh, I'm afraid!" When the *tengu*'s *bota-mochi* were gone, he began to throw in little gold coins.

He called, "Are you still alive?"

When all the cakes and coins were thrown in, he thought the old woman must be dead, so he ran away. The old woman ate the rice cakes, but she decided there was no telling who she would meet up with if she lived there. She went down into the village and lived in comfort with the money.

The Robbers and the Old Woman

SCOTLAND[4]

There was once an old woman, she lived herself in a little wee house in the country, oh, in the back of beyond, but she was turnin' very very old. She was away aboot eighty or eighty-odds, and of course she was getting' a bittie dottled,[*] kind of things, speakin' to herself and one thing and another. But she was supposed to have a lot of money, ye see, hidden in this house—a *lot* of money (she was real miserly-kind, ye know), and there was three men came to rob her that night, three men. And one of these men was missing an eye, but the three of them was going to help each other and get the money—steal the money and murder the old woman and get away with it, ye see, 'cause 'twas in a lonely place. One of these men wanted an eye.

But it happened to be, one way or another, that that night this poor old creature she had the brander[†] (you know the brander she used to keep in her fire and some of them has them yet in the country, real old-fashioned—they used to roast the kippers[‡] and things upon the branders, ye see). And she was—with this old-fashioned brander on—she was roastin' these kippers for her supper. But she was speakin' away to the kippers as if they were human beings, ye see, as dottled folk does, 'cause I've sat and watched them, ye see. She's speakin' away to these kippers, ye see, rockin' herself back and forth, ye see, in an old chair, over this old-fashioned fire,

*dottled: feebleminded
†brander: a ribbed open griddle
‡kippers: herring or salmon

8

ye see, roastin' these kippers and turnin' them, ye see.

But she did not ken* there was three men come to murder her and rob her at night. But one was comin' down the lum† (that was the way that he was goin' to enter, ye see, because the house was all locked up, and he was goin' to enter—comin' down the lum). But she'd this wee bittie o' a fire on, ye see, not very much, two, three sticks, and she's roastin' this kipper. The first kipper, she says, "Ha, ha," she says, "there's three o' ye, and there's one of ye," she says, "goin' away," she says, "soon," she says, "for I'll roast ye and I'll toast ye," she says, "and I'll eat ye for my supper." Ye see.

Now, a lot o' them they says, not only was she a miser, but a lot o' them said that she was an old witch, ye see—well, they believed it in those days, anyway—whether they were or no, they'd only to say it.

But this—there was a story out, oh, years afore, that this old woman was an old witch, ye see. An' this man at this time, was the first one was comin' down the lum when she was roastin' the first kipper, and she's speakin' to the kipper and she's not speakin' to him at all. She did not ken about a man comin' down the lum, so that's what she said.

"Ha, ha," she says, "there's three o' ye, and there's one o' ye is goin' away," she says, "and I'll roast ye," she says, "and I'll toast ye, and I'll eat ye for my supper."

He says, "God bliss us!" he says. "She kens I'm comin' down." He says, "She's goin' to roast me and toast me for her supper." So he's up the lum and out of it. "No, no," he says to the other ones, he says, "Praise God!" he says, "I'm not goin' to rob her," he says, "or kill her—she kens," he says, "that I was comin' down the lum—she kent," he says, "we're here. She said there was three of us and that I was—ye know—one was goin' away, and she was goin' to eat me—roast me and eat me, ye see." So he says, "No, no," he says, "I'm not takin' nothin' today." He's off and away. He got feared.

Ach, down the second one goes, he says, "He's too yellow," ye see. "She's not a witch," and all this and the next thing, but he goes

*ken: know
†lum: chimney

down the lum. Now she's roastin' the second kipper by this time. An' she says, "Ha, ha, there's one o' ye is away," she says, "and this is the second one to come," she says, "but I'll roast ye, and I'll toast ye," she says, "and I'll eat ye for my supper."

But he took a heart-fright too, ye see, and he's up the lum—he wondered what way she kent—'cause nobody seen them goin' near this place, ye see. An' he's up the lum and he tells the other one— "No, no," he says, "that's a witch right enough," he says. "She kent," he says, "that I was comin' an' she was preparin' for to roast me and toast me for her supper. So," he says, "no, no," he says, "I'm not goin' to have nothin' to do with her." So he's away too, runs away too. Now the last one to come was missing an eye. But it just happened to be that her last kipper did not have an eye either—it wanted an eye. Well, we would not pay any notice whether the kipper had an eye or no, but an old dottled bodie* like this sees queer kind of wee ferlies,† they stand out to them. So she puts the kipper on and she's roastin' it and turnin' it, ye know, and down comes this man wantin' the eye, and he's the one that was goin' to murder her. An' he's quite desperate for to kill her, and get her money.

"Ha, ha!" she says, "come on," she says, "come away, I'm just waitin' fur ye!" she says. (But it was her kipper she was speakin' to.) She says, "Just come away," she says, "hurry up and come," she says, "I'm waitin' upon you," she says, "ye're the third one to come," she says, "and ye want an eye."

Now this made it more convincin' to him when he heard her sayin' this. "An'," she says, "the third one wants an eye," she says. "Ye're the third. But," she says, "I'll roast ye," she says, "and I'll toast ye, and I'll *eat* ye for my supper." (She's beginnin' to get high kind now, ye see, wi' this kipper, wantin' the eye.)

So when he hears this, he says, "God bliss us! It's right enough." He says, "She even kens I am missing an eye." So he's up the lum and away. So it was only the poor old dottled woman speakin' to her three kippers that saved her own life.

*bodie: person
†ferlies: strange or unusual sights, wonders

Cauth Morrisy Looking
for Service

IRELAND[5]

Well, neighbours, when I was a youngster about fifteen years of age, and it was time to be doing something for myself, I set off one fine day in spring along the high road; and if anybody asked me where I was goin' I'd make a joke about it, and say I was going out of Ireland to live in the Roer.* Well, I traveled all day, and the dickens a bit o' the nearer to get a service;† and when the dark hour come I got a lodging in a little house by the side of the road, where they were drying flax over a roaring turf fire. I'll never belie the vanithee‡ her goodness. She give me a good quarter of well-baked barley bread, with butter on it, and made me sit on the big griddle over the ashpit in the corner; but what would you have of it? I held the bread to the fire to melt the butter, and bedad§ the butter fell on the lighted turf, and there it blazed up like vengeance, and set the flax afire, and the flax set the thatch afire, and maybe they didn't get a fright. "Oh, musha,** vanithee," says they, "wasn't it the devil bewitched you to let that omadhān†† of a girl burn us out of house and home this way? Be off, you torment, and pursuin' to you!" Well, if they didn't hunt me out, and throw potsticks, and tongs, and sods o' fire after me,

*Roer: a district in Kilkenny
†the dickens . . . to get a service: it had been a fruitless search for a job
‡vanithee: woman of the house
§bedad: oh my gosh!
**musha: used especially to express surprise or annoyance
††omadhān: devilish but likable at the same time, rogue

leave it till again; and I run, and I run, till I run head foremost into a cabin by the side of the road.

The woman o' the house was sittin' at the fire, and she got frightened to see me run in that way. "Oh, musha, ma'am," says I, "will you give me shelter?" and so I up and told her my misfortunes.

"Poor colleen,"* says she, "my husband is out, and if he catches a stranger here he'll go mad and break things. But I'll let you get up on the hurdle over the room, and for your life don't budge."

"I won't," says I, "and thank you, ma'am." Well, I was hardly in bed when her crooked disciple of a man came in with a sheep on his back he was after stealing. So with that he skinned the sheep, and popped a piece down into the boiling pot, and went out and hid the skin, and buried the rest of the mate in a hole in the floor. Well, when he made his supper on the mutton he says to his wife, "I hope no one got lodging while I was away."

"Arrah, who'd get it?" says she.

"That's not the answer I want," says he. "Who did you give shelter to?"

"Och, it was only to a little slip of a girl that's as fast as the knocker of Newgate† since eleven o'clock, on the hurdle."

"Molly," says he, "I'll hang for you someday, so I will. But first and foremost I'll put the stranger out o' pain." When I hear him talk I slip down and was out o' the door in a jiffy; but he was as stiff as I was stout, and he flung the hatchet after me, and cut off a piece of my heel.

"Them is the tricks of a clown," says I to myself, and I making away at the ling of my life;‡ but as luck would have it, I got shelter in another cabin, where a nice old man was sitting over the fire, reading a book. "What's the matter, poor girl?" says he, and I up and told him what happened me. "Never fear," says he, "the man of the mutton won't follow you here. I suppose you'd like your supper." Well, sure enough, the fright, and the run, and the cut heel,

*colleen: little girl
†fast as the knocker of Newgate: sound asleep
‡at the ling of my life: by the skin of my teeth

and that, made me hungry, and I didn't refuse a good plate o' stirabout.*

"Colleen," says the man, "I can't go to sleep early in the night; maybe you'd tell a body a story."

"Musha, an' the dickens a story meself has," says I.

"That's bad," says he; "the fire is getting low; take that bouran† out to the clamp,‡ and bring in the full of it of turf."

"I will, sir," says I. But when I took a turf out of the end of the clamp 500 sods tumbled down on me, head and pluck, and I thought the breath was squeezed out of me. "If that's the way," says I, "let the old gentleman himself come out, and bring in his firing."

So I went in, and had like to faint when I came to the fire. "What ails you, little girl?" says he.

"The clamp that fell on me," says I.

"Oh, but it's meself that's sorry," says he. "Did you think of e'er another story while you were at the clamp?"

"Indeed an' I didn't."

"Well, it can't be helped. I suppose you're tired. Take that rushlight into the barn, but don't set it on fire. You'll find plenty of dry straw for a bed, and come into your breakfast early." Well, I bade him good night, and when I came into the barn, sure enough, there was no scarcity of straw. I said my prayers, but the first bundle I took out of the heap I thought all the straw in the barn was down on my poor bones. "Oh vuya, vuya,§ Cauth," says I to myself, "if your poor father and mother knew the state you're in, wouldn't they have the heart-scald." But I crept out and sat down on a bundle, and began to cry.

I wasn't after cryin' a second when I heard steps outside the door, and I hid myself again under the straw, leaving a little peephole. In came three as ugly-looking fellows as you'd find in a kish o' brogues,** with a coffin on their shoulders. They wondered at the candle, but

*stirabout: porridge
†bouran: three-legged pot
‡clamp: pile of peat, turf
§vuya: an expression of sadness
**kish o' brogues: basket of shoes

they said nothing till they put the coffin down, and began to play cards on it with the dirtiest deck I ever see before or since. Well, they cheated, and scolded, and whacked one another, and in two minutes they were as great as pickpockets again.*

At last says one, "It's time to be goin'; lift the corpse."

"It's easy say lift," says another. "You two have the front, and I must bear up all the hind part—I won't put a hand to it."

"Won't you?" says the others. "Sure there's little Cauth Morrisy under the straw to help you."

"Oh, Lord, gentlemen, I'm not in it at all," says myself; but it was all no use. I had to get under one corner, and there we trudged on in the dark, through knocs, and ploughed fields, and bogs, till I thought the life would leave me.

At last at the flight of night, one of them says, "Stop here, and Cauth Morrisy will mind the corpse till we come back. Cauth, if you let anything happen to the honest man inside you'll sup sorrow—mind what I say." So they left me, and lonesome and frightened I was, you may depend.

But wasn't I frightened in earnest when I heard the corpse's knuckles tapping inside o' the lid. "Oh, sir, honey," says I, "what's troublin' you?"

"It's air I want," says he, "I'm stifling. Throw off the lid, body and bones." I did so, and there was a wicked-looking old fellow inside, with a beard on him a week old.

"Thankee, ma'am," says he, "I think I'll be the easier for that. This is a lonesome place them thieves left me in. Would you please to join me in a game of spoil-five?"

"Oh, musha, sir," says I, "isn't it thinking of making your soul you ought to be?"

"I don't want your advice," says he, "maybe I haven't a soul at all. There's the cards. I deal—you cut."

Well, I was so afeard that I took a hand with him, but the dirty devil, he done nothing the whole time but cursin', and swearin', and cheatin'. At last, says I to myself, "I can't be safe in such com-

*as great as pickpockets again: on the most friendly terms again

pany." So I threw down the cards, though I was within three of the game, and walked off.

"Come back and finish the game, Cauth Morrisy," says he, shouting out, "or I'll make it the bad game for you." But I didn't let on to hear him, and walked away. "Won't you come back, Cauth?" says he. "Then here goes." Well, the life had like to leave me, for I heard him tearing after me in his coffin, every bounce it gave striking terror into my heart. I run, and I bawled, and he bawling after me, and the coffin smashing against the stones. At last, where did I find myself but at the old gentleman's door, and if I didn't spring in and fasten the bolt, leave it till again.

"Ah, is that you, my little colleen? I thought you were asleep. Maybe you have a story for me now."

"Indeed an' I have, sir," says I, an' I told him all that happen me since I saw him last.

"You suffered a good deal," says he. "If you told me that story before, all your trouble'd be spared to you."

"But how could I tell it, sir," says I, "before it happened?"

"That's true," says he, and he began to scratch his wig. I was getting drowsy, and I didn't remember anything more till I woke next morning in the dry gripe of the ditch with a bochyeen* under my head. So—

*bochyeen: block of dried cow dung

Death and the Old Woman

HUNGARY[6]

O nce upon a time, beyond the Seven Seas and even beyond the Glass Mountains, behind the tumbledown oven without even a wall (and where it was good, it wasn't bad, and where it was bad, it wasn't good); at the foot of the "Search-me-not-ask-me-not" Hill, there flowed a river, and on its bank there grew an ancient and gnarled willow tree, whose every branch was inhabited by a flock of fleas! And may he be herd to them all who does not listen attentively to my tale. And if he allow but one of them to escape, then let him be the victim of their bloodthirsty vengeance and be bitten to death!

Once upon a time, nor here, nor there, but somewhere in this world of ours, there lived a very, very old woman, older than the hills and even older than God's own gardeners. She never gave death a thought, even after all her teeth had dropped out, but just kept on working and working, in the hope of becoming rich. She scurried and stumbled and bustled about, gathering up and hiding away everything she could put her fingers on. If she could, she would have stowed away the world, yet she was as lonely as could be and had no one on Earth to take care of. But her zeal was not all in vain. She got richer and richer and fatter and fatter. And there was nothing lacking in her house, from the biggest axe to the smallest.

One day Death chalked his marks on her door and came to fetch her. But the old woman did not want to leave her riches and begged him to grant her just a little more time, just ten years, or five, or even one year more. Death, however, turned a deaf ear on her entreaties and said, "Hurry up and come, else I shall have to use force."

But the old woman went on imploring him to let her live just a wee bit longer, but Death was not easy to persuade. The old woman, however, argued and argued with such persistence that Death at last relented and said, "Very well, I grant you three hours."

"That's awfully little," the old woman replied. "Don't take me today, please put it off until tomorrow."

"That's impossible!"

"But why?"

"Because!"

"Just the same, put it off just a bit longer!"

"Very well," Death said at last, "since you are so determined, you shall have your way!"

"Then I have just one more wish. Please chalk on my door that you will not come until tomorrow. I shall feel safer if I see it written there."

Then Death, wishing to waste no more time in arguing, took a piece of chalk from his pocket and wrote "Tomorrow" on her door, whereupon he went his way.

On the morrow, at sunrise, he reappeared at the old woman's house, to find her still abed.

"Come with me," Death called to her.

"Not so fast," the old woman answered, "see what is written on my door."

And Death, glancing at the door, read the word he had written on it: "Tomorrow!"

"Very well, but I shall return without fail," and so saying he vanished.

Death was as good as his word and returned the next day, only to find the old woman in bed again; and once more she refused to accompany him and pointed to her door, whereon was written "Tomorrow."

This game went on for a week. On the seventh day, having lost his patience, Death said to the old woman: "Enough of this! You won't get the better of me again, I have need of that chalk, and shall take it with me," and wiping the chalk off the door, he continued. "Now mark my words, tomorrow I shall return, and take you along!"

So Death went his way, leaving the poor old woman very much crestfallen, for she realized that willy-nilly she would have to die on the morrow. And in her anguish, she began to shake like an aspen leaf.

Next morning, almost beside herself with terror, she would have sought refuge from Death even inside an empty bottle had that been possible. She hunted high and low for a hiding place, when she suddenly remembered a barrel of honey standing in her pantry and crept into it, so that only her eyes, her nose and her mouth remained visible above the honey.

"But what if he should find me here too? I had better hide inside my eiderdown."

So she crawled out of the honey and into the eiderdown feather. But this did not satisfy her either, so she emerged again to seek safety elsewhere. It was at that very moment that Death put in his appearance. Not recognizing the weird freak which suddenly stood before him, he was so terrified at the sight that he took to his heels and fled; and for all I know he has not dared to approach the old woman again to this very day.

The Story of the Caterpillar and the Wild Animals

MASAI PEOPLE, KENYA AND TANZANIA[7]

Once upon a time a caterpillar entered a hare's house when the owner was absent. On his return the hare noticed the marks on the ground, and cried out, "Who is in my house?"

The caterpillar replied in a loud voice, "I am the warrior-son of the long one, whose anklets have become unfastened in the fight in the Kurtiale country. I crush the rhinoceros to the earth, and make cow's dung of the elephant! I am invincible!"

The hare went away saying, "What can a small animal like myself do with a person who tramples an elephant under foot like cow's dung?" On the road he met the jackal, and asked him to return with him and talk with the big man who had taken possession of his house. The jackal agreed, and when they reached the place, he barked loudly, and said, "Who is in the house of my friend the hare?"

The caterpillar replied, "I am the warrior-son of the long one, whose anklets have become unfastened in the fight in the Kurtiale country. I crush the rhinoceros to the earth, and make cow's dung of the elephant! I am invincible!" On hearing this the jackal said, "I can do nothing against such a man," and left.

The hare then fetched the leopard, whom he begged to go and talk with the person in his house. The leopard, on reaching the spot, grunted out, "Who is in the house of my friend the hare?" The caterpillar replied in the same manner as he had done to the jackal, and the leopard said, "If he crushes the elephant and the rhinoceros, he will do the same to me."

They went away again, and the hare sought out the rhinoceros. The latter, on arriving at the hare's house, asked who was inside, but when he heard the caterpillar's reply, he said, "What, he can crush me to the earth! I had better go away then."

The hare next tried the elephant, and asked him to come to his assistance, but on hearing what the caterpillar had to say, the elephant remarked that he had no wish to be trampled under foot like cow's dung, and departed.

A frog was passing at the time, and the hare asked him if he could make the man who had conquered all the animals leave his house.

The frog went to the door and asked who was inside. He received the same reply as had been given to the others, but instead of leaving, he went nearer, and said, "I who am strong and a leaper have come. My buttocks are like the post, and God has made me vile." When the caterpillar heard this, he trembled, and as he saw the frog coming nearer, he said, "I am only the caterpillar."

The animals who had collected near seized him, and dragged him out; and they all laughed at the trouble he had given.

Serious Laughter

"What are you the most scared of?" the monster asked the little old lady.

"Rice cakes and little gold coins," she answered. [8]

I burst out laughing. I'd read so many folktales, I could see exactly where this was going! I just knew that the monster would try to do her in and that she would end up with lots of yummy rice cakes and piles of gold coins. The title had played on my fear, but the story had taken such an unexpected turn, it made me laugh. Suddenly the world's insurmountable problems seemed surmountable. I made dinner and smiled at my kids. In a vase on the windowsill, a rose gave off the loveliest scent.

My laughter helped me see that I am not alone. This time is not unique. Humans have always lived with fear: fear of becoming jaguar prey, of being caught by the Vikings, or of a nuclear holocaust. For millennia, huddled around campfires as the darkness descended, gathered in cottages as the wild winds of winter howled outside or on bicycles on the way to school, we have told folktales and they have helped us transform our fear into hope and our hope into action. [9]

Other folktales also encouraged me to laugh when confronting fear. They presented laughter as a solution just as seriously as some tales advocated violence or peacemaking or alliances. Among all the world's accumulated wisdom about fear, the first solution folktales gave me was my own laughter.

As I flipped through binders and books of folktales, I found myself seated at a virtual campfire with strangers and friends who each told a story in turn. In the glow of the fire, a Xhosa man widens his eyes and arches his arms above his head. His fingers mimic claws. The children clustered around him gaze openmouthed while the adults smile knowingly; they've heard the story before.[10]

A Kyoto cabdriver, in his prim blue uniform and pristine white gloves, eyed me curiously, "You understand some Japanese, don't you?" Hardly waiting for my yes, he eagerly began, "Mukashi, mukashi . . . A long time ago, a long time ago, as they were building this very temple . . ." He waved his hand toward the bright orange of Heian Jingu temple.

The bedroom lights are off and my children are tucked into their beds. Their dad sits heavily on one of the child-sized chairs. "One morning when I was little, it had snowed and the snow was up to my shoulders and rain had frozen over the top of it all, so we could make tunnels in the snow. My brother and I went outside . . ."

At my virtual campfire, one tale led to another. "Once there was and there was not . . ." a story began. It wasn't the tale I would have told, but I had no stranglehold on which tales were told. As the tales led from one to another, new ideas and new viewpoints intruded. "Laugh!" the folktales said when I had thought they would only make me more afraid. "Laugh!" the folktales said and I was better able to listen.

When I was about eleven, I went to a sleepover party where we stayed up to watch the late movie. I spent the next few years wearing a silver cross and pulling the covers up around my neck to ward off vampires. I don't like being afraid. Give me courage instead. Let me be George Washington, one foot on the prow of the ship, nobly surveying the dangerous shore. Let me be Errol Flynn or Lara Croft leaping into a pack of enemies and emerging unscathed. Not for me the role of the abused/beaten/murdered woman in the first five minutes of the nightly prime-time crime/police/murder show. Not for me the role of the helpless woman screaming in the face of a chainsaw murderer.

As one story and then another unfolded, issues I hadn't thought of arose. Laughter may have eased my fear for the moment, but should I be afraid? Maybe there is a reason for fear.

Magic to Overcome Anxiety: Turtledove Cannot Change Its Nature: What Turtledove Says

DAHOMEAN PEOPLE, BENIN[11]

There was a bird called Wututu,[*] and there was Chameleon, Agama. There was Turtledove whose heart was never easy. She was afraid. Wututu said to her that as her heart was never free from anxiety, he must make a good charm for her.

"When Chameleon is on the road and sees a man, he does not worry, but goes on his way. He does not try to run away," said the Turtledove. "But I, who am larger than Chameleon, even if *I* see a child, I fly away."

Wututu gave Turtledove a magic preparation to eat and recommended to her that if a man approached her, she was to remain until she saw whether the man wanted to catch her or not.

So Turtledove settled herself on the road to see if the charm was good. A man was passing by. When Turtledove saw him from afar, she flew away without letting him come near her at all. She flew to the limb of a tree, and said to herself, "The charm Wututu made for me has not done anything for me. If I do not take care, I will be caught by someone. I must try again, for I must have a charm to protect me."

She went and again settled herself on the road. There was an old woman who was on her way to look for firewood, and she had taken a stick for a cane. When Turtledove saw this, her heart began

---

[*]Wututu: This bird is associated with the god of thunder.

to beat, and she flew away once more. When she felt herself safe this time, as she sat on a tree, she called, "Oh, Wututu! Oh, Agama! The charm you made for me whether it gives fire or does not give fire, all the same my heart beats, beats." And it is this that Turtledove now sings,

Fear is killing me
Little by little.

How Thomas Connolly
Met the Banshee

I R E L A N D [12]*

A w, the banshee,[†] sir? Well, sir, as I was striving to tell ye I was going home from work one day, from Mr. Cassidy's that I told ye of, in the dusk o' the evening. I had more nor a mile— aye, it was nearer two mile—to thrack to,[‡] where I was lodgin' with a decent widdy[§] woman I knew, Biddy Maguire be name, so as to be near me work.

It was the first week in November, an' a lonesome road I had to travel, an' dark enough, with trees above it; an' about halfways there was a bit of a bridge I had to cross, over one o' them little streams that runs into the Doddher. I walked on in the middle of the road, for there was no toe-path[**] at that time, Mister Harry, nor for many a long day after that; but, as I was sayin', I walked along till I come nigh upon the bridge, where the road was a bit open, an' there, right enough, I seen the hog's back[††] o' the old-fashioned bridge that used to be there till it was pulled down, an' a white mist steamin' up out o' the water all around it.

Well, now, Mister Harry, often as I'd passed by the place before,

---

*I have normalized some of Yeats' spellings. See p. 232, note 12, for details of the changes.

[†]banshee: a female fairy that follows the old families and wails before a death

[‡]more nor a mile—aye . . . two mile—to thrack to: he had to go about two miles

[§]widdy: widowed

[**]toe-path: path on the side of the road, footpath

[††]hog's back: the arch of the bridge

that night it seemed strange to me, an' like a place ye might see in a dream; an as' I come up to it I began to feel a cold wind blowin' through the hollow o' me heart. "Musha* Thomas," says I to meself, "is it yerself that's in it?"† says I; "or, if it is, what's the matter with ye at all, at all?" says I; so I put a bold face on it, an' I made a struggle to set one leg afore the other, until I came to the rise o' the bridge. And there, God be good to us! in a cantle‡ o' the wall I seen an old woman, as I thought, sittin' on her hunkers,§ all crouched together, an' her head bowed down, seemin'ly in the greatest affliction.

Well, sir, I pitied the old creature, an' thought I wasn't worth a thraneen,** for the mortial fright I was in, I up an' says to her, "That's a cold lodgin' for ye, ma'am." Well, the sorra ha'porth, she says to that, nor took no more notice o' me than if I hadn't let a word out o' me, but kep' rockin' herself to an' fro, as if her heart was breakin'; so I says to her again, "Eh, ma'am, is there anythin' the matter with ye?" An' I made for to touch her on the shoulder, only somethin' stopt me, for as I looked closer at her I saw she was no more an old woman nor she was an old cat. The first thing I tuk notice to, Mister Harry, was her hair, that was streelin'†† down over her shoulders, an' a good yard on the ground on each side of her. O, be the hoky‡‡ farmer, but that was the hair! The likes of it I never seen on mortial woman, young or old, before nor since. It grew as strong out of her as out of e'er a young slip of a girl ye could see; but the colour of it was a mystery to describe. The first squint I got of it I thought it was silvery grey, like an old crone's; but when I got up beside her I saw, by the glance o' the sky, it was a soart of an Iscariot§§ color an' a shine out of it like floss silk. It ran over her shoulders and the two shapely arms she was leanin' her head on,

*Musha: exclamation esp. showing surprise or annoyance, Well!
†is it yerself that's in it?: I don't feel like myself today
‡cantle: corner
§sittin' on her hunkers: squatting down
**thraneen: something of little or no value, a trifle
††streelin': streel, to trail or float in the manner of a streamer
‡‡hoky: used as a mild curse
§§Iscariot: having the traits of Judas Iscariot, treacherous

for all the world like Mary Magdalen's in a picture; and then I perceived that the grey cloak and the green gown underneath it was
made of no earthly material I ever laid eyes on. Now, I needn't tell
ye, sir, that I seen all this in the twinkle of a bed-post—long as I
take to make the narration of it. So I made a step back from her,
an' "The Lord be between us an' harm!" says I, out loud, an' with
that I blessed meself. Well, Mister Harry, the word wasn't out o'
me mouth afore she turned her face on me. Aw, Mister Harry, but
'twas that was the awfullest apparition ever I seen, the face of her
as she looked up at me! God forgive me for sayin' it, but 'twas
more like the face of the 'Axy Homo' beyond in Marlboro Street
Chapel nor like any face I could mintion—as pale as a corpse, an' a
most o' freckles on it, like the freckles on a turkey's egg; an' the
two eyes sewn in with thread, from the terrible power o' crying
the' had to do; an' such a pair of eyes as the' were, Mister Harry,
as blue as two forget-me nots, an' as cold as the moon in a bog-
hole of a frosty night, an' a dead-an'-live look in them that sent a
cold shiver through the marrow o' me bones. Be the mortial! ye
could ha' rung a tea cupful of cold perspiration out o' the hair o'
me head that minute, so ye could. Well, I thought the life 'ud leave
me entirely when she rose up from her hunkers, till, bedad!* she
looked mostly as tall as Nelson's Pillar;† an' with the two eyes gazin'
back at me, an' her two arms stretched out before her, an' a keen‡
out of her that rose the hair o' me scalp till it was as stiff as the
hog's bristles in a new hearth broom, away she glides—glides
round the angle o' the bridge, an' down with her into the stream
that ran underneath it. 'Twas then I began to suspect what she was.
"Wisha,§ Thomas!" says I to meself, says I; an' I made a great struggle to get me two legs into a trot, in spite o' the spavin** o' fright
the pair o' them were in; an' how I brought meself home that same

*bedad: oh my gosh!
†Nelson's Pillar: a large statue in Dublin
‡keen: a lamentation for the dead uttered in a loud wailing voice
§Wisha: Well! A term of endearment. He's encouraging himself.
**spavin': swelling enormity

night the Lord in heaven only knows, for I never could tell; but I must ha' tumbled agin the door, and shot in head foremost into the middle o' the floor where I lay in a dead swoon for mostly an hour; and the first I knew was Mrs. Maguire standin' over me with a jorum* o' punch she was pourin' down me throat, to bring back the life into me, an' me head in a pool of cold water she dashed over me in her first fright. "Arrah,† Mister Connolly," says she, "what ails ye?" says she, "to put the scare on a lone woman like that?" says she. "Am I in this world or the next?" says I. "Musha! where else would ye be only here in my kitchen?" says she. "O, glory be to God!" says I, "but I thought I was in Purgatory at the least, not to mention an uglier place," says I "only it's too cold I find meself, an' not too hot," says I. "Faith, an' maybe ye were more nor half-ways there, on'y for me," says she; "but what's come to you at all, at all? Is it your fetch‡ ye seen, Mister Connolly?" "Aw, nabo-clish!"§ says I. "Never mind what I seen," says I. So be degrees I began to come to a little; an' that's the way I met the banshee, Mister Harry!

"But how did you know it really was the banshee after all, Thomas?"

Begor,** sir, I knew the apparition of her well enough; but 'twas confirmed by a circumstance that occurred the same time. There was a Mister O'Nales was come on a visit, ye must know, to a place in the neighbourhood—one o' the old O'Nales of the county Tyrone, a real old Irish family—an' the banshee was heard keening round the house that same night, be more than one that was in it; an' sure enough, Mister Harry, he was found dead in his bed the next mornin'. So if it wasn't the banshee I seen that time, I'd like to know what else it could a' been.

---

*jorum: pitcher

†Arrah: Oh!

‡fetch: the phantom double of a living person appearing as an omen of death of the person

§naboclish: don't mind it

**Begor: a mild oath

The Frightened Fox

A fox was running in terror, stumbling and whimpering in headlong flight.

"What's the matter?" people called. "What disaster makes you run like that?"

The fox paused to get its breath. "They are rounding up the camels," he gasped. "They are pressing them into service!"

"Idiot!" they laughed. "Why are *you* fleeing, then? You're not a camel. You don't even look like one."

"Be quiet!" snapped the fox. "I know I'm not a camel, and *you* know I'm not. But this mob behind me don't care for niceties like that. It only takes one of them for spite to shout, 'Look, there's another camel!' and who will hear our few voices among the howls of the pursuers? And by the time it's all sorted out it will be far too late. I'll have died in the desert with a camel's load on my back!"

The Nature of Fear

I have never been afraid of starving to death. I have never been afraid that I would be homeless. I have never been afraid that I would be rounded up like the fox[14] or placed in a concentration camp. My husband has not been to war. My mother nearly died of scarlet fever; I had antibiotics. I was vaccinated against smallpox and polio.[15] I have had the almost unimaginable privilege of living without constant fear for most of my life. However, now that the capability for large-scale destruction has become more democratic, I find myself a captive stranger to fear. It seems as if ours is the generation that will face the end of the world. Yet in every generation, every individual, every group and species, faces death and extinction. Every one of humanity's characteristics has come through millennia of testing and filtering by natural selection. If fear were not a useful emotion, it would have been weeded out of the population generations ago.[16]

It was my third foray into the Australian bush. Tender ferns looked like frothy green mist but were harsh as steel pads. One plant burst from its roots like a green fountain, each gracefully arching stream culminating in a sharp thorn. Rainbow lorikeets darted through the spare branches of eucalyptus trees and screeching flocks of sulfur-crested cockatoos swooped across the sky. My daughter Deirdre caught my sleeve with a sharp jab. "Mom!" I froze. Slithering across the path in the place where my next step would have landed was a brown snake, one of the five most venomous snakes in the world. Odd that a fidgety person like myself found it effortless to stand absolutely still as that snake languidly wound its way across the path and disappeared into the bush. Fear held me motionless. Fear has its uses.

Fear can give you the rush of adrenaline that enables you to slam on the brakes, think of a lie, or run if you've seen the banshee.[17] However, fear can take over. Fear focuses energy to the exclusion of all else in this instant because it is a life-or-death instant. What if this isn't a life-threatening moment and fear blinds us to a more critical moment? We're afraid of sharks and saltwater crocodiles and killer bees, but every day without a second thought, we hop into our cars and hurtle down the highway at sixty-five miles per hour in a ton of metal. We're afraid of the banshee and ghosts, but not of eating junk food and candy. We're afraid of others' weapons, but not of others' poverty.

I once saw a cat snare a pigeon. I only saw the last few seconds of the cat's approach. The successful pounce happened so quickly that I blinked and missed it. I understand why the turtledove has to be afraid.[18] I have also watched the fairy wren's frenetic twitches and cannot imagine living with that continual fear.

One tale led to another. Scheherazade not only knew fear, she also had courage. What do folktales have to say about courage? They tell of the heroine who clamps the dagger between her teeth and dives into the roiling sea to slay the dragon. They tell of the knight in shining armor who charges the enemy lines and single-handedly vanquishes the foes. As we struggle to draw the battle lines clearly so that we know in-group from out-group, so that we know exactly where we stand in this fight, it is to our advantage to be certain and to be courageous in that certainty. Isn't it?

There Is Nothing Anywhere
(That We Fear)

AKAN-ASHANTI PEOPLE, GHANA[19]

They say that there once lived a Leopard and his wife, and that they had two children. Now the mother and the father of these children used to go to the bush every day to catch meat to bring to them. One day their mother and father said to them, "When you rise up, you must cry out and say, 'There is nothing anywhere that we fear, there is nothing anywhere that we fear.'" Then they went off to the bush, leaving their children there. Then Dankwanta, the Nightjar,* came along, and the children cried out:

> *"There is nothing anywhere that we fear.*
> *There is nothing anywhere that we fear!"*

The Nightjar said, "Who told you to cry out such a thing?"
They replied, "It was father and mother who said it."
The Nightjar said, "They are wrong; you must cry out, 'Times soon change, times soon change.'"
Now, as for those infants, their mother and their father returned, and heard their children crying:

> *"Times soon change,*
> *Times soon change!"*

They said, "Who told you to cry out such a thing?"

*Nightjar: a common grayish brown nocturnal bird

32

They replied, "A certain man told us."

Then their mother and their father said, "You must not call out that, you must call out, 'There is nothing anywhere that we fear, there is nothing anywhere that we fear.' " They gave the infants meat and went off.

The Nightjar came back, and he had made two spears. Now at the place where the infants lay stood two trees. When the Nightjar came, he broke the two trees, and he stuck the spears in the stumps. He said to the infants, "You must cry, saying, 'Times soon change, times soon change,' and when your mother and your father return you must say that it is I, who have told you."

The Nightjar flew and alighted on the point of one of the spears. Not long after, the mother and father of the infants returned. They said, "Who told you to cry out this?"

The Nightjar answered, "I did."

The male Leopard was leaping upon him to seize him, when the Nightjar flew off and the Leopard impaled himself on the spear. The Nightjar flew on the second spear. When the female Leopard would have leaped to catch him, she, too, was impaled on the spear. The Nightjar said to the children, "Now, you see you will not get any more meat to eat. That is what I meant when I told you, 'times soon change.'"

This, my story, which I have related, if it be sweet, or if it be not sweet, take some elsewhere, and let some come back to me.

The Boy Who Went
in Search of Fear

GERMANY[20]

A father had two sons. The older was smart and clever and did well in everything. The younger was stupid. He couldn't understand anything. He couldn't learn anything. When people saw him, they said, "He'll be a burden to his father." Whenever there was something to do, the older son had to do it. However, if it was late, or even worse, nighttime, and the father told the older son to go get something and the path wound past the churchyard or some other eerie place, the older son said, "Oh no, Father, I'm not going there, it gives me the creeps." He was afraid. Or, in the evenings, by the fire, when tales were told that made one shudder with fear, often the listeners would say, "Oh, that gives me the creeps!"

The younger son sat in the corner and listened to all of this and couldn't understand what they were talking about. "They always say, 'It gives me the creeps! It gives me the creeps!' Nothing gives me the creeps. That must be a skill I know nothing about."

One day the father spoke to him, "Listen, you in the corner there, you're getting big and strong. You have to learn something so you can earn your living. Look at how hard your brother works, but you, you're a hopeless case."

"Oh, Father," he answered, "I really would like to learn something. Now that you mention it, I really do want to learn how to get the creeps, because I don't understand a thing about that."

The older son laughed when he heard that, and thought to himself, "Dear God, what a dummy my brother is! He'll never amount to anything. You can't make a silk purse out of a sow's ear!"

The father sighed and said, "The creeps! I'll give you the creeps! But you'll never earn a living with that."

Shortly thereafter the sexton paid them a visit and the father complained and told how his younger son was dim-witted, knew nothing, and could learn nothing. "Can you imagine, when I asked him how he was going to earn a living, he actually asked me to teach him how to get the creeps."

"Well, if that's all it is," the sexton answered, "he can learn that at my place. Just give him to me, I'll smooth over his rough edges."

The father was overjoyed, because he thought, "The boy might just get straightened out a bit."

The sexton took the boy to his house and gave the boy the job of ringing the bells. After a few days, the sexton woke the boy at midnight and told him to get up, climb the church tower, and ring the bells. "You'll soon learn to get the creeps!" thought the sexton and secretly went out ahead of the boy. The boy got to the top of the bell tower and turned around to grab the bell pull, when there on the steps opposite the sound hole he saw a white shape. "Who's there?" he called out.

The figure didn't answer, didn't move, didn't budge.

"You better answer me," the boy yelled, "or get out of here. You've got no business here in the middle of the night."

The sexton stood stock-still so the boy would believe that it was a ghost.

The boy yelled at the figure a second time, "What do you want here? Speak! if you be an honest man, or I'll throw you down the stairs."

The sexton thought, "He doesn't really mean that," and stood still as if he were made of stone.

Then the boy yelled a third time, and since that had no effect either, he took a running start and shoved the ghost down the stairs so hard that it fell ten steps and came to a stop lying in the corner. After that, the boy rang the bells, went home, and went—without saying a word to anyone—to bed and to sleep. The sexton's wife waited a long time for her husband, but he didn't come back.

Finally, she got worried. She woke the boy and asked, "Do you know where my husband is? He went ahead of you up into the tower."

"No," the boy answered, "but there was someone standing on the other side of the sound hole by the steps, and since he didn't answer and wouldn't go away, I figured he was a mischief-maker and I shoved him down the steps. If you go to the tower you can see if it was your husband. I'd be sorry if it were."

The wife jumped up, ran to the tower, and found her husband lying in the corner wailing with his leg broken. She carried him down and rushed off to the father of the boy. "Your boy," she screamed, "has caused a terrible accident. He threw my husband down the stairs so hard he broke his leg. Get that good-for-nothing boy out of our house."

The father was shocked. He ran to the sexton's house and gave the boy a tongue-lashing. "What kind of wicked pranks have you been up to? The devil must have put you up to it."

"Father," the boy answered, "just listen to me. I didn't do anything wrong. He stood there in the night like someone who was going to do something bad. I didn't know who it was. And I told him three times to say something or to go away."

"Oh," the father said, "you'll bring me nothing but bad luck. Get out of my sight. I don't ever want to lay eyes on you again."

"Okay, Father, gladly, just wait until it's day. Then I'll leave. And I'll learn how to get the creeps. That way I'll have at least one skill with which I can earn my living."

"Learn whatever you want," the father said, "I couldn't care less. Here are fifty talers.* Go out into the wide world. Don't tell anyone who you are or who your father is, because I'd just have to be ashamed of you."

"Okay, Father, if that's the way you want it. If that's all, I'll be able to remember it."

When day came, the boy stuck his fifty talers into his pocket and walked along the road, continually saying, "If only I could get the creeps! If only I could get the creeps!"

*taler: large silver coin

Along came a man who heard what the boy was saying to himself. When they had gone a bit further and the man could see a hanging tree ahead, he said to the boy, "Look. Here is the tree where seven men married the ropemaker's daughter. Now they're learning how to fly. Sit yourself under here and wait until night comes. Then you'll learn how to get the creeps."

"If that's all it takes," the boy answered, "that's easy. And if I learn how to get the creeps that quickly, you shall have my fifty talers. Just come back tomorrow morning." Then the boy went over to the gallows, sat down, and waited until evening came. He was cold. So he made himself a fire. At midnight, the wind became so cold that the boy couldn't get warm even though he had a fire, and the wind knocked the hanged men against one another so they swung back and forth, and the boy thought, "You're freezing down here by the fire, imagine how they must be shivering and shaking up there." He felt sorry for them. So the boy put up the ladder, climbed up, untied one after the other and lugged all seven down. Then the boy stirred up the fire and blew on it and arranged the seven around it so they might warm themselves. However, they just sat there and didn't move and their clothes caught on fire.

The boy said, "Hey! Watch out, or I'll hang you back up."

The dead men heard nothing, said nothing, and let their rags burn.

The boy got angry and said, "If you won't pay attention, then I can't help you, and I'm not going to burn up with you." And one after the other, he hung them back up. Then he settled himself down by the fire and fell asleep.

The next morning, the man came to the boy expecting to collect fifty talers. "So, did you learn how to get the creeps?"

"No. How would I have learned that? Those guys up there didn't open their mouths. They're so stupid they let the fire burn those old rags they've got on."

At this point, the man realized he wouldn't be walking away with the fifty talers, so he left, saying, "I've never met anyone like that before."

The boy also went on his way and again began to mutter to himself, "Oh, if only I could learn how to get the creeps! Oh, if only I could get the creeps."

A carter who walked up behind the boy heard him and asked, "Who are you?"

"I don't know," the boy answered.

"Where do you come from?"

"I don't know."

"Who is your father?"

"I'm not supposed to say."

"What do you keep mumbling to yourself?"

"Oh," said the boy, "I want to learn how to get the creeps, but no one can teach me."

"Don't talk such nonsense," said the carter. "Come along with me and I'll make sure you get a place to stay."

The boy went with the carter, and that evening they came to an inn where they planned to spend the night. As the boy walked into the room he said quite loudly, "If only I could get the creeps! If only I could get the creeps!"

When the innkeeper heard that, he laughed and said, "If that's what you want, you've got the opportunity right here."

"Oh, be quiet," said the innkeeper's wife. "Too many foolhardy men have lost their lives because of this. It would be a pity if those pretty eyes never saw the light of day again."

However, the boy said, "I don't care how hard it is, I've got to learn it. That's why I left home." He wouldn't let up until the innkeeper explained that not far away there stood a haunted castle where one could certainly learn how to get the creeps. All he had to do was spend three nights inside. The king had promised his daughter's hand in marriage to anyone who risked it and she was the most beautiful girl under the sun. In the castle there was also a vast treasure to be gained, a treasure that could make a poor man rich, but it was guarded by evil ghosts. Many men had gone in, but not one had yet come out again.

The next morning, the boy went before the king and said, "If I may, I would like to spend three nights in the haunted castle."

The king gazed at the boy, and because he liked him, the king said, "You may take three things into the castle with you, but they must be lifeless things."

The boy answered, "I'd like fire, a lathe, and a carpenter's bench with its knife. The king allowed the boy to take all of that into the castle during the day. When night came, the boy entered the castle. He made a bright fire in one of the chambers, placed the carpenter's bench and knife nearby, sat down on the lathe and sighed, "If only I could get the creeps, but I doubt I'll learn it here either." At about midnight, he went to stoke the fire. As he blew on it, a cry burst from the corner. "Ow, miaow! We're freezing!"

"You fools, what are you screaming about? If you're cold, come sit by the fire and get warm," said the boy. Once he'd said that, two huge, black cats leapt with a powerful spring over to the fire. They sat on either side of the boy and stared ferociously at him with their fiery eyes. After a while, when they'd gotten warm, they said, "How about a game of cards?"

"Why not," the boy answered, "but first show me your paws."

The cats stretched out their claws.

"Oh," the boy said, "what long nails you have! Wait, I have to clip them first." With that, he grabbed them by the scruffs of their necks, lifted them onto the carpenter's bench, and screwed their paws into a vise. He said, "I was keeping a sharp eye on you two, and I don't think I want to play cards just now." He killed them and threw them out into the water. After he'd dealt with the cats, he was about to sit down by the fire again when from all the corners and corridors came black cats and black dogs on glowing chains. More and more, they kept coming until he couldn't get out. They screamed horribly. They stomped on the fire. They tore it apart and tried to put it out. For a while, the boy calmly observed all this, but when things got too out of hand, he grabbed his knife and yelled, "Get out of here, you rabble," and he lashed out at them. One group ran away. The other group, he killed and threw out into the lake. When the boy came back; he blew on the coals, started up his fire, and warmed himself.

As he sat there, the boy just couldn't keep his eyes open. He simply had to sleep. Well, he looked around and saw a large bed in the corner. "That's perfect," he said, and lay down. Just as he was about to shut his eyes, the bed started moving on its own. It zoomed around the whole castle. "Hey! Can you go faster?" Then the bed streaked around as if six horses were pulling it—over doorsteps, up stairs and down stairs. Suddenly, plop! It turned upside down and lay like a mountain on top of the boy. He pushed the bed off himself, pitched covers and pillows into the air and said, "Now anyone else who wants a ride can have one." Then he lay down by the fire and slept until it was day.

In the morning, the king came. When he saw the boy lying quite still on the ground, the king thought that the ghosts had killed the boy. "What a shame about that handsome young man," the king said.

The boy heard this, sat up and said, "I'm not finished yet."

The king was amazed but happy and he asked the boy how things had gone.

"Fine," he answered. "One night down. Two to go."

When the boy came to the inn, the innkeeper's eyes bugged out. "I never thought I'd see you alive again. Now have you learned how to get the creeps?"

"No. It's no use. If only someone could explain it to me!"

The second night, the boy returned to the old castle, lit his fire, and began to mumble his oft-repeated refrain, "If only I could get the creeps!" As midnight came, he heard a roaring and rumbling. At first it was faint, then it grew louder and louder. Then all was still. Finally, with a shrill scream, half of a man fell down the chimney and landed in front of the boy. "Hey!" the boy yelled. "There's half missing. That's not enough!" The noise began as before. It howled and wailed and the other half also fell down. "Just a minute," the boy said, "I'll stoke up the fire a bit." When he had finished and looked around, both pieces had come together and a gruesome man sat in the boy's seat. "That wasn't part of the deal," the boy said. "The bench is mine."

The man tried to push him away, but the boy didn't let him. The boy gave the man a big shove and then the boy sat down again in his seat. Then more men fell down, one after the other. They held nine corpses' bones and two corpses' skulls which they set up and played a game of ninepins. The boy wanted to play as well and said, "Hey, can I play too?"

"Yes, if you have money."

"I have enough," he answered, "but your balls aren't round." The boy took the skulls, set them on the lathe, and turned them until they were round. "Now they'll roll better," he said. "Hey! Now we'll have some fun!" He played and lost some of his money, but as the clock struck twelve, everything vanished. He lay down and fell into a peaceful slumber.

The next morning, the king came and asked him. "How was it this time?"

"I played a game of ninepins, and I lost a little money."

"Did you get the creeps?"

"No way," he said. "I had a great time. But, oh, I would like to learn how to get the creeps!"

For the third night, the boy sat down again on the bench and ever so despondently said, "If I only knew how to get the creeps!" When it got late, six large men came in carrying a coffin. Then the boy said, "Hey! That must be my cousin who died a few days ago." The boy crooked his finger and called out, "Come here, Cousin, come on!" The men put the coffin onto the ground; the boy went and took off the lid. There lay a corpse inside. The boy felt the corpse's face. It was cold as ice. "Wait," he said, "I'll warm you up a bit." He went to the fire, warmed his hand and laid it on the corpse's face, but the corpse stayed cold. The boy took the corpse out, set it by the fire and laid himself on the corpse's lap and rubbed its arms so the blood would flow again. When none of this helped, the boy thought, "When two lie together in bed, they warm each other up." So he brought the corpse to the bed, covered it, and lay down beside it. After a while, the corpse became warm and began to move. Then the boy said, "Just think, Cousin, what would have happened if I hadn't warmed you up."

But the corpse yelled, "Now I'm going to strangle you!"

"What?" the boy cried. "Is this all the thanks I get? You're going back into your coffin." The boy lifted the corpse, threw it into the coffin and slammed the lid shut. Then six men came and carried it off.

"I'll never get the creeps," the boy sighed. "I'll never learn it no matter how long I live."

Then a man came in who was bigger than all the others. He was absolutely ghastly, but he was old and had a long white beard. "You little runt," the man yelled. "You'll get the creeps now, because you're going to die."

"Not so fast," answered the boy. "To kill me, you have to catch me first."

"Oh, I'll get you all right," said the monster.

"Easy does it. Easy does it. Don't brag now. As strong as you are, I'm that strong and stronger."

"We'll see," said the old man. "If you're stronger than I am, I'll let you go. Come on, let's see." He took the boy through dark passageways to a smithy. The old man took an ax, and with one fell stroke he drove the anvil into the ground.

"I can do better than that," said the boy, and went to the other anvil. The old man stood close in order to see and his white beard hung down. The boy grabbed the ax, split the anvil with a single blow and jammed the old man's beard into the split. "Now I've got you," said the boy. "Now you're the one who's going to die." Then he got an iron bar and began beating the old man until he whimpered and begged the boy to stop. He'd give the boy great riches. The boy pulled out the ax and set the man free.

Then the old man led the boy back into the castle and showed him three chests full of gold in a cellar. The old man said, "One chest is for the poor, the other is for the king, the third is yours." At that moment, the clock struck twelve and the ghost disappeared. The boy stood in complete darkness. "I can still find my way out of here," he said. He tapped around, found the way out of the room, and nodded off by his fire. The next morning, the king came and said, "Now surely you'll have learned how to get the creeps?"

"Nope," the boy answered. "What on earth is it? My dead cousin was here and a bearded man who took me down below and showed me lots of money, but as for the creeps, nobody told me anything about it."

Then the king said, "You have broken the spell and freed the castle and you shall marry my daughter."

"That's all well and good," the boy answered, "but I still don't know how to get the creeps."

The gold was brought up. The marriage was celebrated. However, the young king, even though he loved his wife and was very pleased, still kept saying, "If only I could get the creeps. If only I could get the creeps."

Finally this annoyed his wife. "He'll soon learn about the creeps." She went out to the stream which flowed through the garden and got a whole bucketful of minnows. That night when the young king had fallen asleep, his wife ripped off the covers, doused him with the bucket of cold water with the minnows, and the little fish wriggled all over him. He woke up and screamed, "Hey! I've got the creeps! I've got the creeps, dear wife! Now I know what the creeps are!"

The Fearless Captain

KOREA[21]

There was formerly a soldier, Yee Man-ji of Yong-nam, a strong and muscular fellow, and brave as a lion. He had green eyes and a terrible countenance. Frequently he said, "Fear! What is fear?" On a certain day when he was in his house a sudden storm of rain came on, when there were flashes of lightning and heavy claps of thunder. At one of them a great ball of fire came tumbling into his home and went rolling over the verandah, through the rooms, into the kitchen and out into the yard, and again into the servants' quarters. Several times it went and came bouncing about. Its blazing light and the accompanying noise made it a thing of terror.

Yee sat in the outer verandah, wholly undisturbed. He thought to himself, "I have done no wrong, therefore why need I fear the lightning?" A moment later a flash struck the large elm tree in front of the house and smashed it to pieces. The rain then ceased and the thunder likewise.

Yee turned to see how it fared with his family, and found them all fallen senseless. With the greatest of difficulty he had them restored to life. During that year they all fell ill and died, and Yee came to Seoul and became a Captain of the Right Guard. Shortly after he went to North Ham-kyong Province. There he took a second wife and settled down. All his predecessors had died of goblin influences, and the fact that calamity had overtaken them while in the official quarters had caused them to use one of the village houses instead.

Yee, however, determined to live down all fear and go back to the old quarters, which he extensively repaired.

One night his wife was in the inner room while he was alone in the public office with a light burning before him. In the second watch or thereabout, a strange-looking object came out of the inner quarters. It looked like the stump of a tree wrapped in black sackcloth. There was no outline or definite shape to it, and it came jumping along and sat itself immediately before Yee Man-ji. Also two other objects came following in its wake, shaped just like the first one. The three then sat in a row before Yee, coming little by little closer and closer to him. Yee moved away till he had backed up against the wall and could go no farther. Then he said, "Who are you, anyhow; what kind of devil, pray, that you dare to push towards me so in my office? If you have any complaint or matter to set right, say so, and I'll see to it."

The middle devil said in reply, "I'm hungry, I'm hungry, I'm hungry."

Yee answered, "Hungry, are you? Very well, now just move back and I'll have food prepared for you in abundance." He then repeated a magic formula that he had learned, and snapped his fingers. The three devils seemed to be afraid of this. Then Man-ji suddenly closed his fist and struck a blow at the first devil. It dodged, however, most deftly and he missed, but hit the floor a sounding blow that cut his hand.

Then they all shouted, "We'll go, we'll go, since you treat guests thus." At once they bundled out of the room and disappeared.

On the following day he had oxen killed and a sacrifice offered to these devils, and they returned no more.

Desperate Courage

One evening a young man was walking with his girlfriend past People's Park in Berkeley, California. Someone confronted the young man, pulled a gun on him, and demanded his wallet. The young man was slowly pulling his wallet out of his pocket, all the while trying to dissuade the thief from stealing it, when the thief shot the young man dead. How useful was that young man's courage? How useful was the desperate courage of the robber, who ended up killing a man for a few dollars? Napoleon promoted the soldiers who were the first to charge across the enemy line. His officers were young, courageous, and short-lived. These people aren't like Lara Croft; these heroes do not emerge unscathed.

Folktales take up the idea of courage and offer nuances. If the fearless captain from Korea had been less courageous, his family might have lived.[22] Was the boy who went in search of fear courageous or simple-minded, or both?[23] Is courage possibly an overrated commodity?

As I read them, the folktales blended together. Each action merged into the many actions and reactions that humans have found and puzzled out in the past and the distant past, and the very distant past and the present. Folktales laud the knight in shining armor who rescues the princess, but the little tailor who brags about killing seven (flies) at one blow also wins the princess. As I read story after story, my definition of courage became a process. Each successive story presented a different shade of courage, like the gray of predawn melting into day. The more I read, the more my heroines and heroes lost those sharp outlines that set them apart from questions, uncertainty, reality. Reluctantly I watched them blur. I read "The Boy Who Went in Search of Fear"[24] and I thought of all the courageous young men

*who filled the armies and died in the trenches of World War I. I thought of
the writer H. H. Munroe, who enlisted at the beginning of the war and
died in France in 1916.*[25] *I thought of the friends Vera Brittain loved and
how each young man died, one after the other.*[26] *I thought of the poet
Wilfred Owen. Those young men went off to war and fought courageously.
However, when they understood courage, it had little to do with the glori-
ous knight in shining armor and more with the irony of a boy courageously
going in search of fear.*

> *If in some smothering dreams you too could pace*
> *Behind the wagon that we flung him in,*
> *And watch the white eyes writhing in his face,*
> *His hanging face, like a devil's sick of sin;*
> *If you could hear, at every jolt, the blood*
> *Come gargling from the froth-corrupted lungs,*
> *Obscene as cancer, bitter as the cud*
> *Of vile, incurable sores on innocent tongues,—*
> *My friend, you would not tell with such high zest*
> *To children ardent for some desperate glory,*
> *The old Lie: Dulce et decorum est*
> *Pro patria mori.**
>
> —Wilfred Owen (1893–1918)[27]

*I tried to think of a time when I was courageous, and nothing came to
mind. Instead, I thought of my little four-year-old standing outside the
door to her French kindergarten. Tales had distracted her through breakfast
and tales had occupied her on the bicycle ride to school. We had walked
down the dull school hallway, our steps slowing as we neared the door. The
morning's last story ended. The moment had come for Colleen to enter the
classroom. Her eyes swept over the children inside the room. I saw panic
begin to rise and watched her stifle it, push it back from her eyes and throat,
force it down into her chest where her body confined it. "It must be hard for
you," I said. She crumpled into my arms and heaved a deep sob, "Mommy, it's*

*Dulce et decorum est pro patria mori: Sweet and fitting is it to die for one's
country.

too long. School is too long," she sobbed. To my four-year-old daughter, three hours in a classroom where she understood nothing was an eternity. I would tell her, "Three months from now, you'll understand. You'll even speak French. It'll be easy." However, three months to her was a length of time she couldn't comprehend. To her, it was a time that would never arrive. I gently urged her to go into the room, and she said, "Mommy, please let me talk to you for just one more minute." A minute later she begged, "Just one more hug, please." I held her close. "Okay," she said. She swiped the tears off her cheeks, faced the door, straightened her back, and walked into the classroom.

Our history, our news reports, our movies focus on heroism in the face of a loaded gun or on the battlefield, and there is courage there. However, it also takes courage to do many of the small things that are the sum of our lives.

Girl Learns to Write by Practising on Frozen Pond

ICELANDIC-CANADIAN[28]

Well, I should probably tell you about the first thing I did, or tried to do, which was of use to me, I was just a wee-little kid then, and I asked Dad to give me an envelope that he had. It was some receipt with his name and address on it. And I think to myself, in the fall, when the pond, which was by our house, was frozen over, and I go and get myself a stick that is the right length, and start writing on—on the pond, on the ice. There was a bit of snow on it, and there I wrote on the pond, the whole pond, completely, this name, completely to the end. It must have been, just about like—like, probably, three or four hundred feet, and . . .

It was Dad's name: Mister Jón Jónsson of Yztagrund in Blönduhlíd, Skagafjördur. And I wrote this whole thing, and, closely, on the whole pond. And then when I had written the whole thing, I—I walked across, see, always across what I had written. And I—blasted off—made a footslide over the whole thing, and then the next morning, light snow had covered everything, and then I could do the same thing, and this was my school; it was a rather cold school.

The Cakes of Oatmeal and Blood

IRELAND[29]

There was an upstart of a fellow one time, who was always arranging a marriage between himself and some girl, but in the end he never married any of them. He couldn't make up his mind which wife would be best for him. There happened to be a funeral one day, and after coming home, a little tipsy, he was invited to a dance in a neighbour's house. He went to the dance; there were lots of young men and women there, and some of his own relatives as well. They asked him had he any thought of getting married.

"I have, and every thought," said he, "but I don't know what kind of wife would be best for me."

"'Twould be better for you to marry me," said one girl.

"Don't, but marry me!" said a second girl.

"I'd be a better wife than either of the two of them," said a third girl.

"Well," said he, "I had a nice blackthorn stick* with me, when I was in the graveyard today, and I left it stuck into the ground near the grave of the old woman we buried. I'll marry whichever of the three of ye will go there and bring me home my stick!"

"You may go to the Devil!" said two of the girls. "We wouldn't go into the graveyard for all the sticks in the wood, not to mention your little, blackthorn one!"

"I'll go there," said the third girl, "if you keep your promise to marry me, if I bring you the stick."

"I promise to marry you," said he.

*blackthorn stick: fairies hide and dance around the blackthorn bushes

She set off for the graveyard, without any fear. She went into it and was searching around for the stick, when a voice spoke from one of the graves.

"Open this grave!" called the voice.

"I won't," answered the girl.

"You'll have to open it!" said the voice.

She had to open the grave. There was a man in the coffin inside.

"Take me out of this coffin!" he ordered.

"I couldn't," said she.

"You can very well," said the man.

She had to take him out of the coffin.

"Now take me on your back!" said he.

"Where will I take you to?" she asked.

"I'll direct you," said he.

She had to take him on her back and took him to the house of one of the neighbours, near her own. He told her not to go any further. She carried him into the kitchen. The family were all asleep. The man stirred up the fire.

"See can you get something for me to eat!" said the man.

"Yerra,* where could I get anything for you to eat?" she asked. "I have as little knowledge as yourself of the way about this house!"

"Go on! There's oatmeal in the room. Bring it here!" said he.

She found the room, and the oatmeal was there.

"See can you find milk anywhere now!" said the man.

She searched but couldn't find any milk.

"See is there water, if there isn't any milk!" said the man.

She looked everywhere for water, but there was none.

"There isn't a drop of water in the house," said she.

"Light a candle!" said he.

She did so.

"Hold that candle for me now!" said he.

He made off to a room where two sons of the man of the house were asleep. He took a knife and cut their throats, and drew their blood. He took away the blood, mixed it with the oatmeal, and

*Yerra: Well!

began to eat it. He urged the girl to eat it also, and when he came near her, she pretended to eat it, while at the same time she was letting it fall into her apron.

"'Tis a great pity," said she, "that this should happen to those two boys."

"It wouldn't have happened to them," said the man, "if they had kept some clean water in the house; but they didn't, and they must take what has happened to them!"

"Is there anything to bring the two young men to life again?" she asked.

"No," said he, "because you and I have eaten what would have revived them. If some of the oatmeal which was mixed with their blood was put into their mouths, life would come back to them, as it had been before. And the two of them would have a good life, if they had lived," said he. "Do you see that field that their father owns?"

"I do," said she.

"Nobody knows all the gold there is in it near the bushes over there," said the man. "You must take me back now to where you found me," said he.

She took him on her back, and when she was going through a muddy gap which led out from the yard, she let the oatmeal which she had hidden in her apron fall down near a fence. She took him along and never stopped till she took him to the grave out of which she had taken him.

"Put me into the coffin!" said he.

She did so.

"I'll be going home now," said she.

"You won't!" said he. "You must cover up my coffin with earth, as you found it."

She started to fill in the grave, and after a while, the cock crowed at some house near the graveyard.

"I'll go now," said she. "The cock is crowing."

"Don't take any notice of that cock!" said he. "He isn't a March cock. Work away and finish your task!"

She had to keep on filling in the grave. After another while, a second cock crowed.

"I'll go now," said she. "The cock is crowing."

"You may go now," said he. "That's a true March cock, and if he hadn't crowed just now, you'd have to stay with me altogether."

She went off home, and by that time, the dance was over. She went to bed, and slept late until her mother called her.

"'Tis a great shame for you to be sleeping and the bad news we have near us at our neighbours!" said her mother.

"What news is that?" asked the girl.

"This neighbour of ours found his two sons dead in the one bed this morning!" said her mother.

"How can I help that?" asked the girl.

"I know you can't," said her mother. "But put on your clothes and go to the wake."

She went off to the wake. She remembered every word that the man had said to her. All the people at the wake were crying, but she didn't cry at all.

"Would you give me one of them as a husband, if I brought them to life again?" she asked their father.

The young man who had sent her to the graveyard for the blackthorn stick was at the wake and he heard what she said.

"I thought you'd marry me," said he.

"Don't talk at all!" said she. "I'm tired enough after all I have gone through on account of you last night! Nobody knows what I have suffered on account of your blackthorn stick!"

"Joking me you are!" said the man of the house. "I know well that you couldn't put the life into them again. I'm troubled enough without you making fun of me!"

"'Tisn't making fun of you I am at all!" said the girl. "I'll put life into them, if I get one of them as a husband, and all I'll ask along with him is that field above the house, the Field of the Bushes. You can give the rest of the farm to the other fellow."

"I'd give you that field gladly," said their father, "if I saw that you had put the life into them again, as they were before."

She went out and found the oatmeal that she had let fall near the fence. She took it in and put some of it into the mouth of each of them. As soon as she did that, the two of them rose up, alive, as well as they had ever been.

After a while, she married one of them and she told him the whole story about her meeting with the dead man. When they were married, she told her husband to go and dig near the bushes—that he might find something there. He did and found a potful of gold. He took it home and emptied the gold out of it, and put it into the bank or some other place to keep. The old pot happened to remain in the house, and there was some kind of writing on it that no one could read. A few years later, a poor scholar called to the house and he saw the pot.

"Who put that writing on the pot?" he asked.

"We don't know," they said. "We don't notice it much."

"I don't either," said he, "but I know what the writing says."

"That's more than we do," said they. "What is written on it?"

"It says that on the other side there is three times as much," said he.

That put them thinking and they remembered where they had found the pot and how much gold was in it. So when the night came, out went the girl and her husband, and they started to dig at the eastern side of where they found the pot. There they found three other pots, all full of gold! You may be sure that they weren't short of anything then! They built a fine house in the corner of that field. And that's how that girl got her money because of the man of the oatmeal.

The Neckbone on the Knife

ICELAND [30]

A certain widow lived on a farm of her own in the north country. She was well off and very capable, so several people asked for her hand, and among others a fellow in the same neighbourhood who was skilled in wizardry—and him she refused. This widow had the second sight, which made it easier for her to protect herself.

Not long after, she was in the larder one day towards evening, preparing food rations for her household, and she was slicing a black pudding. She saw a spectre* making its way in along the passage, and in it came by the larder door. The woman stood there with the knife in her hand, and faced the spectre resolutely and fearlessly. The spectre hesitated and tried to pass to one side of the woman, or behind her, for an unclean spirit never attacks a fearless person from in front. The woman saw that the spectre was quite black, except that it had one white mark. She drove her knife into that spot; there was a loud crash, and the woman lost her grip on the knife, just as if it had been jerked out of her hand. She saw nothing more, and she could not find her knife.

Next morning the knife was found out on the flagged court; the top vertebra from a man's back was stuck on the point of it, and yet all the gates had been closed the previous evening.

---

*spectre: an apparition, ghost, phantom that usually inspires fear

The Death "Bree"

There was once a woman who lived in the Camp-del-more of Strathavon whose cattle were seized with a murrain,[*] or some such fell disease, which ravaged the neighbourhood at the time, carrying off great numbers of them daily. All the forlorn fires and hallowed waters failed of their customary effects: and she was at length told by the wise people whom she consulted on the occasion, that it was evidently the effect of some infernal agency, the power of which could not be destroyed by any other means than the never-failing specific—the juice of a dead head from the churchyard—a nostrum[†] certainly very difficult to be procured, considering that the head must needs be abstracted from the grave at the hour of midnight. Being, however, a woman of stout heart and strong faith, native feelings of delicacy towards the sanctuary of the dead had more weight than had fear in restraining her for some time from resorting to this desperate remedy. At length, seeing that her stock would soon be annihilated by the destructive career of the disease, the wife of Camp-del-more resolved to put the experiment in practice, whatever the result might be. Accordingly, having with considerable difficulty engaged a neighbouring woman as her companion in this hazardous expedition, they set out a little before midnight for the parish churchyard, distant about a mile and a half from her residence, to execute her determination. On arriving at the churchyard, her companion,

[*]murrain: a deadly plague, pestilence
[†]nostrum: remedy

whose courage was not so notable, appalled by the gloomy prospect before her, refused to enter among the habitations of the dead. She, however, agreed to remain at the gate till her friend's business was accomplished. This circumstance, however, did not stagger the wife's resolution.

She, with the greatest coolness and intrepidity, proceeded towards what she supposed an old grave, took down her spade, and commenced her operations. After a good deal of toil, she arrived at the object of her labour. Raising the first head, or rather skull, that came her way, she was about to make it her own property when a hollow, wild, sepulchral voice exclaimed, "That is my head; let it alone!" Not wishing to dispute the claimant's title to this head, and supposing she could be otherwise provided, she very good-naturedly returned it, and took up another. "That is my father's head," bellowed the same voice. Wishing, if possible, to avoid disputes, the wife of Camp-del-more took up another head, when the same voice instantly started a claim to it as his grandfather's head. "Well," replied the wife, nettled at her disappointments, "although it were your grandmother's head, you shan't get it till I am done with it."

"What do you say, you limmer?"* says the ghost, starting up in his awry habiliments. "What do you say, you limmer?" repeated he, in a great rage. "By the great oath, you had better leave my grand-father's head." Upon matters coming this length, the wily wife of Camp-del-more thought it proper to assume a more conciliatory aspect. Telling the claimant the whole particulars of the predicament in which she was placed, she promised faithfully that, if his honour would only allow her to carry off his grandfather's skull, or head, in a peaceable manner, she would restore it again when done with. Here, after some communing, they came to an understanding; and she was allowed to take the head along with her, on condition that she should restore it before cock-crowing, under the heaviest penalties.

On coming out of the churchyard, and looking for her companion, she had the mortification to find her "without a mouthful of

*limmer: scoundrel

breath in her body," for, on hearing the dispute between her friend and the guardian of the grave, and suspecting much that she was likely to share the unpleasant punishments with which he threatened her friend, at the bare recital of them she fell down in a faint, from which it was no easy matter to recover her. This proved no small inconvenience to Camp-del-more's wife, as there were not above two hours to elapse ere she had to return the head, according to the terms of her agreement. Taking her friend upon her back, she carried her up a steep acclivity to the nearest adjoining house, where she left her for the night; then repaired home with the utmost speed, made dead bree* of the head ere the appointed time had expired, restored the skull to its guardian, and placed the grave in its former condition. It is needless to add that, as a reward for her exemplary courage, the bree had its desired effect.

The cattle speedily recovered, and so long as she retained any of it, all sorts of diseases were of short duration.

*bree: brew

Quotidian Courage

This night I watched at my child's bedside. The tentative diagnosis was appendicitis, but her father and I had chosen to keep Deirdre under observation for a while rather than put her through a possibly unnecessary operation. The operating room staff went home. If things turned for the worse during the night, it would be life-threatening. At first all went well. The fever had gone. Deirdre hopped off the trolley and I tucked her into the hospital bed. The lights in the children's ward were turned down. I told Deirdre a story as she drifted off to sleep. Then her temperature began to rise. On the hour, every hour, the nurses measured her temperature. Hour by hour, her fever rose with inexorable regularity. Ten o'clock, eleven o'clock, twelve o'clock. As the temperature inched upward, so too did my certainty that we had made the wrong decision, that she needed the operation, and desperately. She had to make it until morning, when the doctors would arrive. The next minutes became enemies. Every passed minute became a success. I counted the minutes in that night.

Every mother who has ever watched through the night at the bedside of a seriously ill child has faced the demons of fear. Is it because we share this struggle that it is not remembered as courage? Instances of daily courage we push to the back of our minds as if they don't exist—facing the bully at school, cooking and cleaning and taking care of a family day in and day out, being out of work and looking for a job. I've told my girls that if they're ever in a car that's being driven in a reckless fashion, to make up an excuse to get out of the car and call me. "Wherever you are, I'll come pick you up." They nod and say okay. I repeat, "Just do it. I'll come get you." They nod and say okay, but I know that it takes courage to insist on getting out of the car.

Just like curing a sick child, a woman's marriage choice or learning to read and write,[32] *or curing a sick cow can be a matter of life and death. Maybe it's easier for us to imagine ourselves as heroines and heroes on a faraway battlefield we never expect to see rather than to recognize this quotidian heroism. Maybe we ignore our day-to-day heroism because a clement silence is necessary for us to ignore our fear and continue doing what we have to do.*

If we had a keen vision and feeling of all ordinary human life, it would be like hearing the grass grow and the squirrel's heart beat, and we should die of that roar which lies on the other side of silence.

—George Eliot[33]

Folktales are the roar on the other side of silence. Many folktales describe a normal person in a moment of crisis, an ordinary crisis in a mundane existence.[34] *Folktales tell of the courage that enables a seventeen-year-old to say,"Let me out of this car,"and the courage of an eight-year-old scouring the garbage dump for her family's subsistence.*

Although folktales include monsters and ghosts, the folktale begins and ends with ordinary people and our ordinary lives.[35] *Although folktales may be set in a place and time we can't pinpoint, they don't really mean in some faraway place and some faraway time, they mean right here and now.*[36] *Folktales have been told for centuries*[37] *by different tellers—neighborhood children, mothers, fathers, village elders, and professional storytellers. Folktales have been told to different audiences, from the French nobility in the elite salons of Perrault's time to solitary campfires on lonely hillsides the world over.*[38] *All those tellers and all those audiences have molded, refined, and adapted these tales for centuries.*[39] *Although folktales seem simplistic, they've passed the test of great literature. They endure and they cross cultural boundaries. Therefore it should have come as no surprise that I could not control the issues brought up at my virtual campfire.*

I had entered my study with a specific issue in mind. I had read stories about fear and courage. I had been pleasantly surprised by the stories I found, but not too surprised. Just as I was getting comfortable, just as I began to think I'd asked the right question and had gotten all the answers

I needed, the ground shifted beneath my feet. It was as if all those story-tellers from all those places and times gave me a shove. Or maybe the tales themselves decided on a different pattern. At my virtual campfire, a woman remembered teaching herself to write. The excited sparkle of youth flitted across her stolid features and a child's smile played around her mouth. I could well imagine her as a little girl—red, runny nose and cold-stiffened fingers—bent determinedly over the ice. Proudly the woman enunciated her father's name, which she had etched into the frozen surface over and over again.[40] *Following her a woman, still beautiful in her middle age, rose to her feet, calmly and gracefully. Her eyes smoldered with defiance. She asserted her right to refuse marriage, a right she had and would continue to defend.*[41] *One tale led to another, but they didn't remain immersed in fear and they didn't conform to my assumed definition of courage. The storytelling session broke out of my neatly confined discussion. Gently but firmly, the tales shoved fear into the background. Gently but firmly, the stories demanded that I consider alternatives, different solutions, different questions. The folktales began to make me think about my own point of view.*

My book-and-story-filled study no longer offered me the closed safety of a medieval turret and a comfortable distance from my questions. Folktales opened the door and dared me to consider questions I hadn't asked. Like the inept third child in the proverbial fairy tale, I was kicked out of my home. I could feel the dirt road crunching beneath my feet. I felt excited at the prospect of seeking my fortune, going on a quest, opening myself to different questions and strange points of view. It would be fun. Like the fairy tale child, I took on the quest with the confidence that happily-ever-after gives a fairy tale.[42] *However, heroines and heroes in fairy tales meet with shadows in their souls. They meet unforeseen giants and powerful witches. The quest inevitably changes the heroines and the heroes.*

The Snail

AFRICAN-AMERICAN[43]

The snail wuz crossin' de road for seben years. Jus' as he got crost, a tree fell and jus' missed him. He said, "Gee! It's good to be fast."

Different Times Have
Different "Adans"

SUDAN[44]

There was once a Sultan and he was strolling through his lands one day, when he saw a fellah* digging away so assiduously at a small patch of land, that he was unaware of a snake which had crept up to him and started coiling itself round his ankle.

Alarmed, the Sultan shouted a warning. But the fellah merely shook off the snake and, without even attempting to kill it, went calmly on with his digging.

The Sultan was frankly amazed at the fellah's unconcern. "Man!" he said to him. "Don't you realize that that snake could have killed you? Yet all you do is to shake it off as if it didn't matter, and calmly go on with your digging!"

"Your Majesty," said the fellah, "I face death every day of my life; not from a snake, but from this very patch of land you see me digging. For if I do not put into it every ounce of strength I possess, I run the risk of starving to death since what it produces is hardly sufficient for mine and my children's bare subsistence."

The Sultan was so moved by the fellah's wretched circumstances, that he ordered his Vizier† to give him a substantial grant to help him out.

Months later, the Sultan was again strolling through his lands when he perceived the same fellah. This time, however, he was not digging. And though he wore his right arm in a sling, he was well dressed and looked fat and prosperous.

*fellah: peasant
†Vizier: a minister or councillor of state

63

Curious to know how he now fared, the Sultan stopped to talk to him. "And what is the matter with your arm, my man?" he asked.

"Your Majesty," replied the fellah, "last night I pricked my finger on a cucumber thorn, so I thought I would rest my arm this morning."

"Subhan Allah!"* said the Sultan in wonderment. "When you were poor and destitute you weren't mindful of a snake which could have killed you outright. Now that you are fat and prosperous, a cucumber thorn can put you right out of action?"

"O Sultan!" said the fellah unabashed. "Let us not forget that different times have different adans."†

*Subhan Allah!: Glory be to God!
†adan: call to prayer

The Story of the King and the
Four Girls

PUNJAB, INDIA[45]

There was once a king who, during the day, used to sit on his throne and dispense justice, but who at night disguised himself and wandered about the streets of his city looking for adventures.

One evening he was passing by a certain garden when he observed four young girls sitting under a tree and conversing together in earnest tones. Curious to overhear the subject of their discussion, he stopped to listen.

The first girl said, "Of all tastes, I think the taste of meat is the best in the world."

The second girl said, "I do not agree with you. There is nothing so good as the taste of wine."

"No, no," cried the third girl, "you are both mistaken, for of all tastes, the sweetest is the taste of love."

"Meat and wine and love are all doubtless sweet," remarked the fourth girl, "but in my opinion, nothing can equal the taste of telling lies."

The girls then separated, and went to their homes. The king, who had listened to their remarks with lively interest and much wonder, took note of the houses into which the girls went. Having marked each of the doors with chalk, he returned to his palace.

The next morning he called his vizier* and said to him, "Send to the narrow street and bring before me the owners of the four

*vizier: a minister or councillor of state

65

houses which have a round mark in chalk upon their doors."

The vizier went at once in person and brought to court the four men who lived in the houses. Then the king said, "Do you four men have four daughters?"

"We do," they answered.

"Bring the girls before me," said the king.

But the men objected, saying, "It would be very wrong that our daughters should approach the palace of the king."

The king answered, "If the girls are your daughters, they are mine too. In addition, you can bring them privately." So the king sent four separate curtained litters and the four girls were brought to the palace and conducted into a large reception room. Then the king summoned them one by one to his presence. To the first girl he said, "Daughter, what were you talking about last night when you sat with your companions under the tree?"

"I was not saying anything against you, my king," she answered.

"I do not mean that," said the king, "but I wish to know what you were saying."

"I merely said that the taste of meat was the most pleasant taste," she said.

"Whose daughter are you?" inquired the king.

"I am the daughter of a Bhabra," she answered.

"But," the king said, "if you are one of the Bhabra tribe, who never touch meat, what do you know of the taste of it? They are so strict that when they drink water, they put a cloth over the mouth of the vessel lest they should swallow even an insect."

Then the girl said, "Yes, that is quite true, but from my own observation, I think meat must be exceedingly pleasant to the palate. Near our house there is a butcher's shop, and I often notice that when people buy meat, none of it is wasted or thrown away. Therefore it must be precious. I also notice that when people have eaten the flesh, the very bones are greedily seized upon by the dogs, nor do they leave them until they have picked them clean. And even after that, the crows come and carry them off, and when the crows have done with them, the very ants assemble together and swarm over them. Those are the reasons which prove that the taste of meat must be exceedingly pleasant."

The king, hearing her argument, was pleased and said, "Yes, daughter, meat is very pleasant as food. Everyone likes it." And he sent her away with a handsome present.

The second girl was then introduced and the king likewise inquired of her, "What were you talking about last night under the tree?"

"I said nothing about you, my king," she answered.

"That is true, but what did you say?" the king asked.

"I said that there was no taste like the taste of wine."

"But whose daughter are you?" continued the king.

"I am the daughter of a priest," she said.

"That is a good joke," the king smiled. "Priests hate the very name of wine. Then, what do you know of the taste of it?"

Then the girl said, "It is true I never touch wine, but I can easily understand how pleasant it is. I learn my lessons on the top of my father's house. Below are the wine shops. One day I saw two men nicely dressed, who came with their servants to buy wine at those shops and there they sat and drank. After a time, they got up and went away, but they staggered about from side to side, and I thought to myself, 'Here are these fellows rolling about, knocking themselves against the wall on this side, and falling against the wall on that. Surely they will never drink wine again!' However, I was mistaken, for the next day they came again and did the very same thing, and I considered, 'Wine must be very delicious to the taste, or else these persons would never have returned for more of it.'"

Then the king said, "Yes, daughter, you are right. The taste of wine is very pleasant." And giving her a handsome present, he sent her home.

When the third girl entered the room, the king asked her in like manner, "Daughter, what were you talking about last night under the tree?"

"O king," she answered, "I said nothing about you."

"Quite so," said the king, "but tell me what it was you were saying."

"I was saying that there is no taste in the world so sweet as the taste of lovemaking," she replied.

"But," said the king, "you are a very young girl, what can you know about lovemaking? Whose daughter are you?"

"I am the daughter of a bard," she answered. "It is true I am very young, but somehow I guess that lovemaking must be pleasant. My mother suffered so much when my little brother was born that she never expected to live. Yet, after a little time, she went back to her old ways and welcomed her lovers just the same as before. That is the reason I think that lovemaking must be so pleasant."

"What you say," observed the king, "cannot be justly denied." And he gave her a present equal in value to those of her friends and sent her away.

When the fourth girl was introduced, the king put the same question to her. "Tell me what you and your companions talked about under the tree last night."

"It was not about the king," she answered.

"Nevertheless, what was it you said?" he asked.

"I said that those who tell lies, must tell them because they find the practice agreeable," she replied.

"Whose daughter are you?" inquired the king.

"I am the daughter of a farmer," answered the girl.

"And what made you think there was pleasure in telling lies?" asked the king.

The girl answered saucily, "Oh, you yourself will tell lies someday!"

"How?" said the king. "What can you mean?"

The girl answered, "If you will give me two lacs* of rupees and six months to consider, I will promise to prove my words."

So the king gave the girl the sum of money she asked for and agreed to her conditions, sending her away with a present similar to those of the others.

*lac: a hundred thousand

After six months, he called her to his presence again and reminded her of her promise. Now, in the interval, the girl had built a fine palace far away in the forest, upon which she had expended the wealth which the king had given to her. It was beautifully adorned with carvings and paintings and furnished with silk and satin. So she now said to the king, "Come with me and you shall see God." Taking with him two of his ministers, the king set out, and by the evening they all arrived at the palace.

"This palace is the abode of God," said the girl. "But He will reveal Himself only to one person at a time, and He will not reveal Himself even to him unless he was born in lawful wedlock. Therefore, while the rest remain without, let each of you enter in order."

"Be it so," said the king. "But let my ministers precede me. I shall go in last."

So the first minister passed through the door and at once found himself in a noble room. As he looked around, he said to himself, "Who knows whether I shall be permitted to see God or not? I may be a bastard. And yet this place, so spacious and so beautiful, is a fitting dwelling place even for the Deity." With all his looking and straining, however, he quite failed to see God anywhere. Then he said to himself, "If I now go out and declare that I have not seen God, the king and the other minister will throw it in my teeth that I am illegitimate. I have only one course open, therefore, which is to say that I have seen Him."

So he went out, and when the king asked, "Have you seen God?" the minister answered at once, "Of course I have seen God."

"But have you really seen Him?" continued the king.

"Really and truly," answered the minister.

"And what did He say to you?" inquired the king further.

"God commanded me not to divulge His words," the minister readily answered.

Then the king said to the other minister, "Now you go in."

The second minister lost no time in obeying his master's order, thinking in his heart as he crossed the threshold, "I wonder if I am illegitimate." Finding himself in the midst of the magnificent chamber, he gazed about him on all sides, but failed to see God. Then he said to himself, "It is very possible I am illegitimate, for I can see no God. But it would be a lasting disgrace that I should admit it. I had better make out that I also have seen God."

Accordingly, he returned to the king, who said to him, "Well, have you seen God?" Then the minister asserted that he had not only seen Him but had spoken with Him too.

It was now the turn of the king, and he entered the room confident that he would be similarly favored. But he gazed around in dismay, perceiving no sign of anything which could even represent the Almighty. Then he began to think to himself, "This God, wherever He is, has been seen by both my ministers, and it cannot be denied, therefore, that their birthright is clear. Is it possible that I, the king, am a bastard, seeing that no God appears to me? The very thought of this will cause confusion. Necessity compels me to say that I have seen Him too."

Having formed this resolution, the king stepped out and joined the rest of his party.

"And now, O king," asked the cunning girl, "have you also seen God?"

"Yes," he answered with assurance, "I have seen God."

"Really?" she asked again.

"Certainly," asserted the king.

Three times, the girl asked the same question, and three times the king lied without blushing. Then the girl said, "O king, have you no conscience? How could you possibly see God, seeing that God is a spirit?"

Hearing this reproof, the king recalled the girl saying that one day he, too, would lie. With a laugh, he confessed that he had not seen God at all. The two ministers, beginning to feel alarmed, confessed the truth as well. Then the girl said, "O king, we poor people may tell lies occasionally to save our lives, but what had you to fear? Telling lies, therefore, has its own attractions for many people, and to them at least, the taste of lying is sweet."

Far from being offended at the trick which the girl had played on him, the king was so struck with her ingenuity and assurance that he married her. In a short time, she became his confidential adviser in all his affairs, public as well as private. Thus the simple girl came to great honor and renown, and so much did she grow in wisdom that her fame spread through many lands.

The Story of the Demon Who Ate People, and the Child

MASAI PEOPLE, KENYA AND TANZANIA[46]

There was once upon a time a demon who was greatly dreaded by the inhabitants of the country in which he lived owing to his principal food being human beings.

On one occasion he devoured a large number of people and cattle—so many, in fact, that he thought he had exterminated the whole tribe. One woman, however, succeeded in hiding herself with her child in a pit, and after the demon had taken his departure, she returned to the kraal* and collected together all the food that had been left there.

The child was brought up in the pit, and when he was old enough to understand, his mother told him the story of the demon. For some time he did not venture away from the hiding place, but after a while he made a bow and some arrows, and went for a walk. He shot a small bird, which he took back with him to the pit, and asked his mother if that was the demon. On being told that it was not, he went out again and shot another bird, and after that a Thomson's gazelle. He continued his search for a long time, and shot all kinds of things in the hope of killing the demon, but when he showed them to his mother, he found that he had not been successful.

The woman repeatedly urged her son not to leave the pit as they were the sole survivors of the tribe, but the boy was determined if possible to shoot the demon. One day he searched for a number of arrows and spears which he took to the top of a tree.

*kraal: village

72

He then climbed with his mother into the tree and lit a fire in the branches to attract the demon's attention. When the demon saw the smoke, he was greatly surprised, as he thought he had eaten all the inhabitants of the country. Having procured some axes, he went to the spot, and called out to the child and his mother to descend. As they refused to comply with his order, he commenced to cut down the tree. The boy shot him twice with his arrows, but the demon only thought he was being bitten by gadflies. As the arrows continued to hit him, however, he had to give up his intention of cutting down the tree, and shortly afterwards he lay down to die.

When he felt that his end was approaching, he said to the child, "When I am dead, cut off my little finger, and your cattle will be restored to you. Then, cut off my thumb, and you will get back your people. After that cut open my face, and one man will come out."

Having said this, he died, and the boy descended from the tree and cut off his fingers and thumb, from the stumps of which all the people and cattle that had been eaten emerged. The face was then cut open, and one man appeared.

The people returned with their cattle to their former kraals, and held a consultation at which it was decided to appoint the boy chief.

After some time had elapsed, the man who had been taken from the devil's face asked the chief to put him back again. The others argued with him, and told him that he was much better off now that he had been liberated, but their arguments availed nothing, and the chief, seeing that the man would take no refusal, asked to be given a month in which to consider the matter.

Knowing that the discontented man was very fond of tobacco, the chief planted some, and when it ripened, he went to watch it. As he expected, the man saw the tobacco, and picked a leaf. The chief called out to him to return it to the plant, but as the thief was unable to do this, he was taken to the kraal, where a meeting was held. Matters having been explained to those present, the thief was again called upon to replace the leaf. When he admitted his inability to do as he was required, the chief remarked that he too was unable to put him back in the demon's face.

Everybody appreciated the wisdom of the judgment, and they all lived happily together ever afterwards, respecting their chief and loving one another.

De White Man's Prayer

AFRICAN-AMERICAN⁴⁷

Well, it come uh famine an' all de crops wuz dried up an' Brother John had prayed last year for rain an' it rained; so they all 'sembled* at de church an' called on John tuh† pray, an' he got down an' prayed:

"Lord, first thing, I want you tuh understand that dis ain't no nigger talking tuh you. This is uh white man talking tuh you now an' I want you tuh *hear* me. I don't worry an' bother you all de time like dese niggers, an' when I do ast‡ uh favor I want it *granted*. Now, Lord, I want some rain. Our crops is all burnin' up, an' I want you tuh send rain. I don't mean fuh§ you to come in uh hell of uh storm lak you done las' year. You kicked up as much racket as niggers at uh barbecue. I mean fuh you tuh come quiet an' easy. Now, another blessing I want tuh ast of you, Lord. Don't let dese niggers be as sassy as they have in the past. Keep 'em in their places, Lord. Amen."

*'sembled: assembled
†tuh: to
‡ast: ask
§fuh: for

When Common Sense Makes No Sense

I stood on a street in Germany, overwhelmed by my inability to comprehend the babble around me, overwhelmed by my five hours in intensive German class and my clumsy attempts to learn, overwhelmed by my helplessness in the face of this new world, new language, new rules. A trolley rumbled past. "Kann ich Ihnen helfen?" *An unknown woman with a concerned face stared at me as if she'd spoken before. I blinked. Then I realized I was standing still and tears were streaming down my face.* "Nein danke," *I answered. I wiped my cheeks and strode toward the corner.*

Though I'd just tried for five straight hours for five days a week for three months, I still didn't understand this new world. Nor could I make myself understood. I was in a world where no matter how hard I studied, I could not say what I thought or felt. I couldn't mutter wisecracks with the secret smile that makes a friend wake up, her eyes take on a focus, then bubble over as the absurdity creeps in. I'd lost those college rumblings of philosophy—staying up until dawn discussing what it would be like to communicate with dolphins or why we think nothing is more basic than something. I'd lost the sound, the rhythm, the form of my ideas.[48] They'd been replaced by a stamp of my foot and a frustrated frown. I was like the African-American who needed to offer up a white man's prayer for it to be heard by a white god, but I didn't know how.[49]

When I lived in Japan, I learned quickly that there is a strict set of rules in gift-giving. If a neighbor gives you six carnations and six roses on your birthday, you'd better give her six carnations and six roses on her birthday—same colors, just to be safe. About a year into my stay, I was mired in a morass of gift-accepting-and-giving. I brought up my quandary in my daily Japanese class. At first, the teacher was the picture of patience. Gently and at length she began to explain the concept of giri, * why people have to give gifts and what it means to accept a gift and how sometimes you don't repay a gift for a long time, so you can owe even more to the person and honor them with an even greater gift. The more she explained, the more I frowned. When she paused and looked at me expectantly, I lurched into details. "Right now, in my situation, today, how many people do I have to give presents to? What kind of presents should I give to whom? What should I do if I can't afford the right kind of present? Do I really, really have to give presents? What did I do to start this whole mess in the first place?"*

Patiently she waited as my questions tumbled out. Then she began her explanation all over again. Still gently and at length she lectured on the societal context of giri. *I folded my arms over my chest and slouched further and further down in my seat with irritation apparent on my face. The harder she tried to explain, the more frustrated I became. Finally, when the class began to snicker, the teacher raised her very soft voice and said, "Well, it's just common sense!"*

There was a shift in my perspective. I was in a world where common sense made no sense at all. I was in a world where no matter how hard I studied, I just couldn't understand—a world where a snail is fast.[50] My assumptions were a problem. My assumptions weren't necessarily wrong or right, but somehow the answers I wanted to get or give seemed like nonsequiturs. The world wasn't asking the appropriate questions. I'd taken up the fairy tale quest and had gone out into the world, and now my worldview had to adapt. I was the discontented Masai man who is forced to realize that the tobacco leaf cannot be returned to the plant.[51] Nullified were many things I had previously and blithely incorporated into my worldview—things as common as common sense, things as easy as "Hello, my name is . . . ," things as obvious as a friend or an enemy.

---

*giri: Literally it means duty, but it might be better described in English as a way of organizing society that involves a specific tally of anything received and strict rules for repayment.

The Ghost of Farnell

SCOTLAND [52]

Near Brechin, in Angus, there is a small village called Farnell. This village, some three miles from Brechin, has now a bridge over a turbulent stream. In former times it had only a ford. This ford some two centuries ago was haunted by a ghost. He was, so my informer had it, murdered at the ford, both he and his horse. So that it was for his pleasure, or for revenge or otherwise, that he haunted the ford, and some miles around it.

He seemed to take pleasure in giving frights, rather than to cause harm. Some distance from the ford there was a cottage, now a ruin. It was once the home of a young girl, her parents, and her sister. Her sister was married, but her husband was not at home. The night was a stormy one, rain and wind were very cold, for it was early winter. The parents were both old, the father an invalid, and the mother not much better. They had a horse, but it too was old and lame. The storm grew worse, and the sister, who was going to have a child, was near her time. Brechin was a long way off, the ford was high, and the chances of the younger sister bringing help from Brechin in time were, in normal circumstances, difficult. This night, prepared as she was for the road, she did not expect to find her sister alive on her return. Her parents tried to stop her, but she argued. Anyway, she said, she might meet a neighbour, or a traveler.

She was at the door, the wind howling, and the rain battering, when a solitary horseman was seen. They all shouted to him and he looked round.

"Would you be going to Brechin?" they asked.

"No," came the reply. "But ye must be sore in need to travel this night; I can go that way."

They told him their plight. He said nothing, but just nodded his head.

"On you get to the back of my horse," said he to the younger sister. "Are you afraid?" said he.

"I am," said she. "Firstly for my sister, for we love each other, and then for the ghost, for I think I would die if I met him this night."

"Well, to the first," said he, "your sister will be well; the doctor has a change of horse, so you need not fear for that this night. As to the second, well, there are ghosts and ghosts, and that ghost ye will not meet this night!"

On they galloped over the turbulent stream, as if it was not tumbling below them, and soon they came near Brechin. The journey seemed to take no time, she said afterwards. They came to the doctor's house, but the horseman would not stop near the lighted window.

"Well, I will go now. Your sister will be fine," he said.

"Thank you, sir," she said, for now he seemed more than just a traveler. "I was real feared I would meet the ghost."

"There was no fear for that," came the reply, "I myself am the Ghost of Farnell!"

Horse and man vanished on the spot.

The Fox and Her Children and Nekhailo the Loafer

UKRAINE[53]

There was once a man by the name of Nekhailo to whom one of his friends left a small vineyard.

Spring came, and Nekhailo went to the vineyard to see what needed to be done there.

"Tomorrow I'll bring a hoe and weed the grass," said he.

And off he went.

Now, hiding in the grass in the vineyard, was a whole family of young foxes. They heard what Nekhailo had said and were very frightened.

The mother fox came home, and they said to her, "There was a man here, Mother, who said he would come tomorrow and weed the grass. Let us run away!"

"Stay where you are and don't be afraid," said the mother fox. "That was Nekhailo who owns this vineyard. I know him. He won't come soon."

A long time passed before Nekhailo came to the vineyard again. He had a hoe with him and was much surprised to see how tall the grass had grown.

He scratched the back of his neck and said, "Ekh, but I cannot do anything here with a hoe. I think I'll go home and fetch a scythe."

And off he went.

The young foxes heard him and were very frightened. "Let us run away, Mother!" they cried. "That same man was here again and he went off to fetch a scythe. He'll come tomorrow and kill us all!"

"Play your games and don't be afraid!" said the mother fox.

Three months and more passed, and Nekhailo came to the vine-yard with a scythe. He tried to cut down the grass, but could not, so thick had it grown. So then he thought for a moment and said, "I think I'll go fetch some matches and set fire to the grass."

"Come, children, now we'd better run away!" said the mother fox. "For burning the grass is easy, so Nekhailo is sure to do it!"

The Lion Who Drowned
in a Well

UKRAINE[54]

L ong, long ago, there lived in the thick of the forest a Lion so huge and fearful that he had only to let out a roar for all the other animals to start trembling in fright like aspen leaves. And whenever he was out hunting he would tear to pieces everyone he came across and scatter them all around him so that a herd of wild pigs even was not safe from him. Few could run away from the Lion, but no matter how many animals he killed he would eat no more than one.

The animals lived in constant fear for their lives. One day, feeling that such a state of affairs could not be allowed to go on, they got together in order to decide what to do.

The Bear was the first to speak.

"Listen to me, friends!" he said. "The Lion kills no fewer than ten of us daily, and sometimes as many as twenty, but he eats up no more than one or two, at most, which means that nearly all of us die in vain. I suggest that we reason with him and make him change his ways."

"Just you try and do that!" the Wolf burst in. "He'll never listen to us. What's more, he'll kill those we send to him."

"I disagree!" the Bear declared. "The question is whom we are to send."

"Why don't you go, Bear?" the Wolf said. "You are the biggest and strongest of us."

"My being strong isn't going to save me from the Lion's claws," the Bear returned. "Better if you go, Wolf, you are much quicker than I."

"That isn't going to save me if the Lion runs after me. We must think of a better way of doing this."

The Deer stepped forward and said, "The only thing I can think of is to be very polite with the Lion and not anger him by word or deed."

"Well, seeing that you are so wise, what's stopping you from speaking to him yourself, Deer?" his friends asked.

"Oh, no, I couldn't! I only wanted to say that the Lion isn't one of us, and talking to him won't be easy."

"True. But then who is to go?"

"Why not the Fox? She is sly and ought to be able to get on the good side of the Lion."

"A good idea! The Fox can do it if anyone can."

They called the Fox, and the Bear said to her, "We have decided that you must go and talk to the Lion, Foxy. You know only too well how many of us he has killed!"

"Yes, but that doesn't mean I want to talk to him any more than the rest of you do. Why can't we cast lots and let chance decide which of us is to do it?"

"No, Foxy, that won't do at all," the Bear said. "What if the lot falls to someone who is too timid or silly to know what to say? Instead of getting the Lion to soften towards us he might anger him even more! We have definitely decided to send you, and go you shall. We'll kill you if you don't!"

Now, this made the Fox quite unhappy, for whether she went and talked to the Lion or not seemed equally dangerous. So she thought and she thought and then she said, "Oh, very well, I'll go if I must!"

And off she set. She feared the Lion far too much to come near him, and as she wandered around the forest kept thinking how to trick him and avoid being killed by him.

She had not gone far before she stumbled upon a well. "I had far rather drown myself in the well," said she to herself, "than give myself up alive to that horrid old Lion and be torn to pieces!"

She walked all around the well, sniffed and looked down into it, and oh how surprised she was to see a Fox like herself gazing up at her from the water! She nodded her head and stuck out her tongue, and the other Fox did the same.

"I do believe that is my reflection in the water I see there!" she cried. "I think I know now how to fool the Lion."

And off she made straight for the Lion's den. Night was drawing on, but she was far more cheerful now and walked quickly.

The Lion's thunderous roars soon reached her ear, and there he was before her. Frightened despite herself, she said with a bow, "Pray bid me speak, Your Lordship, that I may explain what has brought me here. It was like this, Your Lordship. The animals of this forest knew it was your birthday and sent me and two rabbits early this morning to wish you many happy returns of the day. But we had not gone far when we met a beast who looked very much like you. He stopped us and asked where we were going, and when I told him we were on our way to wish you a happy birthday, he became very angry. He said that it was he who was lord of the forest and not you, that all who lived here had to bow to his will and that he would not let us go any farther. 'But,' said I, 'the Lion might kill us for this! It's his birthday, and he's expecting us.' And can you imagine, Your Lordship, he said, 'What's it to me that it's his birthday! I'll eat him up, that's what I'll do!' It took me half the day to persuade him to let me go——me alone, the rabbits were forced to stay with him."

Now, this made the Lion so angry that he forgot how hungry he was. "Where does that beast live?" he roared.

"Quite near here. In a stone palace."

The Lion jumped up in a rage and gave such a roar that it echoed over the whole forest. It was as if another Lion were roaring at the other end of it.

"Do you hear him roar, Your Lordship? He is teasing you," the Fox said.

The Lion became angrier than ever. "I'll tear the wretch to pieces!" he roared. "How dare he oppose me? This forest is mine. Come, take me to him at once!"

The Fox led the Lion to the well.

They came within sight of it, and the Lion asked the Fox to show him where his enemy was hiding.

"He is in that stone palace over there," said the Fox, pointing at the well. "But I don't want to come any closer, I'm afraid he might eat me up. You will see him if you bend down over the well."

The Lion came up to the well, he bent over it, and what did he see there but another Lion looking up at him! He gnashed his teeth, and the other Lion gnashed his. So then he let out a great roar and leapt down into the well. There was a splash, and he found himself in the water! And the well being wide and its stone walls very smooth, he could not climb out of it and drowned.

The Fox, who had witnessed it all, ran off at once to tell the other animals about it. She beamed as she neared them, and they knew it was glad tidings she was bringing them.

"Have you seen the Lion or haven't you?" they asked her.

"I have, I have! But you can forget all about him now, for he is dead. And you know why? Because I tricked him."

"You tricked him? How did you do that?"

The Fox told them all about everything, and when they had heard her out they began dancing about in joy. Neither tongue can tell nor pen can write how happy they were!

The Tiger, the Brahman, and the Jackal

PUNJAB, INDIA[55]

O nce upon a time a tiger was caught in a trap. He tried in vain to get out through the bars, and rolled and bit with rage and grief when he failed.

By chance a poor Brahman came by. "Let me out of this cage, O pious one!" cried the tiger.

"Nay, my friend," replied the Brahman mildly. "You would probably eat me if I did."

"Not at all!" swore the tiger with many oaths. "On the contrary, I should be forever grateful, and serve you as a slave!"

Now when the tiger sobbed and sighed and wept and swore, the pious Brahman's heart softened, and at last he consented to open the door of the cage. Out popped the tiger, and, seizing the poor man, cried, "What a fool you are! What is to prevent my eating you now, for after being cooped up so long I am just terribly hungry!"

In vain the Brahman pleaded for his life; the most he could gain was a promise to abide by the decision of the first three things he chose to question as to the justice of the tiger's action.

So the Brahman first asked a pipal* tree what it thought of the matter, but the pipal tree replied coldly, "What have you to complain about? Don't I give shade and shelter to everyone who passes by, and don't they in return tear down my branches to feed their cattle? Don't whimper—be a man!"

Then the Brahman, sad at heart, went farther afield till he saw a

*pipal: fig

buffalo turning a well wheel, but he fared no better from it, for it answered, "You are a fool to expect gratitude! Look at me! While I gave milk they fed me on cottonseed and oil cake, but now I am dry they yoke me here, and give me refuse as fodder!"

The Brahman, still more sad, asked the road to give him its opinion.

"My dear sir," said the road, "how foolish you are to expect anything else! Here am I, useful to everybody, yet all, rich and poor, great and small, trample on me as they go past, giving me nothing but the ashes of their pipes and the husks of their grain!"

On this the Brahman turned back sorrowfully, and on the way he met a jackal, who called out, "Why, what's the matter, Mr. Brahman? You look as miserable as a fish out of water!"

Then the Brahman told him all that had occurred. "How very confusing!" said the jackal when the recital was ended. "Would you mind telling me over again, for everything seems so mixed up!"

The Brahman told it all over again, but the jackal shook his head in a distracted sort of way, and still could not understand.

"It's very odd," said he sadly, "but it all seems to go in at one ear and out at the other! I will go to the place where it all happened, and then perhaps I shall be able to give a judgment."

So they returned to the cage, by which the tiger was waiting for the Brahman, and sharpening his teeth and claws.

"You've been away a long time!" growled the savage beast. "But now let us begin our dinner."

"Our dinner!" thought the wretched Brahman, as his knees knocked together with fright. "What a remarkably delicate way of putting it."

"Give me five minutes, my lord," he pleaded, "in order that I may explain matters to the jackal here, who is somewhat slow in his wits."

The tiger consented, and the Brahman began the whole story over again, not missing a single detail, and spinning as long a yarn as possible.

"Oh, my poor brain! Oh, my poor brain!" cried the jackal,

wringing his paws. "Let me see! How did it all begin? You were in the cage, and the tiger came walking by—"

"Pooh!" interrupted the tiger. "What a fool you are! *I* was in the cage."

"Of course!" cried the jackal, pretending to tremble with fright. "Yes! I was in the cage—no, I wasn't—dear! dear! Where are my wits? Let me see—the tiger was in the Brahman, and the cage came walking by—no, that's not it either! Well, don't mind me, but begin your dinner, for I shall never understand!"

"Yes, you shall!" returned the tiger, in a rage at the jackal's stupidity. "I'll *make* you understand! Look here—I am the tiger—"

"Yes, my lord!"

"And that is the Brahman—"

"Yes, my lord!"

"And that is the cage—"

"Yes, my lord!"

"And I was in the cage—do you understand?"

"Yes—no—Please, my lord—"

"Well?" cried the tiger impatiently.

"Please, my lord!—How did you get in?"

"How!—Why, in the usual way, of course!"

"Oh, dear me!—My head is beginning to whirl again! Please don't be angry, my lord, but what is the usual way?"

At this the tiger lost patience and, jumping into the cage, cried, "This way! Now do you understand how it was?"

"Perfectly!" grinned the jackal as he dexterously shut the door, "and if you will permit me to say so, I think matters will remain as they were!"

Friend or Foe?

I never have to worry about myself doing the wrong thing in fairy tales. I can do no wrong, or if I do, it won't matter. I'm the heroine or the hero. I love folktales because I recognize myself immediately and I know I'll be fine in the end. "Once upon a time there was a girl . . ."—that's me. "And they lived happily ever after"—absolutely. Sandwiched between the beginning and the happy ending are all kinds of twists and turns, dangers and defeats, but they are all played out in the safety of a foregone conclusion. With the regularity of an atomic clock, folktale heroines and heroes overcome the enemy.[56] Since the heroes in folktales are well defined, I expected the anti-heroes to be simplistic. However, folktales explore with great nuance the idea of the enemy. I may have been seated at a virtual campfire, but the folktales were real. "Folktales offer a way of deepening reality, not escaping from it."[57]

Because she knows the vineyard owner so well, the mother fox doesn't even have to be afraid. She knows exactly when to disregard his threats and when to run away.[58] A pious Brahman gets into trouble because he acts on what he wants to believe, rather than recognizing how a hungry tiger will actually behave.[59] Good and evil are not the point of the folktale. Often a predetermined hero wins by deceit, like the old lady in " 'What Are You the Most Scared Of?' "[60] Sometimes a princess earns her prince by slamming a hapless frog against the wall.[61] Sometimes the fairies are generous and sometimes they take you away forever. "Think!" the folktales said, and presented me with a malicious ghost who saved my sister's life.[62] "Think!" the folktales said, and told me about Nekhailo, who resorted to a simple but destructive solution. "Think about these things," the folktales cautioned, "because the ending of your story is not a foregone conclusion. You're in the middle of your tale."

Once I traveled to Egypt. It was everything I'd dreamt of and more. I had wandered amid the dust-covered treasures of the Cairo Museum. I had visited Hatshepsut's temple and I had snuck like a tomb robber over the cliffs and down into the Valley of the Kings. I had opened the shutters of my hotel room window and gazed across the Nile at sunrise to the desert beyond and the graceful lines of Hatshepsut's temple in the distance. In the foreground, the poor of modern Egypt were crowded in dilapidated ferryboats as they crossed to the east bank of the Nile. There they would spend the day serving tourists, selling to tourists, and begging from tourists like myself. There was a child, maybe three years old; flies crawled around her eyes and snotty nose. She didn't bother to brush them away. Her dress was torn and dirty. She had no shoes. She raised her dark black eyes and her smudged small hands to me, "Baksheesh,"* she lisped.

For three days we'd walked past a pile of rags with a distorted face, hunched in the shadow of a mosque close to the market in Luxor. I'd spent those passing moments trying not to look. On our last day, my husband, Charley, said, "I think we should give that guy something. Here, give him this." Into my hands Charley shoved a worn, torn, and dirty bill which was worth about five cents.

"You do it," I said,

"No, you have to do it."

"Why?"

"I gave money to a beggar like this in Alexandria and it changes things. Go ahead. Do it. It'll change the way you think."

I took the bill reluctantly and muttered, "Don't you have a coin?"

I inched closer while Charley waited at the curb. My world closed down, it focused on this pitiful, deformed human being. He sat wrapped in a filthy galabia, his feet pulled close up to him. A knob the size of my fist protruded from his face above his right eye and distorted the shape of his face and head. "Oh God. Oh God!" I moaned to myself. I leaned down. Holding one edge of the bill, I laid it where his galabia draped between his knees. At

*Baksheesh: money, a tip

that moment a gust of wind blew around the corner and blew the bill away.
I scurried to catch the money. Only now did the beggar realize that I was
there. He twisted his head over and up, lifting his hunched shoulder with
difficulty, trying to see me. One eyeball was missing. The other was white
and almost vacant, filled with cataracts, or leprosy. I shuddered and felt
puke rising from the fear and revulsion in my gut. Every instinct I had
screamed at me to run away, but I had to give the money to him now. He'd
seen me.

I inched toward him sideways like a crab. I stretched out my arm to keep as
much distance as possible between myself and this misshapen man. As I laid
the bill down, he stabbed at it with the stub that was his hand. His finger-
nails grew out of his knuckles. His hand had no fingers. I snatched my hand
back and narrowly avoided touching his clawlike appendage as he pinned the
bill to his knee. Backing away in horror, I began to sob uncontrollably. I
buried my head in Charley's chest as he led me around the corner.

"Charley, why did we only give him that much? Couldn't we have given
him more?"

"How much? Ten dollars?"

"Yes."

"All the money in your purse?"

"Yes!"

"All the money in our hotel room? All our money?"

"I don't know. I don't know."

Folktales never tire of this scene, they never tire of the issue of poverty
and hunger. There is an old woman sitting by the side of the road, do I
share my crust of bread or should I beware? Each tale represents one version
and one possible solution. As one story led to another around my virtual
campfire, I realized that I'd plunged into the shadows. I'd met the old woman
by the side of the road, and sharing or not sharing the bread was no longer
so simple. The folktales seemed to taunt me: What do you know for sure? Do
you know your enemies? Do you know your friends? Do you even know
yourself?

The Bee and the Ásya

HOPI PEOPLE, NORTH AMERICA⁶³

At Potátukaovi lived the Bee, and at Móngwupcovi lived the Ásya, a species of bird. They were both women and both had children. They were great friends with each other. The Ásya one time was walking around in the peach orchard north of her house and was eating peaches, which she relished very much. One time she was visiting her friend, the Bee, and the latter fed her honey, of which she ate. After she was through eating they conversed together all day. In the evening the Ásya returned to her house, inviting her friend, however, to come and visit her too in the morning, which the Bee promised to do. The next morning the Bee went over to her friend's house, but at that time the Bees had no wings. They walked like the hohóyawuu,* so that she did not get there very quickly.

The Ásya was living in an opening in a rock, which the Bee entered. The Ásya gave her a seat and told her to be seated, and then fed her peaches, which the Bee ate. "Do you like these peaches?" the Bee asked.

"Yes," she said, "I always eat them. I like them very much; I live on them."

"But," the Bee said, "what do you think, shall I make some medicine for the peaches? They are not good," because the peaches at that time were not sweet as they are now; they were sour.

"Very good," the Ásya replied, "make some medicine, then, and

---

*hohóyawuu: stinkbug

I shall have something that tastes good." Hereupon the Bee put some honey on the peaches, and ever since the peaches have been sweet and taste better. The Ásya was very happy and said to the Bee, "I am glad, and I shall give you something too, because you have made my peaches better."

Hereupon she pulled out some of her feathers, made some wings, and attached them to the Bee, saying to her, "Now fly."

But the Bee said, "I do not know how it is done."

"You just extend your front legs."

The Bee did so and moved them, whereupon she could fly and flew away. Ever since that time the Bees can fly.

The Broken Friendship

Once upon a time there was a Raja* and his Dewan† and they
each had one son, and the two boys were great friends,
and when they grew old enough, they took to hunting, and when
they became young men, they were so devoted to the sport that
they spent their whole time in pursuit of game; they followed every
animal they could find until they killed it, and they shot every bird
in the town.

Their parents were much distressed at this, for they thought that
if their boys spent all their time together hunting they would grow
up unruly and ignorant; so they made up their minds that they must
separate the young men so that they would not be tempted to
spend so much time in sport, but would be able to learn something useful; they scolded the youths and told them to give up their
friendship and their hunting, but this had no effect. Then the Raja
told the villagers that he would reward anyone who would break
up the friendship, and the villagers tried their best but effected
nothing.

There was, however, an old woman in the village who one day
said, "If the Raja gave me ten rupees, I would soon put a stop to
their friendship."

This came to the ears of the Raja and he exclaimed, "What is
ten rupees to me! Bring the old woman to me and I will give her

*Raja: Indian prince or king
†Dewan: prime minister of an Indian state

94

ten rupees, if she can put an end to this friendship." So the old
woman was brought trembling before the Raja, and on being ques-
tioned undertook to break up the friendship if she were properly
rewarded; and when this was promised she asked for two men to
be given to her and she took them to her house and there she made
them sling a bed on a pole, such as is used for carrying a man on a
journey, and she hung curtains all round it and drew them close,
and inside, on an old winnowing fan,* they put some rotten manure
from a dunghill.

Then she made the two men take up the bed and she fetched a
drum and she paraded all through the bazaar beating the drum with
the bed following behind her. She told the two carriers not to
answer any questions as to what was in the bed. Thus they passed
out of the town and went in the direction in which the two young
men had gone hunting. When they heard the sound of the drum and
saw the two men carrying the bed, they ran up to see what it was
and told the carriers to put it down that they might look inside; so
the bed was put on the ground and the Raja's son peeped inside the
curtain, but as he caught the smell he jumped back, and the Dewan's
son asked what was the matter and he said, "It stinks. It is dung."
The Dewan's son would not believe him and also looked to con-
vince himself. Then they both asked what the meaning of this was.
The old woman said that she would explain the meaning of it, but
only to one of them, and the one who had heard could tell the other.

So she made the carriers take away the bed and she called the
Raja's son aside, saying, "Come, I will tell you what it means." Then
she put her arms around the neck of the Raja's son and put her lips
to his ear and pretended to whisper to him, but really, she said
nothing. Then she let him go and followed the carriers. The
Dewan's son at once ran to his friend and asked what the old
woman had told him. The Raja's son answered, "She told me nothing at all, she only pretended to whisper."

The Dewan's son would not believe this and pressed him to tell,

---

*winnowing fan: a device used to winnow, to separate the grain from the
chaff

saying, "We have been friends for so long and have had no secrets from each other, why won't you tell me this? If you refuse to tell me there is an end of our friendship! But the Raja's son persisted that he had been told nothing and proposed that they should go and ask the old woman if it were not so; but the Dewan's son said that that was no good because the old woman and the Raja's son had plainly made a plot to keep him in the dark. The quarrel grew hotter and hotter till at last they parted in anger and each went to his own home, and from that time their friendship was broken off.

And being separated, they gave up hunting and took to useful pursuits. Thus the old woman earned her reward from the Raja.

The Lady and the Unjust Judge

TURKEY[65]

Now it came to pass that a certain *chöpdji*, or dust collector, had, in the course of five years of labor, amassed the sum of five hundred piasters. He was afraid to keep this money by him, so, hearing the *cadi** of Stamboul highly and reverently spoken of, he decided to entrust his hard-earned savings to the judge's keeping.

Going to the *cadi*, he said, "O learned and righteous man, for five long years have I labored, carrying the dregs and dross of rich and poor alike, and I have saved a sum of five hundred piasters. With the help of Allah, in another two years I shall have saved a further sum of at least one hundred piasters, when, Inshallah!† I shall return to my country and clasp my wife and children in my arms again. In the meantime you will grant a boon to your slave if you will consent to keep this money for me until the time for my departure has come."

The *cadi* replied, "Thou hast done well, my son. I swear on penalty of having to divorce my wife that this money will be kept faithfully and returned unto thee when required."

The poor *chöpdji* departed, well satisfied. But after a very short time he learned that several of his friends were about to return to their *mamleket*‡ and he decided to join them, thinking that his five hundred piasters were ample for the time being. "Besides," said he, "who knows what may or may not happen in the next two

cadi: judge
†Inshallah: God willing
‡*mamleket*: province

years?" So he decided to depart with his friends at once.

He went to the *cadi*, explained that he had changed his mind, that he was going to leave for his country immediately, and asked for his money. The *cadi* called him a dog and ordered him to be whipped out of the place by his servants. Alas! What could the poor *chöpdji* do? He wept in impotent despair as he counted the number of years he must yet work before he beheld his loved ones.

One day, while removing the refuse from the *konak** of a wealthy pasha, his soul uttered a sigh which reached the ears of the *hanoum*,† and from the window she asked him why he sighed so deeply. He replied that he sighed for something that could in no way interest her. The *hanoum*'s sympathy was excited, however; and finally, with tears in his eyes, the *chöpdji* consented, after much coaxing, to tell her of his great misfortune. The *hanoum* thought for a few minutes and then told him to go the following day to the *cadi* at a certain hour and again ask for the money as if nothing had happened.

The *hanoum* in the meantime gathered together a quantity of jewelry and, instructing her favorite and confidential female slave to come with her to the *cadi*, she told her to remain outside whilst she went in. She also told the slave that when she saw the *chöpdji* come out with his money, she, the slave, was to enter the *cadi*'s room hurriedly and say to her mistress, "Your husband has arrived from Egypt and is waiting for you at the *konak*."

The *hanoum* then went to the *cadi*, carrying in her hand a bag containing the jewelry. With a profound salaam she said, "O *cadi*, my husband, who is in Egypt and who has been there for several years, has at last asked me to come and join him there. These jewels are, however, of great value, and I hesitate to take them with me on so long and dangerous a journey. If you would kindly consent to keep them for me until my return, I will think of you with lifelong gratitude. And in case I never return, you may keep them in token of my esteem."

The *hanoum* then began displaying the rich jewelry. Just at that

*konak: large house
†hanoum: the lady of the house or wife of the pasha

moment the *chöpdji* entered and, bending low, said, "O master, your slave has come for his savings in order that he may proceed to his country."

"Ah, welcome!" said the *cadi*. "So you are going already!" And immediately he ordered the treasurer to pay the five hundred piasters to the *chöpdji*.

"You see," said the *cadi* to the *hanoum*, "what confidence the people have in me. This money I have held for some time without receipt or acknowledgment; but directly it is asked for it is paid."

No sooner had the *chöpdji* gone out of the door than the *hanoum*'s slave came rushing in *"Hanoum effendi!* Hanoum effendi!"* she cried. "Your husband has arrived from Egypt and is anxiously awaiting you at the *konak*."

On hearing this, the *hanoum*, in well-feigned excitement, gathered up her jewelry and, wishing the *cadi* a thousand years of happiness, departed.

The *cadi* was thunderstruck and, caressing his beard with grave affection, thoughtfully said to it, "For forty years have I been a judge, but never before, by Allah, has a cause been pleaded here in this fashion."

effendi: title of respect

Today Me, Tomorrow Thee

KIKUYU PEOPLE, KENYA[66]

Put more wood on the fire, my child," said Grandmother Wanjiri, "for the damp enters my old bones in the time of rain and makes them ache."

Little Ephantus threw on a lot of dry gum wood, which opened the heart of the fire and caused a shower of sparks to fly upward as if to meet the stars that loomed close in the thin, chill, upland air. He did not touch the green, newly cut wood stacked nearby, for he knew it would not burn well until it dried. Leaping higher, the fire shone on the round, thatched huts, the cattle in their bomas* and the weathered, wise face of the old woman seated on her pile of sheepskins. Catching more of the wood, the fire spurted higher still, giving out an aromatic perfume and making a breaking noise that sounded like laughing or chuckling low in the throat.

"Ai." The old woman laughed. "*Komu athinirie kaigu wa nyina* is an old saying of our people; it means 'the dry firewood laughs at the green wood, never realizing that they both come from trees and in time will both have their turn in the fire.'"

"True talk, Grandmother, but is there a hidden meaning in this saying?" asked the child.

"There is indeed," said the old Kikuyu woman thoughtfully. "It reminds me of the tale of Tortoise and Lizard."

Little Ephantus sank himself a little more into his sheepskins, well content, for his grandmother was known far and wide as a

*bomas: pens for animals

great teller of the legends of long ago that held both the sweetness of honey and the sting of bees.

"In a long-ago time the rains did not come, neither the short rains nor the long rains, so the maize and millet dried in the fields, and animals died for lack of food and water. A great famine was on the land and bellies withered with hunger. Tortoise and Lizard were neighbors then. Tortoise worked hard to feed her family, but Lizard was lazy and preferred to live by his wits.

"When there was no more food in the neighborhood, Tortoise decided to make a long trip to distant fields and forage for her little ones. Lizard lay in the sun and slept, but his cunning mind was busy.

"Tortoise set out as soon as there was enough light for her to see. She hunted all day, found some food, and at dusk started the slow trail homeward, carrying such edibles as she had been fortunate enough to gather in a bundle on her back. When Lizard heard his neighbor coming he set out on the trail ahead of her, with wicked thoughts in his heart.

"At last he came to a big fallen log by the trail. Tugging and pushing, he just managed to place it squarely across the narrow path along which Tortoise was making her weary way."

"But, Grandmother," protested Little Ephantus, "a little lizard couldn't move a big log."

"This one could," retorted his grandmother. "Don't forget, he was a very wicked lizard, and wickedness is like chilies in the belly; they make the blood hot and the hands and feet restless. Surely you know that!"

"You are right, Grandmother," said the little boy, remembering the time he had eaten a whole, fiery chili to prove himself a man.

"So," said the old woman, with a sharp glance at him, for Kikuyu children are not encouraged to interrupt their elders, "this villainous lizard then hid himself in the bush and waited.

"Along came Tortoise, staggering with the weight of her bundle, until she encountered the log straight across her path.

" 'Oh, by all that is unfortunate,' she moaned. 'How am I to get over this log? I cannot go underneath; and my bundle will be lost if I try to crawl through this thick bush with it. What can I do?'

"Studying the situation, she decided that the only thing left was for her to push the bundle over the log, then force her way through the dense bush beside the path and pick up her burden again on the other side. With a great effort she heaved the bundle up and over the log.

"No sooner had it landed than Lizard, grinning with glee, slithered out of his hiding place and sat down on the bundle. When Tortoise appeared, she saw him there and gasped at his impudence. 'What are you doing with my bundle?' she demanded.

" 'It is my bundle,' he retorted.

" 'How can it be yours when it is mine?' argued Tortoise, trying to be polite.

"At this crisis, Rabbit, out for an evening hop, jumped over the log and heard them arguing. Tortoise appealed to him for justice. 'But, Madame Tortoise,' he said, 'it certainly can't be your property, for Lizard is sitting on it.'

" 'Of course, anyone can see that,' said Lizard smugly.

" 'Who ever heard of anybody letting another sit on his property?' asked Rabbit.

" 'But—but—' stuttered Tortoise. She was completely ineffective against Lizard's pointed tongue and Rabbit's blind view of justice. So she had to stand on the path and watch Lizard disappear with the food that belonged to her hungry children. But her heart burned at this unjust treatment, and secretly she decided to bide her time and pay back Lizard for his misdeeds.

"She set herself to study Lizard's habits carefully, and by and by observed that her enemy, when entering a hole, invariably left his tail outside, wagging in the air. One day Rabbit came by and she passed the time of day with him. Then she suggested casually that they go for a walk. Purposely she led him to Lizard's house, and there, as she had hoped, was Lizard's tail, wagging gaily in the air, while the rest of him was inside. Immediately Tortoise seized the tail in a firm grasp and hung on determinedly.

"'Let go: let go of my tail!' shrieked Lizard.

"'This is my tail,' asserted Tortoise, 'even though someone in the hole is contradicting me.'

"'And you?' shouted Lizard frantically. 'Have you lost your five wits so that you cannot recognize another's property?'

"Now Rabbit, who was not a fool, understood the whole situation in a moment. 'Be quiet, Lizard,' he said. 'It definitely can't be your property, or you would have it with you in the hole.'

"'It certainly is my property; it's my tail!' screamed Lizard, making violent efforts to free himself.

"'Here, Madame Tortoise,' said Rabbit politely, 'I will take my sharp knife and restore to you what is lawfully yours.' Happy to make amends for his former mistake, he quickly severed Lizard's tail."

"What happened to Lizard then, Grandmother?" inquired Little Ephantus.

"Oh, he lived a long time, but he was in disgrace with all the animals, for the story spread about how he had lost his tail. He had the name of a liar and a thief, and nobody respected him after that. Justice, as you see, has a way of triumphing."

"What did Madame Tortoise do with Lizard's tail?" asked Little Ephantus drowsily.

"She fed it to her little ones for their supper, and then put them to bed," said Grandmother Wanjiri. "And I know someone else who is ready to go to bed."

Ole Sis Goose

AFRICAN-AMERICAN[67]

Ole Sis Goose wus er-sailin' on de lake, and ole Br'er Fox wus hid in de weeds. By um by ole Sis Goose swum up close to der bank and ole Br'er Fox lept out an cotched* her.

"O yes, ole Sis Goose, I'se got yer now, you'se been er-sailin' on mer† lake er long time, en I'se got yer now. I'se gwine‡ to break yer neck en pick yer bones."

"Hole on der', Br'er Fox, hold on, I'se got jes' as much right to swim in der lake as you has ter lie in der weeds. Hit's des' as much my lake es hit is yours, and we is gwine to take dis matter to der cote-house§ and see if you has any right to break my neck and pick my bones."

And so dey went to cote,** and when dey got dere, de sheriff, he wus er fox, en de judge, he wus er fox, and der tourneys,†† dey wus foxes, en all de jurrymen, dey was foxes, too.

En dey tried ole Sis Goose, en dey 'victed‡‡ her and dey 'scuted§§ her, and dey picked her bones.

Now, my chilluns, listen to me, when all de folks in de cotehouse is foxes, and you is des' er common goose, der ain't gwine to be much jestice for you.

*cotched: caught
†mer: my
‡gwine: going
§cotehouse: courthouse
**cote: court
††tourneys: attorneys
‡‡'victed: convicted
§§'scuted: executed

Lost

In an inexpensive backpackers' hostel in the backstreets of Tokyo, I joined the other foreigners in the common room. The walls were a dingy yellow. I sat on the threadbare couch. Another foreigner, a woman, slouched in an armchair. Tired sunlight shone through a dirty window and the dust caught in the sunbeams hovered in the air like dust inside a tomb. The young woman had been reticent and other foreigners more eager to share their stories had taken the floor in turn, then left as they finished. We two remained. When she began to speak, her words were suspended in sadness like the dust. She had been a member of the Canadian Peace Corps.

"That's nice," I said to encourage her. It almost made her stop.

"You think so?"

I said nothing but waited.

When she went on, she didn't talk about the village in some strange country or the three years she'd spent there. She talked about going home to Canada. "I was a teacher," she said numbly. "I couldn't take it. I left. I don't know where I'm going or how long I'll go."

"They must have been real brats!" I said.

She smiled sadly. "No, it was me. Every day I went in to teach them and they didn't care. They didn't understand. They were healthy. They had food. It wasn't them. It was me. Every day I got more and more angry. I wanted to grab them and shake them. I wanted to scream at them, 'Don't you know how lucky you are? Don't you know what it means to be able to get an education? Don't you know that children are dying because they can't even get what you are throwing away?' I wanted to shake them till their teeth rattled, till they understood. So I left. I couldn't watch. It wasn't them. How could they know? It was me. It was me." She sat quietly suspended in the sunbeam like the dust, between worlds, not resting, not flying, with nowhere to be and nowhere to go.

As the sands shifted beneath my feet and certainties slipped my grasp, I wondered if I were too trusting of my culture's ideas of common sense, of good versus evil, of universal justice. Maybe justice, like common sense, varies from culture to culture. It's important to know how far to trust an ideal. I read story after story, and in the glow of the campfire, strangers and friends told their tales. A short Kikuyu grandmother with a twinkle in her eye said that justice triumphs.[68] Following her, an African-American woman from Texas directed a twinge of cynicism at my pale skin. The virtual story-telling session countered every certainty I had. You believe in justice? What if you're Sis Goose and all the folks in the courthouse are foxes?[69] What if there is no justice for you? What if you can be right only if you first accept society's definition of your being wrong? Where is the justice in that? You believe in friendship? Look how easily friendship can be destroyed. Maybe some friendships should be destroyed.[70] With their magic wand, folktales could make or unmake anything and I could recognize the truth in each situation. Justice may be served, justice may be violated. Enemies may be friends. Friends may become enemies. The answers are rarely clear; life is rarely simple.

I felt like I was battling an ogre who could take on any shape he wanted. As I listed my certainties one by one, the ogre shifted his stance. If I was a mouse, he became a cat. If I was a lion, he became a mouse. And my certainties became questions, endless questions, suspended in a sunbeam somewhere between truth and lies.

"Fine!" I yelled. "I'll choose what I believe. I don't care if it's true or not!"

The ogre's laugh rumbled deep in his chest. "Yes, and when you have found an ideal to trust, when you know what is really important in your life, how do you defend it? When you are weak and crying out for help, does it matter whom you ask?"

The Tale of the Emir's Sword

During the latter part of the nineteenth century," began Zarif Khan* one evening, stirring his green tea with a silver spoon, "at the time when the rivalry between the Emir Sher Ali Khan and Mohammad Afzal Khan was at its height, the Emir of Afghanistan sent a summons to the jirga† of the Kuki Khel Afridis. The tribesmen reached the capital after a journey of seven days from their homes in Tirah, and on the following day attended the Emir's Durbar‡ in the *Arg*§ at Kabul.

"For their ceremonial meeting with the Emir, the members of the jirga wore their best clothes, consisting of an embroidered green waistcoat over a clean white shirt, with baggy white trousers; and because it was winter each carried wrapped round his shoulders a voluminous blanket to protect him from the cold. When the tribesmen had seated themselves on the big carpet in the inner courtyard of the Citadel, the Emir made his entry with suitable pomp, and the whole Durbar rose and made a deep obeisance to him. He sat down immediately in front of the jirga and bade them all be seated.

"The Emir was anxious to win the Afridis to his side, so he addressed them in a very friendly fashion, ending with the words,

*Khan: local chieftain or man of rank
†jirga: council of Afghan tribal leaders
‡Durbar: public audience or levee, court, held by the ruler of a country or his representative
§*Arg*: citadel

'If I were to have but one half loaf of bread, I would share it with you, my brothers.' When he had finished speaking, one of the Elders, named Sher Afzal, rose to his feet and said, 'Ala Hazrat, we have seen in Kabul much of the glory of your kingdom; why then do you speak to us of half loaves? We know that you are the master of many treasuries, and are the king of a great country. If it ever happens, which God forbid, that you possess only half a loaf, we poor tribesmen out of our scanty provisions will give you bread to eat. The present time, while you are king and we are poor, is the proper moment for you to bestow rich gifts upon us.'

"The Emir was very angry that his kind words had been treated so lightly, and he retorted, 'You Son of Satan, I am beset on either side by the rulers of two powerful kingdoms, who have their eyes fixed on this small stretch of land. I am gathering strength for the hour when one of them attacks me. On that day come to me, and I will be liberal in my generosity to you.'

"Sher Afzal answered, 'Ala Hazrat, at this time when your kingdom is at peace and there is ample time for eating, you give us nothing, while you and your Kabuli Wazirs* live in the greatest luxury. On the day that your kingdom is soaked in blood you will have to excuse us, for then there will be no time for eating.'

"The Emir was so infuriated by this reply that he rose in haste, and strode unceremoniously out of the Durbar, leaving behind on the carpet beside his chair his sabre in its gold-encrusted scabbard. Now the Afridi who had been seated nearest to the Emir's chair was a certain Amin Khan, who, when he noticed that the Emir had left his sword behind, stealthily slipped it beneath the folds of his blanket. Then having made sure that his action had not been noticed, he rose and joined his fellow tribesmen as they left the courtyard.

"Amin Khan's position at the very edge of the carpet, and the unhurried manner in which he had secured the sword, caused him to be the last member of the jirga to file through the gate of the

*Wazir: vizier, a minister or councillor of state

Arg. Unfortunately for Amin, a vigilant sentry was on duty there. This man noticed a gleam of gold where the point of the curved scabbard protruded from the folds of the blanket. He therefore seized the Afridi by the arm, tore the blanket from his shoulder, and exposed the sword to view. Amin struggled desperately to free himself, but to no avail. At the sentry's urgent cry for help, the commander of the Guard came running with the other soldiers, and Amin was quickly overpowered.

"The Guard Commander, confident that his sovereign would reward him generously for recovering his sword and arresting the man who had had the effrontery to steal it, took Amin at once into the presence of the king. When the Emir had heard exactly how his sword had been stolen, he flew into a terrible rage, and shouted at Amin, 'You Afridis are just as wicked in your ways as you are in your talk. You Son of Satan, there is no crime worse than to bite the hand that has fed you. I therefore order you to be blown from a gun this evening as soon as the sun has set. There, in the place of execution, the pariah dogs shall feast upon the shreds of your flesh.' Amin Khan, seeing that no appeal for mercy would alter the Emir's decision to destroy him, remained silent, and at a nod from the Emir he was led away.

"Amin was taken from the *Arg* straight to the mound just outside the city wall where, in those days, stood a piece of artillery much used by the Emir for the execution of criminals. Amin's wrists were securely tied to posts on either side of the gun, and he was left with the muzzle of the gun poked hard against his stomach. An hour or so remained till sunset, and Amin looked forward to spending them in acute discomfort.

"A little before sunset, when the shadows were already lengthening across the hills, a member of the jirga named Agha, with whom Amin Khan had long been at enmity, happened to take a stroll outside the wall of the city. When he came to the mound he was astonished to see Amin tied to the gun of execution, and called out to him, 'Amin Khan, what are you doing?' Amin turned his head toward his fellow tribesman and replied in a calm tone of voice, 'I am committing an impropriety with this unspeakable gun, which has blasted the lives of many Afghans. I am busy. Go your way. I will follow you soon.' Agha Jan was deeply perplexed by these strange words, and drawing closer, said, 'What has happened to you? Surely you are not doing this for pleasure?'

"Amin Khan replied, 'For God's sake leave me alone. This is no time to disturb me.'

"Agha Jan now realized the gravity of the situation, and he set off at once for the Caravanserai* where the Afridi jirga was staying. There he reported to the Khan how he had found Amin fastened to the gun of execution, and the strange words uttered by him. When the members of the jirga realized the terrible fate which was about to overtake Amin, a deep despondency fell on them all. The Khan, however, at once rose to his feet and hurried to the *Arg* to seek an audience with the Emir, for he knew that the order for Amin's execution could have been given only by the king himself.

"The Khan, on reaching the *Arg*, made his obeisance to the Emir, and cried out, 'O Ala Hazrat, it is not customary for a member of the jirga to be blown from a gun.'

"The Emir replied, 'I am executing the man for stealing my sword.'

"The Khan answered, 'O King, you know well that we Afridis can resist every sort of temptation save that of securing a worthy weapon, and the possibility of acquiring thy sword, O King, would tempt even me from the path of righteousness.'

"The Khan's words greatly pleased the Emir, and after pondering for a few moments, he called one of his ghulambachehs[†] to his side and ordered him to go straight to the Commander of the Executioners and tell him to release the Afridi who was due to be blown from the gun at sunset.

"The Khan returned, well pleased, to the Caravanserai, where he told the members of the jirga the happy news of Amin's impending release.

*Caravanserai: an inn where caravans rest at night
†ghulambacheh: a palace servant

"When Amin reached the Serai, the Khan spoke to him severely. 'O Amin,' he said, 'how foolish you were not to send word to one of our tribe that your life was in danger. And when Agha Jan chanced to pass by, and asked you what had happened, why did you give him such a rough and meaningless answer?'

"Amin replied, 'Khan, have you forgotten the old Pushtu verse which runs,

> *Let me be buried in an unknown grave*
> *But never let men think I was not brave . . . ?*

I did not wish Agha Jan, whose family has a longstanding feud with mine, to be able to boast that he had saved my life. I preferred, O my Father, death to such a fate as that.'"

The Revolution

MAYAN PEOPLE, CENTRAL AMERICA[72]

At the beginning of the war, one group of Obregonists was gathered at the graveyard. Another group was gathered at Window Pass.

Now while they were eating, they were discovered by Pineda's soldiers. Pineda's soldiers killed them all.

There were heaps of meat, beef, mutton, chicken left uneaten. Is there anyone who would eat chicken like that—cooked in lard in a frying pan!

It looked fine, if you don't know fear, of course!

I was eleven years old. My neighbor's son had some sheep. We stuck the sheep in the pen. We came right home, since the bullets were sputtering at the top of Horned Owl House Hill.

Pineda's soldiers were coming to kill us. We hadn't a chance of going anywhere. "Forget it, let's each of us lie down at home. We can't say we don't know about the shooting," we said.

They took all the animals. There were twelve sheep, three cows. The cows that had already been killed were tossed up on the horses. The sheep were hung up and skinned. All the meat was left at the courthouse. The soldiers divided it up amongst themselves. But the food that was already cooked—it made no difference who took it.

By the cross above Blessed Spring we went to stick the sheep in the pen. There were two chickens cooking, each one in a frying pan.

Now I really didn't want to take the other frying pan. "Shall I just take the piece of liver to eat?" I said to myself. I took it, but I was looking around behind me. I was scared.

But the owner was an Obregonist in one of those advance groups that was destroyed at Window Pass. There were only three men left to bury the dead. Their arms were wounded. Their legs were wounded. One was wounded in the lung.

The next day we opened the pen for the sheep. It was probably ten o'clock when the fighting broke out.

The fields were ripe with corn.

"Why did we take our chickens home for our mothers to eat? We should have eaten them here by ourselves!" said my companion. "Let's go look at the fire over there to see if there is any food left."

Ooh, a pot was bubbling away on the fire. A pot of chicken.

"Come here! See how good the food is! Let's eat!" he told me.

"Where will we get the tortillas for it?"

"Look! There are tortillas stacked at the foot of the fence!" he said.

We each ate two pieces of chicken. We drank its broth. Whatever we couldn't finish eating we took home. Four pieces for me, four pieces for my companion. We stuck the sheep in their pen. I carried the meat in the little old pot. My companion wrapped his up in a tortilla. We were lucky!

The next day the countryside was deserted. The governor's soldiers were gone. "That's probably how it will be. Old Pineda was able to take the town," we said.

Four days later the government came in force. Who knows how many soldiers. But they had no mercy.

We had a few tortillas among us. We had some watermelon squash flavored with chili. We had cut it in chunks to eat. The Obregonists scooped out the watermelon squash. They took our tortillas and ate them. It didn't matter if you died of hunger yourself!

They found the sheep hanging up. They roasted them and ate them. They surely were satisfied with that! If they hadn't found them hanging there, if there weren't someone guarding them at the courthouse, who knows!

More sheep-stealing and chicken-thieving began. The governor's soldiers only ate stolen food. They'd scarcely buy it!

I had a hen turkey crouching in the tall weeds. They made a path through the weeds and grabbed the turkey. They took away two chickens too. My turkey and my chickens, they did go!

On the fourth day, my pots went, my bowls went. They stole a ball of wool. They sold them at a store. I saw my bowls there. They were huge. What good were they now?

I had a chest. I had some books. They stole them all.

"God, how will we be freed from our hardship, mother, suffering as we do?"

"Never mind, daughter! We'll see what we'll live on," said my mother.

In the end, they returned more than they stole. One day Obregón's soldiers came to our house to ask a favor. They had stolen a mule-load of flour at the pass. "Do you want a third of the flour in exchange for making tortillas for us to eat?" asked the soldiers.

"We do!" we said. A sack of flour!

We made a huge stack of wheat tortillas every day. Every day they ate them.

A half straw mat of flour was used up. They ate it and we ate it.

"If you will still be so kind as to make tortillas, we'll get some more flour," they said.

"Bring it!" we said. One of them brought another bag. "We'll store up the rest," said my mother. "We'll be happy to eat it when we haven't any corn." We put it away. The straw mat was empty.

"What can I do with the straw mat? Take it!" the soldier told us.

"It's probably payment for our firewood, mother."

One day he brought two turkeys. Probably Chamulans' turkeys!

"Fix the turkeys for us to eat," he said. "You eat half, we'll eat half."

My mother fixed a whole turkey. He had said that he would just eat half. But he was carrying the whole turkey off, together with my pot.

"I told you, ma'am, 'One today, one tomorrow.' But never mind. Since there are three of us eating, you'll just have to figure it out."

So he took six pieces of turkey and our little pot. He left the big pot with our own portion.

Other times he would bring a chicken or a rooster. We would fix the food and his tortillas. Our pay was half a bag of flour. We lived on it.

"The trouble is, my firewood has run out," my mother told him.

"There's a lot of firewood," he said. "Take it from the paths! Take it from the fences!" They warmed themselves with the fences!

"But my neighbor will scold me! Don't you see, it's my neighbor's fence," I said.

"What does it matter to you?" he said. "Don't be scared to steal!"

He had brought a bag of green broad beans for us to cook.

"But I don't know how," said my mother.

"Do you know how we should eat them, mother? We'll shuck the pods and then we'll boil them."

"What if they don't eat them that way? What if they only eat them fried," she said.

I shucked the pods. I boiled them until they were good and soft, like corn. "Do you eat them like this?" we asked.

"Ah, these are better!" he said.

He had an enormous bowl. We filled it up for him. "There's enough here for supper and breakfast," he said. He took the beans. He took his wheat tortillas. We ate wheat tortillas for more than a month.

Then the soldiers were sent off to fight. One rooster, two legs of mutton, roasted in the oven, were left at our home. There was still a quart of corn. That became our pay, of course!

Pineda's soldiers came. They marched along the tip of Raven House Mountain. They blew their bugles. Their bugles sounded good.

But the advance force met them at the cemetery. Pineda's soldiers were chased across the top of the mountains. They ended up at the Church of Guadalupe in San Cristóbal. They fled. They fled to this day. Obregón was established. There haven't been any more battles. That was the last battle, indeed!

The Stone Coat Woman

IROQUOIS PEOPLE, NORTH AMERICA[73]

L ong ago four men went to hunt in a far part of the northern
woods where they had never been before. One of the
hunters brought his wife and child with him. Each day the four
hunters went in different directions while the woman stayed behind
to take care of the camp and her small baby.

One morning, while her husband and the others were out seeking
game, the wife went to the spring for water. When she came back,
she thought she heard singing coming from their elm bark lodge.

> "A-uwah
> So good to eat.
> A-uwah
> So good to eat."

The woman was very frightened for she had left her baby sleeping in the lodge. She crept closer and she could hear her baby's
voice, first cooing happily and then screaming each time the song
stopped.

The mother looked into the lodge. There, next to the fire, sat a
huge woman whose skin seemed to be made of stone. In her arms
she rocked the small baby, singing her song. "So good to eat, so good
to eat," she sang as she rocked it. Each time she stopped singing she
would lean down and bite a piece of flesh from the baby's cheek.
Then, as the baby screamed, she would rub the cheek with her finger, healing it completely, and begin the song once more.

The mother was terrified. She thought of running away, but she could not leave her child. Even if she did find her husband, what could he do against a being whose very skin was flint. Her only hope was to use her wits. Boldly she walked into the lodge.

"Grandmother," she said, speaking to the Stone Giant Woman, "I am glad you have come to visit us. You are welcome to stay as long as you wish."

The Stone Coat Woman looked at her and smiled a smile that was wide enough to bite the head off a moose.

"Ah, Grand-daughter," said the Stone Coat Woman, her voice rumbling like great stones rolling down a hill, "I am glad that you welcome me this way. I have come to you because my husband does not treat me well. Now that you have welcomed me as a relative, I can stay with you and help you."

She handed the baby back to its mother. Holding her child, the mother sat down across the fire from the Stone Coat Woman, waiting for her husband to come back, not at all certain what it meant to have this very special guest.

Meanwhile, in the woods to the north of the elm bark cabin, the woman's husband was having no success. Animals were very hard to find.

"Wah-ah," he said, "perhaps it is true that there are Stone Giants in these woods. It is as if something has eaten all the game."

Even as he spoke, he began hearing a sound which he thought at first to be thunder. But as the ground began to shake and the noise came closer and closer, he knew what it was. It was the sound of great stone feet pounding the earth as they walked. There was a hollow tree close by and he crawled into it, leaving his bow and arrows behind him. As he watched through a knothole in the fallen tree, he saw two huge Stone Giants come into sight, pushing the trees aside with their shoulders as if they were reeds in a marsh.

"Ehh?" said one of the stone giants. "I thought you said you saw something good to eat, my brother."

The other stone giant looked slowly around. "It is so," he said. "I am sure it was here. Noh-KWEH! Look!" And with that exclamation of excitement, he reached down and picked up the hunter's bow—which looked like a tiny twig in his hand. "You see, there is good food nearby."

Within the hollow log the hunter held his breath. He prayed that the punky wood of the log would cover his scent.

"I cannot smell him, Brother," said the first stone giant, sitting down on the log which creaked beneath his weight. "Perhaps the food has moved on."

"Let us be certain," the second stone giant said, sitting down on the hollow log beside his brother. It cracked ominously beneath his weight and the hunter was sure he would soon be flatter than a leaf, but the log managed somehow to hold beneath them. "This," said the stone giant, "will tell us where the good food is." Then, as the hunter watched through the knothole, the second stone giant reached into the pouch which hung at his waist and pulled out a single finger. He placed it on his right palm and it stood upright, quivering like an arrow shot into a tree. "Pointing Finger," said the second stone giant, "show us where the good food is hiding."

With that the Pointing Finger bent to point at the hollow log. The Stone Giant reached for one end of the log, but before he could plunge his arm in the hunter ran out the other end and scooted into the trees. Putting the magic finger back into his pouch, the second stone giant gave chase and his brother followed.

The man was very swift of foot, but he knew he was no match for the long legs of his pursuers. Wherever he went the magic finger would point out his hiding place. What could he do? Then an idea came to him. In front of him was a very tall tree with a thick branch which extended out over the trail. Quick as a red squirrel, he went up the tree, crawled out onto the branch and lay very still.

Soon the two stone giants reached the tree, but when they saw the trail ended there, they did not know what to do. Their necks were too stiff for them to look up and they were not smart enough to guess the reason why the human's trail ended so abruptly. Finally, after talking it over for some time, they remembered the magic finger. The second stone giant pulled it from his pouch. He placed it on his palm and it stood straight up, quivering like an arrow which has been shot into a tree.

"Pointing Finger," he said, "show us where our food is." But since he was holding the finger directly under the branch where the man was hiding, the finger did not move.

Now the stone giants were very confused.

"Hunh-uh," the first one said, "I knew we should have gone to hunt for moose."

"Quiet!" said the second stone giant. "I cannot think while you talk."

"Ha-a-ah," said the first one, "you cannot think while you talk either."

"What do you mean by that?" asked the second stone giant.

"Perhaps if I am quiet you will understand," said the first one.

So they quarreled as the man watched from his hiding place. Soon the first stone giant began to beat the ground with his club. Not to be outdone, the second stone giant placed the magic finger on the ground and began to beat the earth with his club, too. They continued arguing. Realizing it was his chance, the hunter slid down the tree, grabbed the magic finger and ran.

"Little Food," the second stone giant shouted, "come back with my finger." But the hunter did not stop.

The stone giants ran after the hunter, but with the Pointing Finger showing him their direction the hunter was able to fool them. At last he reached a stream. Holding the magic finger high above his head, he swam across. When he reached the other side of the stream, he looked back. There were the stone giants, standing on the other bank.

"Little Quick One Good To Eat," said the second stone giant, "bring me back my finger."

"Do you mean this?" the hunter said, holding it on his palm.

"Nyoh," said the second stone giant, "bring it back over here. Then we will be very happy before we eat you."

"You are very stupid, Brother," said the first stone giant. "He will not bring it back if you tell him that we're going to eat him."

"Nyoh," said the second stone giant, "Little One Who Looks So Tasty, bring back my magic finger and I will not tell you that we are going to eat you."

"Truly," said the first stone giant, "you cannot think when you talk, Brother."

"Neh," said the hunter from the other side of the stream, "I do not want to get wet again. I will lean over and hold the finger out to you. If you lean forward you can grasp it."

"Nyoh!" said the second stone giant, "that is very good. I can use the magic finger to find you and eat you later."

The stone giant leaned over, reaching for the magic finger which the hunter held out at arm's length. He had almost reached it, when the hunter drew it back a little. The stone giant stretched further, and again the hunter drew the finger back. Three times this happened and on the fourth time, just as the stone giant was about to grasp the magic finger, the hunter snatched it quickly away. Losing his balance completely, the stone giant gave a great yell and fell into the water headfirst straight down to the bottom, and was killed. Then, leaving the first stone giant raging in anger on the other shore, the hunter stuck the magic finger into his belt and headed back to the lodge.

"My wife," he began as he entered the door, "I have such a story to tell." His words failed him when he saw Stone Coat Woman sitting on the opposite side of the fire from his wife and their little baby.

"Dah-djoh, Husband," said the wife, "our grandmother has come to visit us. Bid her welcome."

"Ee-yah," said the man, coming into the lodge slowly and then sitting down beside his wife and child without taking his eyes off the huge woman. "Grandmother, you are welcome indeed."

The Stone Coat Woman smiled. "I am glad that you welcome me," she rumbled, "for I can see you must be a strong warrior. That magic finger which you now carry belonged to the brother of my husband. If you have it, then you must have killed him. I have indeed come to the right lodge to ask for help."

Then Stone Coat Woman told her story. Her husband had been cruel to her and beaten her. Since she no longer wished to live with him, she had searched for help. If they would allow her to stay, she would help them.

One by one the other three hunters returned and, heeding the words of the hunter's clever wife, they greeted Stone Coat Woman as a relative. She was very pleased and slept that night before their door to guard them from any danger.

The next day, Stone Coat Woman asked to go with them when they hunted. "Use the pointing finger to show the way to the game animals," she said. "I will do the rest."

So the hunter brought forth the magic finger. "Pointing Finger," he said, placing it on his right palm where it stood quivering like an arrow shot into a tree, "where can we find many beavers?" The finger pointed towards the west and the hunters went in that direction.

After a time they came to a large pond covered with ice. All over the pond were many beaver lodges. With one blow of her fist, Stone Coat Woman made a hole in the ice.

> *"A-uwah, A-uwah*
> *Beavers come out,"*

she sang. One by one many beavers came out of the hole in the ice and, as the beavers came out, Stone Coat Woman killed each one. The hunters skinned them, keeping the pelts and the tails and some of the meat for themselves for stew. Stone Coat Woman ate the skinned carcasses raw and was very pleased.

The next day they hunted for raccoons. Pointing Finger led them to a tall hollow tree. With one hand, Stone Coat Woman broke the tree. As it crashed down many raccoons scrambled off. Stone Coat Woman killed them all. The hunters skinned them out, keeping the pelts and some of the meat for themselves. All the rest Stone Coat Woman ate raw and was happy indeed.

Each day when they finished hunting, Stone Coat Woman would

make four piles of the skins and the meat the hunters saved. Then she would rub each pile with her hands until it became small enough to put into a pouch.

"Now these will be easy to carry," said Stone Coat Woman. "Only throw each pile on the ground when you reach home and they will return to normal size." And so they did.

Thus it went for many days. Each morning the hunters went with Stone Coat Woman and caught many animals. Each night she slept in front of the door of their elm bark lodge to guard them.

One morning when they woke, the hunters found Stone Coat Woman standing in front of the door. "Be silent," she said to them. "I am listening." The hunters stood in silence, waiting.

"My husband is coming," she said at last. "I hear his footsteps off to the north. He knows I am here. He intends to kill me and eat you all. If you are brave, you may be able to save your lives. You must cut four long basswood poles and sharpen them. Harden them by placing the pointed ends into the fire. Then go hide behind the great stone. When my husband comes I will fight with him. If he throws me to the ground, you must come up behind him and thrust the poles into him.

The hunter's wife put her baby into a canoe. Then she rolled up four bundles of skins to look like her husband and friends, and then paddled out into the middle of the lake to watch. The four hunters made their basswood spears and hid behind the great stone. Before long, the ground began to shake as if there were an earthquake. Smashing the trees down before him, Stone Coat Woman's husband came rushing out of the forest. He saw the figures in the canoe far out on the lake and began to wade into the water. Then Stone Coat Woman came out to meet him and they fought.

The Stone Coat Woman's husband pulled a great pine tree out of the ground to use as a club. Stone Coat Woman uprooted a great hemlock tree for the same purpose. They struck each other terrible blows with their clubs until both of the huge trees were shattered. Then they threw rocks at each other which were larger than full-grown bears. Neither one seemed able to defeat the other.

Then Stone Coat Woman caught her foot on a root and fell. Immediately her husband leaped on top of her to kill her, but before he could do so, the four men ran out from behind the great stone. They thrust the basswood spears deeply into the stone giant and he died.

"Nyah-weh," said Stone Coat Woman, rising to her feet, "you have saved my life and your own. Now there are no more stone giants here to trouble you. It is time for me to go on my own way again."

Before Stone Coat Woman left, she gave a present to the hunter's wife to thank her for her hospitality. It was a piece of animal skin which had on it the hairs of many animals.

"Pull out just one hair," said Stone Coat Woman, and your hunter will catch that animal on that day."

With the magic finger and the piece of skin, they went back to their village, taking also the pelts of many animals and much meat. There they all lived well for many years. They used their possessions to help others, always remembering they owed their good fortune to the hospitality which the first hunter's wife showed that day to a Stone Coat Woman.

A Swirl of Probabilities

"Can I really befriend a giant who eats humans?" an Iroquois woman at my virtual campfire asked in her tale. The child in her lap played with her mother's long black braids as the woman's eyes darkened with thought. In calling the giant "Grandmother," she had gained an ally, but at the same time she had accepted a child-eater into her home.[74] The Afghan tribesman chose to die rather than put himself in debt to an enemy even within his own tribe.[75] To him, the alliance meant compromising too much of himself. However, the Mayan mother and daughter chose to work for the enemy and stay alive.[76]

My fairy tale quest had lost its quaint appeal. I'd wondered whether to share my bread with a leper. I'd wondered who was my enemy and who was my friend. Now I was wondering whether it was better to be an uncompromising martyr or a compromised survivor. And yet all this shape-shifting, this uncertainty, had some appeal. Though unsettling, it was also comforting. These were questions and possible responses, not absolutes.

After September 11, I watched news reports every day. I watched them the way I watch a movie, guessing or not guessing the outcome, but unable to stop someone else's vision on its inexorable march to their, not my, conclusion. I watched the television replays and news updates and I saw an immutable fact, the buildings crumbled, with attendant causes and future consequences. A chain of events stretched backwards to certain individuals and actions and forward to certain individuals and actions, like a fifth grader's timeline. The line had a dot representing the present and was labeled "September 11, Now." From that dot, the line stretched all the way to the left side of the paper with an arrow at the end to show that the facts of the past continued far into the past, farther than I could draw. The line laid out not only a certain past, but on the other side of that "Now" the line stretched all the way to and beyond the right side of the paper as well. The line laid out a certain past, a certain present, and a future, solid, straight, immutable. This timeline definition of the tragedy cut out so many alternatives, I felt hemmed in and powerless. That, I suspect, was the source of my fear, not fear of bodily harm, but fear in the face of a worldview in which I was a victim and pawn, not a participant.

On the other hand, my children saw the tragedy as a possibility that had occurred with all sorts of continuing interactions. Their world, like folktales, was a swirl of probabilities stretching through past, present, and future. They searched for different solutions and interpretations, like a brainstorming session with the craziest ideas. My children were having a discussion with the present, exploring all sorts of ways of looking at it to open up alternatives, and not just future alternatives, but present alternatives. Their stories were like folktales in which facts may be changed like a frog into a prince by some twist of fate or a magic wand or even by some past occurrence which only becomes known at the moment of transformation.

In the spinning room, an old woman leans forward and raises her finger in warning. The girls' busy hands unconsciously pause. The girls listen as if their lives depend on it, and maybe they do.[77] We think of folk and fairy tales as frivolous childhood fantasies, yet folktales have influenced how we think about very basic concepts, not only throughout individual lifetimes, but over centuries and across cultures.[78] However, folktales are not untouched and untouchable icons. We all take part in the shaping of the tales; folktales are inherently democratic. They are shaped by their tellers and listeners, their centuries and their place, and folktales continue to be adapted to explore new options and solutions with each new telling.

In reading tales from all over the world and seeing many different images of the world, I felt as if I could see the shapes of worlds to come, worlds that had come, worlds that might come from each vision. And I felt responsible for the vision I chose, its benefits and repercussions.

The Devil's Little Joke

ISRAEL[79]

Our wise men relate that when the good Lord was about finished with His work of creation He sat atop a mountain surveying the creatures before Him as they roamed through the fields and forests and waters. Even the worms crawling underground did not escape His divine eye.

At this serene moment, Lucifer or Lilith[80]—I am not sure which—happened along and mockingly said, "Why not create an animal that could be any of the others at will?"

The Lord pondered and pondered and played with the soft cold clay under His feet and shaped a funny-looking animal without wings and without fins, without feelers and without claws, and with only two legs instead of four. And that is how man was born.

And, while all the other animals were created in pairs, the good Lord created only one of this strange being, for a joke is only a joke and there is no need to carry it too far.

"Go hence," said the Lord to man. But man lay still, so the Lord bent over the earthen form, and blew some life into the mouth of clay. It is because of that wisp of breath that man ever since has considered himself to be some sort of divine creature.

And from that day of the devil's sardonic suggestion, man has been versed in the art of putting himself into the skin of other animals. While a fox is a fox and a wolf is a wolf and a bear is a bear, man can be a lamb today and a wolf tomorrow, play dove in the morning and hawk in the evening.

Solomon and the Vulture

TURKEY[81]

Oﾠne day Allah sent Azrail[82] to the Emperor Solomon telling
him that he had come to take his life. Solomon was a ruler
who had great power and also the ability to understand a great
many things about life. When Azrail told him that he had come for
his life, Solomon said, "Very well, but who is going to rule after I
am dead? Will the ruler who comes after me be a good one or a
bad one? I have lived for five hundred years. How can I leave my
realm without knowing what the world will be like after I die? I
am entitled to know this."

Azrail thought him right and went back to Allah and repeated to
him what Solomon had said. Allah listened to Azrail's report and
said this: "I shall give him forty more days of life. Go and tell him
that in that time he must find out what has happened in the past.
Why should he want to live longer? When he sees what has happened in the past, maybe he will change his mind."

Azrail returned to Solomon and told him that he had been given
forty more days by Allah. "During these forty days, you are to travel
around the world to find out what has happened in all of the past."

Solomon consulted with his wise men about which creature had
the longest life span in the world. He was told that the Ak Baba,
the vulture, was the creature that lived longest. Solomon went out
and found a vulture that was fifteen hundred years old. Solomon
said to the vulture, "I have lived five hundred years and Allah has
given me forty more days of life. During this time, I must find out
what has happened during the past. Can you tell me this?"

To this the vulture said, "I have lived only fifteen hundred years. Go and talk to my brother, who is two thousand years old and lives on the other side of yonder mountain."

Solomon went around the mountain and there he found the vulture that he was looking for. He asked the vulture about the past, but this vulture said to him, "I am only two thousand years old, but I have a friend who is a vulture who lives at the river here who is two thousand and five hundred years old. Go and talk to him."

Solomon went to the place where the vulture of two thousand and five hundred years lived and explained to him his mission. "O vulture, tell me what remarkable experiences you have had in your life."

The bird said, "In my long life I had a series of memorable experiences and I will tell you of the most important of these. Once I was caught up in a terrible winter during which I almost starved to death. During this winter I landed one day on top of a minaret which was made of gold. When I looked down, I saw that there was a service in progress in the mosque to which the minaret was attached. Men with white beards were sitting in the front row. Ones with black beards were standing behind them in a row, and the shaven men were in the rear. When they finished praying, the congregation looked up and saw me standing on the minaret. One of them said, 'Poor bird. He is perhaps hungry. Let us kill an ox and give it to him to eat.' They killed an ox and gave it to me to eat. After eating it I was happy and I flew away.

"One hundred years later there was another terrible winter. I flew to a strange country during that winter and I landed on the silver minaret of a mosque, and there I looked down and saw that a service was in progress. Black-bearded men were standing in the front row. White-bearded men were behind them, and the shaven ones were at the rear. When the service was over they looked up and saw me, and one of them said, 'This poor bird must be hungry. Let us kill a sheep and give it to him.' They killed the sheep and gave it to me. I ate it and flew away.

"One hundred years later there was another long and terrible winter. This time I found a mosque with a minaret that had a bronze top. I landed on the top of the minaret and looked down. I saw a service in progress. Shaven men were in the front; black-bearded ones were behind them; and the white-bearded men were at the rear. When the service was over the people saw me there on the minaret. In great excitement they said, one to another, 'Look, there is a bird on the minaret. Bring a gun and let us shoot it.' Everyone went home for his gun. When I realized that I was in danger, I flew away and thus saved my life.

"As you can see from this, the world does not get any better. After you die it will be a worse place than when you lived in it. Go back to your kingdom and accept Allah's will."

The Landlord and His Son

ISRAEL[83]

Many years ago in a small hut within a forest in Lithuania there lived a gentle old woman. Many thought that she was a witch. She lived on mushrooms and on water from the well close by. She did not like human company and used to repeat all the time a single sentence, "One day you will find yourself." Nobody knew the meaning of these words.

The old woman often paid visits to a Polish landlord in the neighboring village. From time to time he gave her some food. In the course of time the landlord began to hate the old woman, and one day he decided to get rid of her. He baked for her a beautiful cake but put within it some poison.

That day the landlord talked with his guest in a very friendly fashion, and the conversation went longer than usual. The old woman whispered again and again, "One day you will find yourself."

"Yes," thought the cunning man within his heart, "shortly she will find herself or the Angel of Death will find her." And he delivered the cake to the old woman. "Such a cake you have never tasted before," he assured her.

The old woman took the cake, thanked the merciful host, and went home.

On the same day that the old woman visited the landlord, his young son participated in a big hunt in the woods. He and his servants lost their way and so came across the hut where the old woman lived. He told her how thirsty and hungry he was, and she invited him to have a piece of cake, which she had not yet touched.

The young man fell down after his first bite. When the servants saw the master dead, they sent immediately for the father. Only then, when the landlord fell down on his son's body, weeping bitterly, did he understand what the old woman's words meant—"One day you will find yourself."

You see how true is the Jewish proverb, "The man who makes holes falls into them himself."*

*Psalms 7:16

Old Man and Old Woman

BLACKFEET PEOPLE, NORTH AMERICA[84]

Long, long ago, there were only two persons in the world: Old Man and Old Woman. One time when they were traveling about the earth, Old Woman said to Old Man, "Now let us come to an agreement of some kind. Let us decide how the people shall live when they shall be on the earth."

"Well," replied Old Man, "I am to have the first say in everything."

"I agree with you," said Old Woman. "That is—if I may have the second say." Then Old Man began his plans. "The women will have the duty of tanning the hides. They will rub animals' brains on the hides to make them soft, and scrape them with scraping tools. All this they will do very quickly, for it will not be hard work."

"No," said Old Woman, "I will not agree to this. They must tan hides in the way you say; but it must be very hard work, so that the good workers may be found out."

"Well," said Old Man, "we will let the people have eyes and mouths, straight up and down in their faces."

"No," replied Old Woman, "let us not have them that way. We will have the eyes and mouths in the faces, as you say, but they shall be set crosswise."

"Well," said Old Man, "the people shall have ten fingers on each hand."

"Oh, no!" replied Old Woman. "That will be too many. They will be in the way. There will be four fingers and one thumb on each hand."

So the two went on until they had provided for everything in the lives of the people who were to be.

"What shall we do about life and death?" asked Old Woman. "Should the people live forever, or should they die?"

Old Woman and Old Man had difficulty agreeing about this. Finally Old Man said, "I will tell you what we will do. I will throw a buffalo chip into the water. If it floats, the people will die for four days and then come to life again; if it sinks, they will die forever."

So he threw a buffalo chip into the water, and it floated.

"No," said Old Woman, "we will not decide in that way. I will throw this rock into the water. If it floats, the people will die for four days; if it sinks, they will die forever."

Then Old Woman threw the rock into the water, and it sank to the bottom.

"There," said she. "It is better for the people to die forever. If they did not, they would not feel sorry for each other, and there would be no sympathy in the world."

"Well," said Old Man, "let it be that way."

After a time, Old Woman had a daughter, who soon became sick and died. The mother was very sorry then that they had agreed that people should die forever. "Let us have our say over again," she said.

"No," replied Old Man. "Let us not change what we have agreed upon."

And so people have died ever since.

The Moon Goddess

CHINESE-VIETNAMESE-AUSTRALIAN [85]

O nce upon a time in China there was a very fierce king who treated his people very cruelly. He taxed them very heavily so that he could have plenty of money for himself. Those who couldn't pay were severely punished and some families had to sell their children to raise the money to satisfy the king's tax collectors. Every family had to send a male member, a father or a son, to spend part of the year working for the king without pay, repairing roads and canals so that his army could reach every part of the kingdom. The work was often so hard that men fell ill and died, then their families found it hard to work the land without them and were punished when they could not pay their taxes. The people became poorer and poorer while the king became richer and richer. But the king didn't care that his people were hungry and cold as long as he had the best of everything and a well-fed army to carry out his commands.

From time to time some of the officials of his court were alarmed to see the people of the country in such a wretched state and tried to persuade the king to ask less of his subjects and show mercy to those who couldn't pay their taxes, but he simply became furious with them and had them put to death.

His wife was as gentle as he was fierce and as kind as he was cruel. She wept sometimes to see how the people suffered and begged the king again and again to change his ways, but he didn't listen to her pleas.

One day, when he realized that he had more wealth than he could ever use, the king decided he wanted something more. He wanted to live forever. He gathered his officials and army officers before him and announced, "I wish to become immortal. You must all help to find herbs that will allow me to achieve this."

It happened that a very learned doctor discovered some herbs which, if mixed together, would give immortality to anyone who swallowed them. The doctor was put to death so that he could never give his secret to anyone else and the medicine was brought to the king. He took it with him to his bedroom and showed it to his wife. "At last I have achieved everything I desire," he told her. But before he ate it he fell asleep and his wife thought, "If the medicine really works and he becomes immortal, the people will suffer forever. How terrible." To prevent this, she quickly swallowed the medicine. "Now he is sure to die like any other person and things may then get better for the people of this unhappy country," she said to herself. Then she quietly and quickly left the palace to hide in the countryside.

When he awoke and discovered that the medicine and his wife were both gone, the king was enraged and ordered his soldiers to search for his wife throughout the land. He joined in himself as the army looked for her in the shops, homes, streets and fields all over the country. Eventually, he caught up with her, hiding in a forest. When he saw her, he called her name, "Chang Her," but she ran with all her might. As she ran, she found that her feet were not touching the ground and she began to rise into the air almost as though she could fly. In front of the king and his soldiers, she rose higher and higher until she reached the moon. She has been there ever since and is known now as Chang Her the Moon Goddess.

Xueda and Yinlin

HUI PEOPLE, CHINA[86]

O nce upon a time, in a remote place, sat a mountain named Gancialin. Near its foot was a bend in the river and a very beautiful place. Fertile soil was there, and many flowers grew and bloomed.

On the land lived thirty poor families. All had come and settled after having fled from calamities elsewhere. These thirty families shared everything, comforts and hardships, and they worked with one heart and mind to support themselves by hunting and planting.

Among the villagers was a lad named Xueda, who had come to the River Bend area with his parents when he was still a child. A few years later his parents died and he became an orphan.

After that misfortune the villagers treated him as their own kith and kin. Among the villagers lived a widow who had an only daughter whose name was Yinlin. The widow and her daughter were especially kind to Xueda. Xueda regarded the villagers as his relatives; he viewed the widow as his mother and Yinlin as his little sister.

While he was still very young, Xueda was diligent and brave. By the time he reached eighteen he had become far more handsome and strong; he was very skilled in the martial arts. Shooting with bow and arrow was his favorite sport—a hundred shots for him meant a hundred bull's-eyes. When he came upon wild animals he never missed.

One day Xueda went hunting in the mountains. He met an old and white-haired man who gave him a bow and three golden arrows. After that, no matter who the wild animals were—tigers, lions, even demons and spirits—none of them could avoid his golden arrows.

When Yinlin reached the age of about fifteen she became very beautiful and intelligent. The birds and flowers which she embroidered appeared like real and living ones. Cotton cloth which she wove sold well. Aside from that she was good at singing and the people enjoyed her songs very much.

One day, when she was gathering firewood in the mountains, a very kind grandmother approached her and gave her a wonderful flute. No matter how tired one was, whoever heard the music that she played on her flute would forget his or her weariness entirely. Xueda and Yinlin often enthusiastically helped the villagers. They often gave away to them the bundle of firewood which they had collected. They would offer a helping hand to whoever was in need. And so Xueda and Yinlin were living with the villagers pleasantly and peacefully.

One year some people in the village became infected with a disease that gradually enlarged the patients' bellies. It spread across the village and there was an increasing number of sick people. They suffered severely from that lingering illness and groaned with pain.

Xueda and Yinlin were deeply grieved by the people's suffering and decided to bring relief. In the village lived an educated man by the name of Ma, he had studied some medicine. And so Xueda and Yinlin came to ask him what kind of illness it was and how it could be cured.

Mister Ma said, "It is potbelly disease which is not easily treated. But I have been told that there is an effective remedy. It is a pity that we do not have the primary herb that is needed. It is the small iris. The other medicine is leopard gallbladder. If you cannot find these two medicines within three months, the patients will die."

Then Xueda and Yinlin asked where the two medicines could be found, so that they each could go and look for them. Mister Ma said, half remembering and half lost in thought, "It has been said by old people that in the fairy cave, at Rock Cliff, there lives a leopard who comes forth only once a year, and only during hot days. Nobody dares to go there because an evil spirit returns to the cave soon after that happens. The place where the small irises grow is called Flower Mountain. To get there you must pass through Birds Cave. But no one can approach that cave without endangering his life."

What Mister Ma said did not frighten Xueda or Yinlin. Instead, it strengthened their resolve firmly to find the medicines, even to the point of risking their lives.

Xueda and Yinlin set out on their journeys, separately, leading four boys and four girls, respectively.

Days and nights Xueda and his four fellows walked straight toward Rock Cliff. In order to get there they had to go over six high mountains and cross six deep streams. Faced by the steep mountains and the deep rivers the four fellows were frightened and would go no further. Only Xueda was left to continue his journey. After countless hardships, and after crossing mountains and streams, he reached Rock Cliff.

In the gully by Rock Cliff grew many types of flowers and trees which he had never seen anywhere else. Birds and small animals of all kinds were playing happily and freely. Yet, Xueda had no time to enjoy this beautiful scenery. Immediately he hid himself in a cave opposite the rocky cliff to wait for the leopard. When he was thirsty and hungry he simply drank spring water and ate some wild fruits. In this manner he waited and watched. There was nothing to be seen of the leopard.

One day, while looking out with his sharp eyes, right and left, he noticed startled birds flying from trees and small animals on the ground escaping. After that the entire Rock Cliff became silent again.

Relying on his hunter's sensitivity, Xueda knew that a wild beast was approaching. He lost no time getting his golden bow and arrows and his hunting knife ready, all the while watching carefully. After a while he noticed a beam of red light streaming from the cave in Rock Cliff; it shone brilliantly over the entire valley. From that brilliant light emerged a very wild leopard spirit.

In excitement Xueda raised his bow and successfully shot two arrows at the two eyes of the leopard spirit. Being in great pain, and blinded, the leopard spirit roared terribly and leaped up and down while trying to flee for its life. Xueda seized the chance and rushed at it with his dagger and killed it. He skinned the leopard and took out its gallbladder. And having been successful he began his return journey.

After parting company with Xueda, Yinlin led the four girls and journeyed in the direction of the small irises. After a long trip they arrived at the Birds Cave at last.

The four girls looked inside and found it to be dark, and deep; and a variety of weird sounds came from it that made their blood curl and their hair stand on end. By the cave some ferocious and gigantic birds stood guard, looking at them fiercely. The four girls were absolutely terrified and retreated from this threat; they went back home. Yinlin also was terrified. But, thinking of the death which threatened the villagers she encouraged herself to approach Birds Cave.

She took out her bamboo flute and began playing on it. When these weird birds heard the beautiful sounds they gradually fell asleep. Yinlin seized the opportunity and passed through the cave and thereby entered another valley.

She felt hungry and intended to find something to eat when, suddenly, she caught sight of a small thatched hut ahead, on a nearby hill. By the cottage sat a kindly looking old man. Yinlin walked up to greet him and begged him for something to eat while, at the same time she asked the way to Flowers Mountain.

The old man said nothing but went into the hut and soon returned with a bowl of soup and a large cake. When she had finished eating the old man pointed Yinlin the right way and disappeared, together with his hut.

Yinlin walked three full days along the road shown by the old man before she finally arrived at Flowers Mountain. She looked ahead and found it to be a truly beautiful mountain, covered with many different flowers and plants which she had never seen before. Yet, Yinlin was not in any mood to enjoy them but began to search intensively after small irises. After having searched a while she saw some that grew halfway up the mountain.

With great delight Yinlin climbed up the mountain. When she got there she discovered that the small irises were in a basket carried by a girl wearing a red skirt. Two pink flowers adorned her head. The girl looked at her with a smile and asked her about the purpose of her coming. Yinlin explained her purpose. Then the girl, seeing the bamboo flute, asked Yinlin to play. This she did.

Unexpectedly her flute playing attracted dozens of young girls in red, and boys in blue. They surrounded her and requested that she play once more. This time Yinlin played a sorrowful piece, expressing thereby the miserable sufferings of the villagers. This caused the girls and the boys to shed sympathetic tears. Quickly they gathered all small irises into one large basket and brought them to her.

Afterward a girl led Yinlin to the edge of a cliff. Yinlin looked in the direction into which the girl pointed and saw that there were even more patients in the village. Most of them were already at the verge of death, and moaning voices could be heard throughout the entire village. Seeing this situation, Yinlin felt even more grieved and worried. How she wished she could fly back quickly to the village with her herbs!

The girl had already read Yinlin's mind. She asked her to close her eyes and then blew a puff of air towards her. Within a minute Yinlin had flown back to her village.

And so the diligent and brave young people, Xueda and Yinlin, overcame many difficulties and finally obtained leopard gallbladder and small irises within the required three months. They returned the critically ill villagers to life and thereby saved the whole village.

Later, everybody in the village agreed to hold a grand wedding ceremony for Xueda and Yinlin. They got married, and the villagers lived happy lives ever after.

The World We Travel Toward

"I'm not stupid!" Colleen screamed, her face red with anger and streaked with tears. My little girl screamed to me at the top of her lungs, resisting, with all the depths of her soul and every bit of strength she could muster, the hole she was being shoved into by the people around her. Every Friday during the spelling lesson, the teacher announced, "Colleen, put down your pen. That's your quota." Colleen was forced to put down her pen as all the other students went on with quotas of fifteen, twenty-five, and thirty words. Every week, she had to face this humiliating public evaluation of her intelligence. She wanted to try more words, she knew she had to learn faster, she knew she could do more, and she didn't know how it was all going so wrong. Something she had not doubted before, her own ability, was denied at school daily. As she felt herself beginning to internalize the deadly message, her last best effort to contradict it was to scream—wrestling with a devil, trying to keep it separate from herself and raging against its insidious infiltration of her own soul.

Rarely have I seen so apparent a struggle for a personal vision of a world. Usually the struggles are ill defined, unrecognized. They are won or lost, and the result becomes us before we even realize there might be a them and an us. Rarely do we recognize that we participate in the definition. Rarely do we take responsibility for our creation of that vision. Maybe we can change our lives by what we watch on television, which videos we rent, whether or not we smile at the harried grocery clerk, whether or not we let others call us stupid. Maybe we can change our lives by the stories we tell and the stories we believe.

It affects my actions if I believe that the world is shaped by forces outside of my control.[87] *It shapes my life if I believe that my evil actions will boomerang and directly hurt me, like the landlord's poison cake.*[88] *It changes my life if I believe that a small action like swallowing a drink can change the world.*[89]

Years ago on my parent-participation day at Colleen's preschool, the teacher had just finished reading a book to a semicircle of three-year-olds. "Who were you?" the teacher asked the group. The boys and several girls waved their hands in the air and called out. They had identified with the hero of the story. One little girl, however, inched forward, opened the book, and began turning the pages. Finally she found the page for which she had been searching. "There I am!" she cried triumphantly and pointed to a picture of a little girl in a crowd, the only little girl pictured in the book.

In choosing which tales to tell and which tales to believe, we build a vision of the world for ourselves. Like any other adaptation, folktales define who we are and how we behave. They influence our world and our survival. The quality and number of different tales we tell could be as significant in creating our future as the quality and number of weapons we manufacture.[90]

Im ʿAwwād and the Ghouleh

PALESTINIAN ARAB PEOPLE[91]

Once upon a time there were some women who agreed to
meet on a certain day to go wash their clothes at the spring
on the edge of town. As they were discussing the matter, a ghouleh*
who had hidden herself behind a retaining wall nearby heard what
they agreed to do that day. On the appointed night, toward dawn,
she came to the one among them whose house was on the outskirts
of town and made as if she were one of the women who had promised to go to the spring. The woman to whose house she had come
was called Im ʿAwwād. Calling out from the outside door of the
house, the ghouleh said, "Hey! Im ʿAwwād! Let's go! Tie your dirty
clothes in a bundle, and let's go do the laundry!"

"Who is it?" asked Im ʿAwwād.

"I'm Im So-and-So,"† answered the ghouleh.

"All right," said Im ʿAwwād.

It was the middle of the month, and the moon was bright.
Thinking it was daylight already, she put her laundry in a tub and
lifted it.

"Bring your son with you," suggested the ghouleh. "We might be
a while."

She brought her son with her, and the two women walked, with
the ghouleh in front. When they had gone just beyond the last

*ghouleh: ghoul
†I'm Im So-and-So: rather like saying, "I am Mrs. So-and-so," the ghouleh
can take on any form she wants

houses in town, Im 'Awwād looked and saw that the feet of the woman walking in front of her were making sparks. Realizing the woman was a ghouleh, Im 'Awwād was afraid.

"I want to go back," she said.

"Why?"

"I forgot my husband's tunic," she replied, "and he'll kill me if I don't wash it. Here! Take this boy and go ahead, and I'll catch up with you."

Putting down the washtub, and the boy by its side, she went running back to her husband.

"Heat up the oil, you whose house is in ruins!" she cried out, knocking on the door. "Now she'll come and eat us before anyone can come to our help."

By the time the ghouleh had finished eating the boy, she came back to eat Im 'Awwād and her husband.

"O Im 'Awwād!" she cried out from behind the outside door. "Here's 'Awwād's little prick! Make it into a little wick!"

When the man heard this, he said to his wife, "What you've been saying is true, damn your parents! This is a ghouleh!"

The ghouleh dug under the door until she could stick her head and neck inside, and Abu 'Awwād poured the boiling oil over her head.

"Do it again!" she cried out, and he answered, "My mother didn't teach me how."*

The ghouleh's head exploded, and she died.

Its dust has scattered, and now for another one!

---

*Do it again! . . . My mother didn't teach me how: a ghoul must be killed with one blow

An Evil Being Appears
at an Appointment Instead of
the Right Person

PAPUA NEW GUINEA[92]

One day the Dáru people arranged to go fishing early on the morrow. At sunset a woman went outside the house, where a friend of hers lived, and called out to her, "Tomorrow we go catch fish," and the other woman replied, "We go." The two women were overheard by a *híwai-abére*.*

In the night, when the moon was shining, the *híwai-abére* appeared outside the same house and called to the woman, "*Árao*,† you come quick! I go first time, you come behind." The *híwai-abére* went on ahead, and the woman, who thought that it was her friend, jumped up, took her fish-trap, and ran after her. The *híwai-abére* led the way out on to the beach. "*Árao*," she cried, "you come quick, people will be finished," and the woman hastened after her. In order not to be found out, the *híwai-abére* walked at a quick pace and as she went picked up an old fish-trap which somebody had thrown away. When they arrived at the fishing place, the woman said to her, "*Árao*, no people here."

"We no can catch fish?" the *híwai-abére* replied. "You and me come catch plenty of fish, no good if plenty people come." She urged the woman to go into the water.

"Better you go catch fish, I cannot go along water, I get sick, by and by I get too cold." The evil woman did not want to go into the

híwai-abére: monster
†*Árao*: friend

water herself, so she deceived her companion. The girl waded out and caught fish, which she threw on shore, and the *híwai-abére* swallowed them up. She said to the girl, "You catch plenty of fish, throw them on shore, I kill them here and keep them," but she devoured them all.

At last the girl became suspicious, thinking to herself, "I do not hear her hammer that fish." The next time she threw a fish on shore, she found out what the *híwai-abére* was doing. "Oh, she swallowed it down. She isn't putting fish along the rope. That is a devil-woman. No good if I take fright. I'll catch plenty of fish, make her belly full. Then I'll run, she can't run quick when her belly is full."

The girl kept on catching fish, which the monster devoured. At last she noticed that the *híwai-abére* found it difficult to swallow any more. "Oh, that woman she swallowed one fish but the tail stayed along the mouth, she swallowed two times. Oh, her belly is full now. Close up I run away." Then she caught a large rock-fish and asked the *híwai-abére*, "*Árao*, you come help me."

"I cannot go there," the evil woman replied, "I get cold. You catch him yourself, you are a strong woman."

The girl brought the fish on shore saying, "*Árao*, you come help me pull," but the *híwai-abére* replied, "No, no, I cannot go."

When the fish was landed, the *híwai-abére* came and seized it. Passing behind the monster, the girl put down her fish-trap and ran away. The *híwai-abére* was occupied with the fish, and on seeing the trap beside her thought to herself, "The woman is standing up there close to it." But the girl was running away at the top of her speed. At last she reached the village, climbed up the ladder of her house, went quickly to her bed, and lay down. She did not tell anyone of her adventure.

The *híwai-abére,* who was eating the rock-fish, had not noticed anything. When at last she became aware of the girl's flight, she cried out, "Oh, that woman she has run away," and started in pursuit, scenting out the way which the girl had taken. But when she came to the ladder of the house, the girl was already inside and the *híwai-abére* could not follow her thither.

At dawn, when the wild fowl began to cry out, the people got up. The girl who had run away from the *híwai-abére*, was secretly watching them from her place. Her friend came and called her, "*Árao*, some people have gone, you come quick!" The girl pretended to be ill and replied, "I cannot go, I got too much cold all over my body." She remained indoors, and was asked to look after her friend's children while the mother went fishing. The people found the tracks of two persons on the beach. "Oh!" they exclaimed. "Two women went here, they left a track! Plenty of fish have been caught here. Somebody has killed fish here." And they asked everybody, "Which woman went and caught fish in the nighttime?" One woman had heard the *híwai-abére* calling the girl in the night and told the others so. "Some woman, she stopped by a house, somebody sang out in the nighttime." They tried to find out who that had been. "Did you sing out? Did you sing out?" they asked each other, but nobody had called the girls.

A man coming from the men's house asked the girl who had remained in the village, "Why didn't you go catch fish?"

"I cannot go," she answered, "I got sick, how should I go?"

In the evening the people returned to the village with fish. The woman whose children the girl had looked after, came to her and gave her some fish. "Why didn't you come?" she asked her friend.

"I cannot come," the girl answered, "I wasn't sick, I was afraid. In the nighttime one *híwai-abére* sang out, fooled me. We two caught plenty of fish, the devil-woman swallowed them all. That's why I couldn't go." Her friend went and told the people, and then they understood. "Oh, that's why we saw the track."

Since then the people do not go and call each other in the night, but on the previous evening arrange the details of meeting. At the time agreed upon, the one friend walks into the other's house to waken him or her up, sometimes the caller whistles outside or knocks against the ladder with a spear. The *híwai-abére* never do so.

The Outwitted Ghost of the Forest

ARAWAK PEOPLE, NORTHWEST AMAZON BASIN[93]

Once upon a time a family was invited to a festival. Everyone went except the daughter, who refused to go. She stayed at home all alone.

Late in the afternoon, a friend whom the girl hadn't seen in a long time came for a visit. At least the girl thought it was her friend Dai-adalla, whom she had exchanged names with long ago.* Really, however, the girl's visitor was a ghost of the forest. This ghost had taken on the form and looks of the girl's friend in order to do his evil deeds. Since they were such good friends, the ghost of the forest casually called the girl Dai-adalla, and asked her what she was doing all alone in the house. When the girl said that she hadn't wanted to go to the festival with everyone, the ghost of the forest said, "Oh, that's good! I'll stay here tonight and keep you company."

In the evening as it became dark, they heard a bunch of frogs croaking. The girl asked her friend if she liked to eat frogs and the friend answered that she loved to eat frogs. So the two went right out to catch some frogs.

Together they went out into the darkness, then each went in a different direction, and after a while they began to call to each other and ask how many frogs the other had caught. The ghost of the forest answered, "Lots, but I eat them as quickly as I catch them." The girl was shocked by this answer, that the other was eating the frogs raw, and the girl suddenly realized the real nature of

*exchanging names: Among the Arawak, intimate friends were accustomed to trading names.

148

her supposed friend. The ghost of the forest called out, "Dai-adalla! How many have you caught?" The girl answered, "Lots, but I'm putting them all into my calabash."

The whole time the girl kept thinking how she could escape her companion. The girl knew quite well that despite the darkness, the ghost of the forest knew exactly where she stood from the sound of her voice. When the ghost of the forest called to her once more, she answered, "Be still! Don't talk! Don't make any noise! The frogs will get scared and I won't be able to catch any more." When once more silence reigned, the girl stole quietly back to the house. She crawled inside and turned all the pots in the house upside down without making the smallest noise. Then she threw the frogs away and climbed onto the roof to wait for what would happen next.

It didn't take long. After the ghost of the forest had waited a while and had received no answer to its call, it realized that it had been tricked and raced back to the house. There it tapped around in the darkness and turned over one pot after another, but its prey was not under any of them. "Oh!" it called out loudly enough for the girl to hear. "If I had thought that she would escape me, I would have eaten her right away like I did the frogs."

It searched, but in vain—there were a lot of pots there—until the dawn came and it had to leave. The girl came down from the roof and waited for her parents. When they came, she told them how the ghost of the forest had come in the form of a friend. Then the girl's father said, "Next time, when we say you should come with us, you'll obey us."

Using Speculation Machines

In Strasbourg, France, we stood at a bus stop but were unsure of the number of the bus we needed. The buses lined up along the stop in no particular order and they left quickly. I waited with Colleen and Deirdre while my husband darted quickly into the street, then hopped back up onto the curb and rushed up the busy sidewalk. "This one!" he shouted. Before I could grab her, my older daughter, Colleen, rushed after him. She knew she wasn't allowed in the street, so she ran, balancing, along the curb. In slow motion, I watch the first bus begin to pull away from the curb. I see my little girl's ankle twist. She catches her balance. She doesn't fall, the bus doesn't hit her. I retrace my mental steps. Before I can grab her, Colleen rushes after her dad. In slow motion, I watch the first bus begin to pull away from the curb. The woman with the big handbag drops something. As she bends over, she inadvertently knocks my little girl into the path of the bus. No. It doesn't happen. I retrace my mental steps. Before I can grab her, Colleen rushes after her dad. I lunge. I grab her wrist. I pull her back and tell her, "There's no need to rush. If we miss this bus, there will be another one. Go on the sidewalk this way." Colleen darts into the crowd on the sidewalk and runs after her dad. No, it doesn't happen. I retrace my mental steps.

It's a nightmare, my brain replays the situation over and over again with slight changes in each replay. Like a speculation machine, my mind recreates the past, present, and future. My brain does what folktales do: both explore options and alternatives. Each folktale has variants. Much of the story remains the same, but some phrase or detail or small section varies and the tale takes on a different cast.

As tales pass through different storytellers, generations, and cultures, parts of the stories remain the same: There is danger. What have we done? What shall we do? Parts of the stories change: Talk to your neighbor, ask for help, know your enemy, throw your spear. The three previous stories from very different parts of the world have very similar plots. A monster comes disguised as a friend. If the heroine doesn't do something, it will kill her. She escapes, but how will we all avoid this danger in the future? Will we organize the community to kill the monster, or should we form a neighborhood communication scheme, a community watch, or should we all go places together?

The folk narrative is probably the most ancient, most successful method of transferring ideas and information across generations. Tales may be almost as ancient as language itself.[94] *As tales were told and retold around campfires by successive generations, fundamental aspects of the human brain were evolving.*[95] *We can tell because our brains seem to be most comfortable with narrative.*

One cold day in France, we were riding home from school. I rode my bicycle with Deirdre perched up in the child's seat on the back. Colleen pedaled her little pink bicycle beside us. "Mom, can you tell me a story?" Colleen asked.

I sighed. I didn't think I could summon up the energy to tell stories on the way home as well as all through the difficult morning. "Honey, I'm cold and hungry and I just want to get home."

She begged, "Please, please, please!"

As I searched my brain for yet another tale, a small voice behind me, Deirdre's voice, narrated softly. "Once tupon ta time, there was a little girl go walking in the forest. And . . . and . . . and . . . and there was a ghost and . . . and . . . and . . . and then she went home." Deirdre was only three, but her mind was already building stories, because that was definitely a tale, with a beginning, a middle, and an end.

Cross-cultural, multigenerational brainstorming sessions have blossomed into folktales that operate on many levels.[96] *Thanks to folktales, we don't have to expend all the time and take all the risks that would be necessary to test all the solutions to all the problems we encounter.*[97] *Some other warrior has already encountered that weapon, some other woman has already prepared that food during a drought, some other hunter has already tracked* that animal, and we hear their stories. Folktales are survival tools. They are cultural extensions of our speculation machines, our brains.

It seemed ages ago that I had entered my study and felt the comfort of a quiet and dark book-and-story-filled room. It seemed ages ago that I had thought reading folktales would be a safe retreat. The stories at my virtual campfire had made me laugh, but had moved me quickly away from simple questions about fear and courage. I'd gotten mired in a demon's maze of questions. Folktales led me into the maze, but they wouldn't leave me there alone and hopeless. I've learned to use these tales as speculation machines. I'll sit here now and let the folktales do their job. Let them take the risks as I consider my options. Because of September 11, I am afraid. What can I do? What are my options? What are the repercussions?

Still Another Spook

MAYAN PEOPLE, CENTRAL AMERICA[98]

Long ago there were a great many Spooks. The Spooks would steal chickens. They would steal money. They would go from house to house to steal women away.

We couldn't go anywhere. We couldn't go out to gather firewood or fetch water. From three o'clock in the afternoon until eight o'clock the next morning we were closed up inside the house. At nine o'clock we could go out, but only nearby, and never alone. We couldn't go far because it was dark under the trees. They would be squatting there, waiting to grab us as we were gathering wood or drawing water.

Once a Spook came to the house of one of my neighbors. "Nanita, won't you please do the favor of preparing my meal?" asked the Spook, carrying a stolen turkey with him.

"Give it to me! Come in! Sit down!" said the woman. She put her pot of water on top of the fire. When the boiling water was bubbling, she dipped the turkey in it. She put another pot on the fire. "Wouldn't you like to drink some *posol** while you wait for your meal?"

"I would!" said the Spook.

While he was drinking his *posol*, she threw boiling water on him. He was scalded like a chicken.

But it didn't kill him. He just rolled out the door. He was rolling around the whole day at the door, since he was burnt. But in three

posol: a Spanish-American drink made of cornmeal, water, and sugar

153

days he was well again and walking around. He tried to grab a baby girl.

You see how tricky they were. They would grab whatever they could get. There weren't any good Spooks. They were wicked.

"Forget it," said the woman when she saw that the awful Spook couldn't be killed.

"But we shouldn't be scared. We should be brave now that there are several families nearby," said the women of Zinacantán.* "Now that he has seen our houses, there's no time left."

The women gathered together. The Spook arrived again.

"Nanita, Nanita. You gonna make dee meal!" said the Spook in his awful Spanish.

"But he's a countryman of ours. Don't believe he's a Spook. He's fooling us," said the women, trying to humor him.

"Give it to me! Where is it? Come on! We'll fix it! If you want to eat a meal, I will grind the corn. I will make the tortillas," said the woman of the house.

"Grind it. I'll wait, Nanita!" said the Spook.

She patted the tortillas. She cooked the chicken. He ate.

"If you want a little coffee, I'll make it," she said.

He was in the midst of drinking his coffee. Then he was shot at; God, he didn't die from the bullets.

The women attacked him with a machete. He was cut up properly. They didn't cut his body into just two pieces. He didn't get just a single blow!

But he was sewn up. He revived, since he just wouldn't die.

A week or two later he returned again. He brought two hens and a crate of bread along with him. "Nanita, fix dee meal. I eat!" said the Spook.

"Ah, give it to me! If you are hungry, I'll fix it. I'll rinse my corn and make the tortillas."

"Oh, his horrible eyes, his horrible teeth. They'd give you a fright!" said the woman who told me about it.

*Zinacantán: the town this story came from

"His horrible wide eyes were red. You'd be scared of him. You certainly wouldn't eat with him."

"Did you eat with him?" I asked.

"I ate with him," she said, "because we had already decided what to do."

The tip was sharpened. She served his meal, her meal, and her children's meal. They finished eating.

The gentleman burped. "Ahh!" he said. "Burr! Well, Nanita, thank you for the meal. Do your children have enough to eat?"

"They do," she told him.

"Fine! Spend a good night, Nanita!" said the Spook. He stretched his legs and went out the door.

He landed on a sharpened stake. It went up his ass, came out his mouth. He was spitted.

"Now we'll roast him on the fire."

They roasted him on the fire the way we roast a rabbit. Wouldn't he die of that?

They turned him over from side to side. They used up eight logs.

They cooked him until he was well-done. Then they set him afire. They poured kerosene on him so that he would die. Die for good.

The Spooks have disappeared to this day. There are very few left. Only where a road is being made or a bridge is being built do we hear of Spooks. But we don't see them much anymore. Long ago we couldn't even go outside. It was scary because we were killed by Spooks.

The Oyster and the Shark

MUᴎKAN PEOPLE, AUSTRALIA⁹⁹

At one time Min Wára, older and younger brothers, lived at Wa:tama. They were sitting on the beach one day when Té:'alédyan the shark passed by them, hunting stingray.

The oyster brothers called out to him, but he went on looking round, looking round, taking no notice of them. After a while he came up to the beach where they were sitting.

The oyster brothers stole his stingray when his back was turned. By and by the shark came back to find it: "Where's the fish? Those two must have taken it from here! They must have a grudge against me."

He didn't follow them up straightaway, but went another way round. He got his spear ready for them, tightening the barbs with gut and smoothing the gum over the barb on his wooden palette. "Tomorrow I'll look for them!" he said.

He slept there. Early in the morning he left and found those two still lying asleep. "What fish is this you've been eating? Why did you steal my fish?"

"We called to you and you wouldn't answer!"

"I didn't hear you!"

"We were hungry and we called out to you!"

"There were plenty fish swimming in the river! Why couldn't you spear them for yourselves? There's plenty of room for us both!" The shark struck the youngest oyster brother with his spear-thrower.

The elder brother said: "Why do you hit my young brother?"

"You took the stingray from me!"

"You struck first with the club!"

"I'll strike you with a spear presently!"

They went on quarrelling. The shark picked up a spear, balanced it on his spear-thrower and hooked it ready to throw. The oyster hit back the spear with his spear-thrower.

They take to wrestling on the ground, knocking each other over. The shark picks up ashes from the fire and throws them over their bodies; their heads, faces, and arms are covered with ashes. The oyster picks up hot sand and throws it in the shark's eyes: "I can't see!"

The shark picks up a spear. He spears the older brother with two spears. The younger brother takes his brother's part. The shark hits the older brother hard with his spear-thrower and flattens his nose; blood runs from the older brother's nose.

The younger brother chased the shark southwards along the beach. He picked up his boomerang and threw it after the shark— hitting him in the back. Té:'alédyan ran away altogether, with the boomerang still sticking in his back.*

The younger brother came back up. He cried over his older brother. The older brother could do nothing for himself; the spears were hanging down from his back, and he couldn't get up. The younger brother looked after him; he caught the lice in his brother's hair for him.

The two brothers went down to the water's edge to find a place where they could stay. They came to a small island, Pikta. "This is our place! Tomorrow we'll go down here, my young brother!" said Wára. "We will stay here and sink down under. Our children's children will eat us for food!"

They sank deep down under the water. Just there is the *auwa*† of the oyster.

---

*boomerang still sticking in his back: this has become the shark's fin
†*auwa*: place from Dreamtime

Mr. Fox

ENGLAND[100]

Lady Mary was young, and Lady Mary was fair. She had two brothers, and more lovers than she could count. But of them all, the bravest and most gallant, was a Mr. Fox, whom she met when she was down at her father's country-house. No one knew who Mr. Fox was; but he was certainly brave, and surely rich, and of all her lovers, Lady Mary cared for him alone. At last it was agreed upon between them that they should be married. Lady Mary asked Mr. Fox where they should live, and he described to her his castle, and where it was; but, strange to say, did not ask her, or her brothers to come and see it.

So one day, near the wedding day, when her brothers were out, and Mr. Fox was away for a day or two on business, as he said, Lady Mary set out for Mr. Fox's castle. And after many searchings, she came at last to it, and a fine strong house it was, with high walls and a deep moat. And when she came up to the gateway she saw written on it:

BE BOLD, BE BOLD.

But as the gate was open, she went through it, and found no one there. So she went up to the doorway, and over it she found written:

BE BOLD, BE BOLD, BUT NOT TOO BOLD.

Still she went on, till she came into the hall, and went up the broad stairs till she came to a door in the gallery, over which was written:

BE BOLD, BE BOLD, BUT NOT TOO BOLD,
LEST THAT YOUR HEART'S BLOOD SHOULD RUN COLD.

But Lady Mary was a brave one, she was, and she opened the door, and what do you think she saw? Why, bodies and skeletons of beautiful young ladies all stained with blood. So Lady Mary thought it was high time to get out of that horrid place, and she closed the door, went through the gallery, and was just going down the stairs, and out of the hall, when who should she see through the window but Mr. Fox dragging a beautiful young lady along from the gateway to the door. Lady Mary rushed downstairs, and hid herself behind a cask just in time, as Mr. Fox came in with the poor young lady, who seemed to have fainted. Just as he got near Lady Mary, Mr. Fox saw a diamond ring glittering on the finger of the young lady he was dragging, and he tried to pull it off. But it was tightly fixed, and would not come off, so Mr. Fox cursed and swore, and drew his sword, raised it, and brought it down upon the hand of the poor lady. The sword cut off the hand, which jumped up into the air, and fell of all places in the world into Lady Mary's lap. Mr. Fox looked about a bit, but did not think of looking behind the cask, so at last he went on dragging the young lady up the stairs into the Bloody Chamber.

As soon as she heard him pass through the gallery, Lady Mary crept out of the door, down through the gateway, and ran home as fast as she could.

Now it happened that the very next day the marriage contract of Lady Mary and Mr. Fox was to be signed, and there was a splendid breakfast before that. And when Mr. Fox was seated at table opposite Lady Mary, he looked at her. "How pale you are this morning, my dear."

"Yes," said she, "I had a bad night's rest last night. I had horrible dreams."

"Dreams go by contraries," said Mr. Fox, "but tell us your dream, and your sweet voice will make the time pass till the happy hour comes."

"I dreamed," said Lady Mary, "that I went yester morn to your castle, and I found it in the woods, with high walls, and a deep moat, and over the gateway was written:

BE BOLD, BE BOLD."

"But it is not so, nor it was not so," said Mr. Fox.

"And when I came to the doorway over it was written:

BE BOLD, BE BOLD, BUT NOT TOO BOLD."

"It is not so, nor it was not so," said Mr. Fox.

"And then I went upstairs, and came to a gallery, at the end of which was a door, on which was written:

BE BOLD, BE BOLD, BUT NOT TOO BOLD,
LEST THAT YOUR HEART'S BLOOD SHOULD RUN COLD."

"It is not so, nor it was not so," said Mr. Fox.

"And then—and then I opened the door, and the room was filled with bodies and skeletons of poor dead women, all stained with their blood."

"It is not so, nor it was not so. And God forbid it should be so," said Mr. Fox.

"I then dreamed that I rushed down the gallery, and just as I was going down the stairs, I saw you, Mr. Fox, coming up to the hall door, dragging after you a poor young lady, rich and beautiful."

"It is not so, nor it was not so. And God forbid it should be so," said Mr. Fox.

"I rushed downstairs, just in time to hide myself behind a cask, when you, Mr. Fox, came in dragging the young lady by the arm. And, as you passed me, Mr. Fox, I thought I saw you try and get off her diamond ring, and when you could not, Mr. Fox, it seemed to me in my dream, that you out with your sword and hacked off the poor lady's hand to get the ring."

"It is not so, nor it was not so. And God forbid it should be so," said Mr. Fox, and was going to say something else as he rose from his seat, when Lady Mary cried out:

"But it is so, and it was so. Here's hand and ring I have to show," and pulled out the lady's hand from her dress, and pointed it straight at Mr. Fox.

At once her brothers and her friends drew their swords and cut Mr. Fox into a thousand pieces.

Mereaira and Kape Tautini

MĀORI PEOPLE, NEW ZEALAND[101]

Ngāti Awa chief, Te Keepa Toihau, did marry and fathered a daughter who became famous in this area, Mereaira Rangihoea. In time she was betrothed to a young Whakatōhea chief known as Kape Tautini, from Ōhakana Island in the Ōhiwa Harbour. These people were known to have been frequent enemies of Ngāti Awa. Tautini lived with his wife Mereaira under the mantle of her father, Te Keepa Toihau at Tauwhare pā, and a child was soon born to the couple. But during his stay here Tautini became restless and moody among the Ngāti Awa people and without notice made his way back to his Whakatōhea tribe. Mereaira was bereft at her husband's departure and became inconsolable, fearful of what might happen.

Her fears were realized when, not long after, a flotilla of Whakatōhea war canoes was seen approaching Tauwhare pā, and Kape Tautini was sighted on board. Whakatōhea had become resentful of Ngāti Awa's presence on Te Moana o Tairongo and sought to drive Ngāti Awa back over the hills. Mereaira and her people were totally unprepared for the attack and rallied around their chief Te Keepa Toihau for advice, Mereaira begging her father to plea for peace. Ngāti Awa had no choice but to huddle on a hill above the beach, helpless and passive.

The Whakatōhea warriors began to perform their *haka** on the mud flats below Tauwhare, reciting the remembrance of past insults

*haka: war dance

162

and wounds cast upon them by Ngāti Awa. However, before they had a chance to assail the relatively undefended pā, Mereaira, filled with love and terror, stood on the edge of the cliff above the warriors, holding her infant baby above her head. She cried out to her husband and his warriors so that all could hear: "The child I am holding is the symbol of the union between our two tribes and could make for peace or for war. What use is it living together if the price to be paid is always in blood? Has not the sea sufficient for all? Who, then, shall say it is theirs? Unless the killing is stopped now and forever, I shall throw my child on the rocks and his blood shall be on your hands and will become your eternal disgrace."

Kape Tautini and his Whakatōhea people were filled with shame and their hearts brimmed with admiration for Mereaira. Their aggression towards Ngāti Awa subsided, and peace was made between the tribes. Kape smiled. A light shone from his eyes, and he was no longer grim and forbidding. He approached his young wife and took her and the infant lovingly in his arms.

On Death's Payroll[102]

I had edited an anthology of folktales featuring heroines. These heroines were courageous mothers, clever young girls, and warrior women who saved their villages from monsters, ruled wisely over kingdoms, and outwitted flying heads, thieves, and tigers. The breadth of these heroines' responses to threats amazed me. They sang, they ran, they used gossip as well as daggers and magic. They danced. They used kindness, intelligence, and determination to overcome the obstacles they faced.[103] "Women have so many different solutions to problems," I said to my husband. "Men just fight."

We were making sandwiches for lunch and he didn't even have to stop spreading the mayonnaise to think of his answer. "But how do men fight?" he said. "Do you know how many ways there are to fight and kill the enemy? Do we use spears or swords or guns? Organize armies or fight single-handedly? Do we use germs or technology? Ambush or frontal attack? There are lots of ways to fight a battle and it's important for men to think about what they'll do. You only think women have more solutions because you understand those solutions better."

I took my sandwich and retreated to my study to thumb through more folktales. At my virtual campfire, a Mayan woman, her face lined by famine and war, efficiently enumerated how not to kill a spook. Don't scald or burn him. Don't shoot him. Don't slice him up. Roast him on a spit. Next a thin, dark-skinned man from northern Australia leapt to his feet. He danced the battle between the oysters and the shark. With strongly punctuated stamps and staccato movements, he threw the spear, the boomerang, the sand into his opponent's eyes. Then he sank backwards onto his imaginary spear.

In early tribal wars, groups of maybe fifty men loosely gathered on either side of an undrawn but easily perceived line. One man stepped into no-man's-land and heaved his spear which ineffectually skidded along the ground as a few opponents sidestepped it. In modern wars, hundreds of thousands are grouped on jagged lines across the globe and one finger on a button is equivalent to that step into no-man's-land and the spear hurled is the death of thousands rained from the skies.

As population rises, killing has become more effective. This violence might be an evolutionary answer to overpopulation, but it is also a threat to our survival. Maybe warfare has outlived its usefulness now that we face nuclear devastation. Regardless of the answer, taking responsibility for our world requires the admission that violence has always been an option.

We killed about 55 million of ourselves from 1941 to 1945.[104]

We killed about 18 million of ourselves from 1914 to 1918.[105]

We killed about 5 million of ourselves in the Vietnam War.[106]

We strangled, drowned, burned, and beheaded at least 100,000 of ourselves, mostly females, in Europe from 1500 to 1700.[107]

We killed 8 million of ourselves on Haiti from 1492 to 1555.[108]

Violence has always been an option.

The Poles of the House

The poles of the Igogau's house were quarreling. Said the floor supports to the poles who were quarreling, "What can you do if I am not?" "What can you do if I am not?" said the footboards to those floor supports who are quarreling. "What can you do if I am not?" said the cross supports to those floor supports who are quarreling. "What can you do if I am not?" said the cross supports to those footboards who are quarreling. "What can you do if I am not?" said the floor to those cross supports who are quarreling. "What can you do if I am not?" said the wall to the floorboards who are quarreling. "What can you do if I am not?" said the beams to the wallboards who are quarreling. "What can you do if I am not?" said the *pongo** to the beams who are quarreling. "What can you do if I am not?" said the woven bamboo[†] to the *pongo* who are quarreling. "What can you do if I am not?" said the end pole to those woven bamboo who are quarreling. "What can you do if I am not?" said the *salabáwan*[‡] to those end poles who are quarreling. "What can you do if I am not—who am *legpet*?"[§] said those *legpet* to those *salabáwan*. "Though you are *legpet*, you can do nothing if I am not," said the *gakot*,[**] "because you fall," said the *gakot* to the *legpet* who

*pongo: Several native names which have no exact English equivalents are used here.

[†]woven bamboo: woven bamboo used on ceilings, daplat

[‡]*salabáwan*: native name with no exact English equivalent

[§]*legpet*: native name with no exact English equivalent

[**]*gakot*: native name with no exact English equivalent

are quarreling. "And what can you all do if I am not, who am grass? You all decay if I am not," said the grass roof to those who are quarreling. "Therefore we are all the same use to the house of the Ipogau; we will unite our thoughts and breath, so that in the same manner the thoughts of the Ipogau are united, who live in us," said those who are quarreling. And they united their thoughts and breath. After that the Ipogau who were sick were cured, those who lived in the house. It was as if there was nothing bad for that family.

The Dead Moon

ENGLAND[110]

Long ago the Lincolnshire Cars were full of bogs and it was death to walk through them, except on moonlight nights, for harm and mischance and mischief, bogles* and dead things and crawling horrors came out at nights when the Moon did not shine. At length the Moon heard what things went on in the bog when her back was turned, and she thought she would go down to see for herself, and find what she could do to help. So at the month's end she wrapped a black cloak round her, and hid her shining hair under a black hood, and stepped down into the boglands. It was all dark and watery, with quaking mud, and waving tussocks of grass, and no light except what came from her own white feet. On she went, deep into the bogland and now the witches rode about her on their great cats, and the will-o'-the-wykes† danced with the lanterns swinging on their backs, and dead folks rose out of the water, and stared at her with fiery eyes, and the slimy dead hands beckoned and clutched. But on she went, stepping from tuft to tuft, as light as the wind in summer until at length a stone turned under her, and she caught with both hands at a snag nearby to steady herself; but as soon as she touched it, it twisted round her wrists like a pair of handcuffs and held her fast. She struggled

*bogles: goblins, evil creatures

†will-o'-the-wyke: ignis fatuus, a light that sometimes appears in the night, usually over marshy ground and often attributable to the combustion of marsh gas, also called will-o'-the-wisp

and fought against it, but nothing would free her. Then, as she stood trembling she heard a piteous crying, and she knew that a man was lost in the darkness, and soon she saw him, splashing after the will-o'-the-wykes, crying out on them to wait for him, while the Dead Hands plucked at his coat, and the creeping horrors crowded round him, and he went further and further from the Path.

The Moon was so sorry and so angry that she made a great struggle, and though she could not loose her hands, her hood slipped back, and the light streamed out from her beautiful golden hair, so that the man saw the bog-holes near him and the safe path in the distance nearly as clear as by day. He cried for joy, and floundered across, out of the deadly bog and back to safety, and all the bogles and evil things fled away from the moonlight, and hid themselves. But the Moon struggled in vain to free herself, and at length she fell forward, spent with the struggle, and the black hood fell over her head again, and she had no strength to push it off. Then all the evil things came creeping back, and they laughed to think they had their enemy the Moon in their power at last. All night they fought and squabbled about how best they should kill her, but when the first grey light before dawn came they grew frightened, and pushed her down into the Water. The Dead Folk held her, while the Bogles fetched a great stone to put over her, and they chose two will-o'-the-wykes to guard her by turns, and when the day came the Moon was buried deep, until someone should find her, and who knew where to look?

The days passed, and folk put straws in their caps, and money in their pockets against the coming of the new Moon, and she never came. And as dark night after dark night passed, the evil things from the bogland came howling and screeching up to men's very doors, so that no one could go a step from the house at night, and in the end folk sat up all night, shivering by their fires, for they feared if the lights went out, the things would come over the thresholds.

At last they went to the Wise Woman who lived in the old mill to ask what had come of their Moon. She looked in the mirror, and in the brewpot and in the Book, and it was all dark, so she told them to set straw and salt and a button on their doorsills at night, to keep them safe from the Horrors, and to come back with any news they could give her.

Well, you can be sure they talked, at their firesides and in the Garth* and in the town. So it happened one day, as they were sitting on the settle at the Inn, a man from the far side of the bogland cried out all of a sudden, "I reckon I know where the Moon is, only I was so 'mazed I never thought on it." And he told them how he had been all astray one night, and like to lose his life in the bogholes, and all of a sudden a clear bright light had shone out, and showed him the way home. So off they all went to the Wise Woman, and told what the man had said. The Wise Woman looked in the Book, and in the pot, and at last she got some glimmer of light and told them what they must do. They were to set out together in the darkness with a stone in their mouths and a hazel twig in their hands, and not a word must they speak till they got home, and they must search through the bog till they found a coffin, and a cross, and a candle, and that was where the Moon would be. Well, they were main feared, but next night they set out and went on and on, into the midst of the bog.

They saw nothing, but they heard a sighing and whispering round them and slimy hands touching them, but on they went, shaking and scared, till suddenly they stopped, for half in and half out of the water they saw a long stone, for all the world like a coffin, and at the head of it stood a black snag stretching out two branches, like a gruesome cross, and on it flickered a tiddy† light. Then they all knelt down and they crossed themselves and said the Lord's Prayer, forward for the sake of the cross, and backward against the bogles, but all silently, for they knew they must not speak. Then all together they heaved up the stone. For one minute they saw a strange beautiful face looking up at them and then they stepped

*Garth: yard, enclosure
†tiddy: tiny

back 'mazed with the light, and with a great shrieking wail from all the horrors, as they fled back to their holes, and the next moment the full Moon shone down on them from the Heavens, so that they could see their path near as clear as by day.

And ever since then the Moon has shone her best over the bog-lands, for she knows all the evil things that are hid there and she remembers how the Car men went out to look for her when she was dead and buried.

Legend of Sway-Uock

D eep in the forest among the tallest fir trees lived an evil witch, who was known as Sway-Uock.

The very mention of her name alarmed parents and spread terror among children. She was as tall as the trees in the forest, and she could step over village houses with ease. She had a giant basket, deeper than a child was tall. Sway-Uock was greatly feared because she used the cover of darkness to slip into villages and steal children. When her giant basket was filled with screaming and crying children, she would return to her shelter and eat them for her dinner. Because of her great size, the people of the village were powerless to stop her.

Sway-Uock came out of the forest only when she was hungry. The evil witch would never bother grown-ups; children were her favorite food.

One night when Sway-Uock was very hungry, she raided a small village near the beach. As she went from house to house, she snatched boys and girls from their beds and dropped them into her huge basket. After filling her basket, the evil witch disappeared into the forest.

Sometime later, Sway-Uock made a return raid on the little village. During the second visit, many of the parents took special note of old Sway-Uock's face. Although it was dark, the fire pits threw enough light for the villagers to see her frightening features.

Her hair was matted and unkempt, her face was long and thin; and she had a crooked nose. When Sway-Uock opened her mouth, they noticed that two of her front teeth were missing.

"Those front teeth were lost when she was not careful to remove the bones," a medicine man told the people. "Her evil deeds have distorted her face and made her the ugly person she is today."

As the medicine man was talking, Sway-Uock approached the village to look for more children. The giant witch was said to have poor eyesight, but had excellent hearing. When she came to the village, Sway-Uock would creep about very quietly. Sometimes even the adults did not know she was making a raid until they heard the screams of the children in her basket.

Sway-Uock stood motionless at the edge of the forest listening for children who were making noise instead of sleeping. Every time she heard laughter or whispering, she would make a mental note of which houses contained children. When the evil witch thought she had located enough children, she went into the village and scooped them up.

During this raid Sway-Uock had a little hunchbacked boy among the children she had placed in her basket. Before starting, the witch swung the basket onto her back and secured it with braided cedar bark. While she was trudging along the trail leading through the forest, the little hunchback tried and tried to escape from the basket, but the sides were too high. He noticed that sometimes limbs of trees would brush through the basket. As one fir bough slid over Sway-Uock, part of the limb dipped low into the basket. When the limb came within reach of the little hunchback, he firmly grasped the branch and used it to swing himself out of the basket. Sway-Uock did not notice that one of her prisoners had escaped, and she continued her journey.

The boy, who was left high in the fir tree, could see very far from this vantage point. He could see the witch work her way down the hill to her house. Once home, she threw wood on her fire until the flames leaped high in the air. Then she danced around and around the fire.

Through the branches, the little hunchback could see Sway-Uock place the children on red-hot rocks at the edge of the fire.

After they were cooked, the boy saw the evil witch eat every one of them.

The little hunchback could hardly believe what he had witnessed, so he was anxious to tell the people of his village. Climbing down from the fir tree, he ran home. The little boy repeated exactly what he had seen, over and over, until everyone had heard the news and all the villagers were sad.

Months later, Sway-Uock returned to the same village. During this trip, the witch filled her basket with children as she had during previous visits. But, by chance, all the children she had stolen were girls. This had never happened before, as she usually had boys in her basket as well.

As Sway-Uock lumbered along with the basket tied to her back, the girls inside worked on a plan to save themselves. "Quiet in there," the ugly witch would order. But the girls continued to plot, speaking only in low whispers.

Soon Sway-Uock arrived at her home, and after loosening the rope knots, she dropped the basket to the ground. Then the giant witch rekindled her fire and kept adding firewood until the flames leaped high. The cooking stones near the fire began to heat.

As the cooking stones got hotter and hotter, the witch decided to remove her catch from the basket and see what kind of a dinner she would have. As each girl was removed, Sway-Uock lined her up near the roaring fire. "This group will make a fine dinner," the witch said after depositing the last girl on the ground.

Sway-Uock was very pleased with her catch and began to sing and dance around the fire. "Rocks, get red hot for the little children," the witch repeated over and over as she danced.

The girls decided they would put their plan into action as the witch danced around the fire. When Sway-Uock danced by them, they planned to push her into the hot flames.

Sway-Uock had sharp hearing and overheard part of the girls' conversation. "Did I hear you say you are going to push me into the flames and destroy me?" the witch asked.

"You must have misunderstood," the little girls assured her. "We are too small to push someone as large as you into the fire." This answer satisfied Sway-Uock, and she continued to sing and dance.

When the witch danced to about the center of the row of girls, one gave the signal. As planned, they all helped topple the cruel witch into the roaring fire. When they had made sure that she was dead, the girls returned to their village.

The village was in deep mourning when the girls arrived home. Their parents were at the beach weeping, for they thought surely their children had been eaten by Sway-Uock. Laughter replaced tears when the mourners saw that the girls had survived, and they shouted triumphantly: "Sway-Uock is dead—Sway-Uock is dead!"

Happiness spread through the village, and to celebrate the occasion, the people decided to hold a great festival. Indians say this was the beginning of the potlatch celebration, where Indians get together for feasting and the giving of gifts.

The Indians found a lesson in the conquering of Sway-Uock. Despite the witch's great size, she was destroyed through the combined efforts of small girls. Working together, they were able to accomplish something that one of them working alone could never have accomplished. Women of the village proudly point out that it was girls, not boys, who were able to outsmart the cruel witch.

How the Young Maidens Saved Guam Island

CHAMORRO PEOPLE, GUAM[112]

Guam Island has an odd shape. It is about thirty miles in length and about five or six miles wide, and it is narrow at the middle. From an airplane, it looks as though large bites had been taken in the island from both sides, at the Bay of Agana on the western side and at Pago Bay on the eastern shore.

How did Guam get that form? The Chamorro people of the island tell an old legend about it.

Long ago, before the Guamanians of today came to Guam Island, a race of superhuman people lived there. They were called the Tao-tao-mona. It is said that they were more clever than people of today, and that they used many kinds of magic.

Once, they discovered a strange thing. The center of their island was being eaten away on both sides. Day by day, the land between Agana Bay and Pago Bay was becoming more narrow.

"If this keeps on, the island will be cut in two," the people said to each other. "We must do something to stop it."

A meeting was called, and all the wisest persons came. "What shall we do?" they asked each other, but no one knew a good answer.

As they talked together, a messenger brought word that a giant fish had been seen cruising along in Pago Bay, nibbling and nibbling. The shores of Guam have many high cliffs, but the fish passed by them until it came to softer spots. There it bit deeper and deeper into the soil. It was eating through the island.

"The great fish must be destroyed," said the Tao-tao-mona leaders. "Every strong man of Guam Island must go to Pago Bay and try to kill it."

So the strongest and bravest of the men brought bows and arrows, war clubs, spears, hatchets, knives, hooks, poles, and their fastest canoes. They went together to Pago Bay to kill the monster that was destroying their island.

Pago Bay was covered with their canoes. They paddled in the lagoon and sailed outside the coral reef into the ocean, looking everywhere for the enemy fish. They did not find it, for it had hidden itself when they came.

The men hunted for many days, but they had to give up and return to their homes in the villages. "Our island will be eaten in two," they said.

"Maybe the fish will eat up the whole island," some of the people said.

"Perhaps it will, and all of us besides," said others.

The bad news passed from village to village. It was heard by some of the young maidens of the island. Every day, they used to gather at a large, deep pool called Agana Spring. It was in the hills, some distance from Agana Bay.

They went there to bathe and swim, to sing songs, and to talk and laugh together. They washed their long hair in the cool, clear water. Then they rinsed it with the juice of lemons. When they had finished, they threw the lemon peelings into the spring.

One day, after the maidens had washed their hair, the lemon peelings were found floating in Pago Bay, on the other side of the island. That could mean but one thing. "Water is passing from the spring to Pago Bay," the people said. "The fish is eating the land from underneath. If this goes on, the island will fall to pieces."

The young girls talked together at the spring. "Our men can do nothing," they said. "Perhaps we can be more clever than this fish."

"The lemon peelings were found in Pago Bay," one of them said. "Now surely, if lemon peelings can go outward, the fish can swim inward."

"Yes, yes!" cried the other girls. "Let's get him in here. Maybe we can catch him."

One of the girls thought of a way in which it might be done and she explained it to the others. "Let's do it!" they cried.

They cut off some of their long, beautiful hair and wove it into a fishnet. It grew and grew and spread out in every direction. Then the girls sat down around it, holding it. They began to sing.

They sang sweetly. The fish, cruising along in Pago Bay, heard the sound. He swam into the underland waters to hear more clearly. The maidens sang all their known songs. Then they invented new ones. The giant fish swam nearer and nearer. He swam farther and farther under the island, toward Agana Spring. At last, he came to the place where the maidens sat and sang.

Suddenly, they all dived into the pool, spreading the net. The great fish plunged into it and became tangled in it.

Some of the girls called the Tao-tao-mona men, who came with their weapons and killed the monster. The young maidens of Guam had saved their island. With the magic of their lovely hair and beautiful singing, they had done what the strongest men could not do.

A Shared Destiny

1910. "The miners in Greensburg, Pennsylvania, went on strike for more wages. Their pay was pitifully low. One day a group of angry women were standing in front of the mine, hooting at the scabs that were taking the bread from their children's mouths. The sheriff came and arrested all the women 'for disturbing the peace.' While the judge was sentencing them to pay thirty dollars or serve thirty days in jail, their babies set up a terrible wail so that you could hardly hear the old judge. Two mounted police were called to take the women and their babies to the jail, some ten miles away. The sheriff took them upstairs, put them all in a room and let [Mother Jones] stay with them for a long while. [She] told them to sing the whole night long. They sang the whole night and the people complained about the singing, and the women would not shut up, and the babies would not shut up, and nobody would shut up. The next morning, [Mother Jones] came with milk and fruit for the children. The sheriff said angrily, 'Mother Jones, make them stop. Those women howl like cats!'

"[Mother Jones scolded,] 'That's no way to speak of women who are singin' patriotic songs and lullabies to their little ones. You telephone to the judge to order them loose.'

"[The second night, the women sang. They sang the whole night long. The third night and the fourth night they sang.] Finally after five days in which everyone in town had been kept awake, the judge ordered the women's release."[113]

This sounds just like a folktale, maybe like the maidens singing to save Guam or the little girls uniting against Sway-Uock.[114] *However, this is history. It happened.*

You will not have read this story in your history book. You won't have heard of the women who sang their way out of jail because our history consistently focuses on an individual and identifies a revolution or war or movement with that person. History looks back at the American Revolution and sees George Washington. History looks back at India's independence and sees Gandhi. Yet these were both movements like the women's rights movement of the last century or the abolitionist, union, and civil rights movements of the 1800s and 1900s. Our history still reflects the message of the monarchies, remembering the highest, the most powerful, singling out and glorifying one person.

The idea of democratic government where people pledge their "lives, fortunes and sacred honor"[115] to each other may be new, but it reflects another idea often lost to the history books: the idea of cooperation. For centuries, folktales have been our visionary guides. Folktales speak for the people: a group of women singing, laughing and talking together, a neighborhood that sets out together to rescue the Moon, or a group of small prisoners who work together to overcome a monster. Although we might have forgotten, folktales are still there to remind us of the importance of cooperation.

It was a sun-drenched day. We'd splurged and rented a little motor scooter and set off, out of the city and into the dry hills of Crete. Charley knew how to ride a motorcycle, so he drove and I sat behind, holding on to his waist and gazing at the landscape, dry yellow grass on one side, a drop-off into a rock-strewn valley on the other. It was a dirt road, lots of twists and turns, always the pebbles crunching under the wheels and a cloud of dust behind us. At one turn, three crosses, one askew, marked a deadly drop-off. We rounded the corner and tried to accelerate up the steep incline when our scooter stalled. Charley put his feet onto the ground to hold the scooter still as he restarted it, but he couldn't get a good footing on the dirt and gravel incline. Since I was wearing our heavy pack, I couldn't hop off to lighten the load. Inch by inch, the motor scooter slid backward toward the crosses. I could see the edge of the cliff right behind us. Only Charley's feet on the ground kept us from plummeting over the edge, so he couldn't lift a foot to put on the brake, but he also couldn't stop us from slowly slipping and the motor wouldn't catch. Then I could see the bottom of the valley. In desperation, I jammed my leg forward between his and stomped on what I hoped was the brake. It was.

The Meatballs' Leader

O nce upon a time, there was a dish of meatballs, sizzling in the oven.

"Oh, oh, oh, who will save us from this terrible scorching heat?" cried the meatballs.

"I will save you," said a large meatball in the middle of the tin. "Think of me as your leader, and I can promise you beds of fine white rice upon which to lie, and a cooling sauce to cover your sizzling sides."

So all the meatballs with one voice agreed to follow the large meatball in word and deed, and unanimously they chose him as their leader.

No sooner had the vote been taken, than the Cook opened the oven door and laid the meatballs upon large plates of gleaming white rice.

"O Excellent Meatball Leader," they cried, as the Cook poured a rich, red tomato sauce upon them, "You have indeed led us out of danger, into this cool, refreshing place of rice and sauce."

But at that moment, several of the meatballs were forked onto plates, and felt themselves being swallowed by humans.

"Perfidious Meatball," cried the remainder, "You have led us into acute danger. How can you explain this horror and degradation which now faces us. You have deluded and deceived us, who gave you all our loyalty and devotion!"

"I knew that the next step in all our lives was from the oven onto cooling beds of rice," said the large meatball, "and look, even as I speak I go the way of all meatballs, for is it not our ultimate destiny to be eaten?" And he slipped down a human throat as easily as a meatball which has been chewed usually does.

The Maiden Who
Lived with the Wolves

SIOUX PEOPLE, NORTH AMERICA[117]

T he early Sioux Indians moved camp frequently when they
were traveling to their summer hunting grounds. The journey from the winter camp to the summer area was many miles and
took months of travel.

During these expeditions, the people carried most of their food
supplies. When game and other edibles found along the trail
became scarce, the Indians would use food from their reserves. If
wild fruit and berries were plentiful in an area, sometimes the
migrating band would camp nearby to replenish their food supply.

It was on such a halt that a young maiden decided to leave the
camp for a few hours to gather food. Once away from the camp,
she became lost and could not find her way back. After several days
of wandering about, the young maiden finally found the campsite,
but her people had struck their tepees and departed, leaving her to
survive by her own means.

She was terrified as to what the future might hold, so she sat
down on a large rock to calm her nerves and to think out a plan.
While she was seated there, a large wolf walked by and sensed that
she was very worried.

He felt sorry for her and came to her side. At first the girl
thought he would attack, but his friendliness overcame her fears.
She followed him to the top of a high butte, where the wolves of
that region had their den.

The wolves seemed to welcome her, and she made her home with them. Soon she began to understand their ways and then their language. They learned to understand her ways too.

When she was hungry, the maiden would tell the wolves, and they would send a hunting pack to the valley to kill a buffalo for her. They would then drag the best pieces of meat up to the den for the maiden to eat.

The maiden lived with the wolves through the cold winter months. Early the next spring she looked down on the valley below and noticed a band of Indians had set up a camp. She asked the wolves to scout the camp to see if they were her people.

The scouting party returned to report the Indians camped below were her people. She thanked them for taking care of her and departed to the valley.

At the camp she had a joyful reunion with her people and told the story of how wolves had saved her from starvation and cold. She revealed how wolves shared responsibilities, stalked their prey, and hunted as a pack.

"We can learn from the wolves," the chief told his people after listening to the maiden's story. "When our hunters kill an animal for themselves, they can kill another for those who are unable to hunt. All will benefit, and our hungry elders, widows, and children will always have a source of food."

This plan was passed on from band to band until it became a practice of the Sioux people. The lessons gained from the experiences of the maiden who lived with the wolves provided a way to feed many who were unable to hunt for themselves.

The Tale of Nung-kua-ma

CHINA[118]

A woman was once taking some cakes to her parents. On the way she met a man-eating Nung-kua-ma, a monster with a body like a bull, a head like a measure of rice, and sharp teeth and claws. Its eyes gleamed, and its coat was shaggy and thick. The monstrous beast roared with laughter, and said, "Give me all your cakes to eat." The woman said timidly, "I can't do that; they are for my parents."

"Good," said Nung-kua-ma, "I will come back this evening and tear your flesh and crunch your bones and eat you up." The woman began to scream with terror. Fearing that men might come and catch it, the monster fled into the hills like an arrow shot from a bow.

The woman was frightened nearly to death. She did not go to her parents, since her heart was beating like that of a hunted deer. She sat in the doorway and wept. To everyone that passed she told her story and begged for their help, but everyone turned pale at the very word Nung-kua-ma and were too frightened even to reply. Naturally, no one could help her, and she began to cry even more.

Finally, a peddler came by with two bamboo baskets on his carrying pole and a little clapper in his hand. He was surprised to see a woman weeping bitterly, surrounded by a gaping crowd, and asked, "Woman, what are your troubles that you cry so bitterly?" Between her sobs the woman replied, "The Nung-kua-ma is coming to eat me . . . this evening."

"My dear woman, don't weep," said the old man, "I will give you twenty needles to stick in the door. When the Nung-kua-ma arrives, it will prick itself." The peddler gave her the needles and then continued on his way, beating his clapper as before. But the woman thought that twenty needles would do little harm to the monster, and continued to sit weeping in the doorway.

Then a man arrived who collected swine, dog, and cattle dung, as manure for the fields. Seeing the sobbing woman, he asked the reason. "Don't worry," he said when she told him, "I will give you some dung, which you must stick on the door. When the Nung-kua-ma arrives, it will soil itself and run away." The woman accepted the gift, but she was still not comforted and continued to weep.

A little later a snake catcher came by with a basketful of snakes. He walked slowly along, crying, "Snakes for sale." At the sound of weeping, he also asked the reason and was told the whole story. Then he said to the woman, "You needn't be anxious. Nothing will happen." But she begged him to help her. He said, "I will give you two big snakes which can climb trees and are terribly poisonous. You must put them in the water pot, because when the Nung-kua-ma comes in with dirty hands, it will certainly want to wash them, and then the snakes will bite it to death. You see you needn't worry." Then he put the two enormous green bamboo snakes into the pot, but after his departure the timorous woman began to weep again.

Next a fishmonger arrived, who saw that the woman's face was swollen with tears. He did not dare to question her himself, but he soon learned from other people what the trouble was. He was sorry for her and, putting three pounds of round fish into the cooking pot, he said, "Don't weep, my woman. Pay attention to me, and you need have no fear. Take this pot with the round fish, but don't put any water in or they won't bite. If the Nung-kua-ma is bitten by the snakes, it will go and wash in the cooking pot. The fish will bite it, which ought to frighten it away at least, if it doesn't finish it off." But when the fishmonger had gone, the poor woman began crying again.

Next an egg seller appeared, calling, "Eggs. Good fresh eggs. Eight for ten cents." He also saw the weeping woman, and asked,

"Good woman, why are you weeping? It breaks my heart to hear you. Have you quarreled with your husband, or your mother-in-law, or your sister-in-law?" The woman told him her sad story, though she never imagined that such a man would be able to help her. At any rate, it could do no harm, she thought. However, the egg seller said, "Don't worry. Don't weep. I will give you ten eggs to hide in the ashes on the hearth. When the Nung-kua-ma is bitten by the snakes and the fishes, it will try to stop the bleeding with ashes. Then the eggs will burst in its eyes and blind it." But the woman was still frightened and did not stop weeping.

Finally, there came a man who sold millstones and iron goods. When the weeping woman confided in him, he also promised to help her. "I will give you a hundred-and-twenty-pound millstone," he said, "which you must hang on the framework of the mosquito netting around your bed. Prop it from beneath, and fasten it to the bar with a wire; and when you hear the Nung-kua-ma coming, cut through the wire, and it will be crushed by the stone." Then he added, "I will also give you an iron tool. If it is still not dead, you can finish it off with that. Now there is nothing more to be done. Just follow the instructions carefully." Now the woman was finally consoled, and she went into the house to prepare everything before evening came.

She lay alone in the pitch darkness, with the iron tool clasped in her hands in case the monster arrived. The first and second night watches went by, but although she strained her ears listening she could hear nothing. The third watch began at midnight. The sky was blue, with scarcely a star to be seen, since the bright moon shone into her room and lit up the floor. A cool, refreshing wind sprang up. She was so tired that she soon fell asleep. Suddenly she heard a noise. It was footsteps, and she knew the Nung-kua-ma had arrived. Hardly daring to breathe, she listened carefully and clasped her iron tool more securely.

"Open the door!" shouted the beast. "If you don't open it, I will eat your bones." With three kicks, it broke down the door. A scream and a curse followed, as it scratched itself on the needles and got the dung all over its hands. "What's all this?" it roared. "You've made me get my hands all dirty, you filthy woman." The door was now open, but it said, "I must first wash my hands. There is time enough afterward." It went across to the water jar. But as soon as it dipped its hands, the green bamboo snakes bit it in the finger and it screamed with pain as the red blood flowed out.

With all its strength, the monster shook off the snakes and then went across to the cooking pot, thinking to itself that the water there must be safe and clean. The moment it touched the water, something else bit it in the finger, which made it cry out even more loudly, "Another of this hag's tricks! I will smash all her bones. But first I must quench the blood at the hearth." While it was burrowing in the ashes, all the eggs exploded and bits of shell flew into its eyes and blinded it. "Damnation!" he cried. "Things are going from bad to worse. I have never met such a woman. I can't stand it."

Now it no longer cared about the pain, but burst screaming into the bedroom in such a fury that it tore off its eyebrows on the door beams, though with its mind full of revenge it did not feel the pain. It bellowed, and threatened, "You filthy old hag! All your tricks can't kill me. Now I am in your room. In a little while, I shall eat you up, bones and all. Only then will I get my revenge." With these words, it grabbed the mosquito netting. The woman cut through the wire with her knife, and bang! The heavy millstone dropped on the beast's head. Its bones were crushed and the blood gushed out like a river. It began to scream in agony, whereupon the woman beat it with the iron tool until it was quite dead.

In this way she escaped being eaten. Instead of being devoured herself, she had killed the monster. She sold it for a great sum of money, and bought everything she wanted.

Consider the Source

In the movie The Princess Bride,[119] the Dread Pirate Roberts is scaling the Cliffs of Insanity. Suddenly a rope drops from the top of the cliffs and dangles enticingly beside him. However, the rope had been thrown down and was held by the Spaniard, who was waiting to kill the pirate. We hold on to facts like a lifeline—"I heard it on the news . . ." "Experts say . . ." "I read it . . ." As we grab our lifeline, as we use facts to make the decisions that shape our future, it's important to ask who is throwing the line our way and why, because a fact, just like the rope, is only as dependable as the person throwing it. The meatballs' leader was right about what would happen, but he wasn't leading, nor was he saving the meatballs from danger as they anticipated. Because the maiden had lived with wolves, she was the one who could teach her people about the wolves.

As we make the transition from mono-culture to global culture, the filters our information comes through—language, media, reporters—leave us less capable of understanding the motives behind the purveyors of the "facts." My children believed the fact that the Twin Towers went down, but then my children created their own stories. I watched the television and took that as my story. However, television has its own motives and sources of income that have very much to do with making sure I turn on the television regularly so the sponsors can sell me more products day after day.

It was July 2. The evening news ran a long story about the dangers of fires on the Fourth of July. People were exhorted to take care because of all the firecrackers and sparks and barbecues. There were even reports about various fires which had broken out in previous years. Then there was a commercial break. The first commercial was for fire insurance. I'm not normally a cynic and I try hard to give people the benefit of the doubt, but this was too much for me. I turned off the television, unplugged it, and stuck it into the bottom of the closet where it stayed for about two years.

Television will use comedy, star power, even fear if that will be most successful in getting me to tune in tomorrow. In this way, television and other modern media differ greatly from folktales. Folktales have been a highly successful adaptation because their goal of helping me understand an issue and my goal of survival are the same goal. Unlike television, folktales encourage us to take an active role in assessing information and acting upon it.

One story followed another. In the glow of my virtual campfire, a Japanese grandmother, her back bent parallel to the ground from years of working the rice fields, had made me laugh in the face of fear.[120] A little story about a snail had reminded me that there are other points of view.[121] From there the folktales had bogged me down in uncertainty. We were well into the night. A chilled silence hung over the virtual campfire. Then a slender Chinese girl stood stiffly and narrated in a loud voice her vision of a present world where the Moon Goddess has saved us all from an evil tyrant.[122] My fear began to become hope. There I thought I could stay, but I was wrong. Folktales launched me back into the real world and encouraged me to connect my hope with actions. The woman whom Nung-kua-ma threatened to kill sat and cried most of the day. However, in the end, she had to set up all the traps and watch through the night herself in order to defeat the monster and survive.[123]

My alarm rings. I roll over and smack the top of the clock. The noise stops. I get up and shuffle around the kitchen, packing lunches for Charley and the girls as the sky outside the window turns pink and gold. Most mornings I drop the girls off at school and immediately take refuge in a local coffee shop where they let me sit and write for as long as I like. A couple of hours later, I run errands or do the grocery shopping, call my mom or dad, clean the house, or pay the bills. I pick up the girls in the afternoon and drive them to dance and music lessons and soccer practice and make dinner. Maybe Lara Croft has time to save the world, maybe Mereaira stood on a cliff, held her baby above her head, and stopped a war, but I don't exist on that scale, my actions are not as dramatic. Yet folktales insist on action.

Baling with a Sieve

A pretty and clever girl was married to a half-witted fellow, and lived alone with him in the home of his ancestors. She was skilled in weaving, and once, when she had finished a web of fine linen, she wanted to sell it; but she feared that if she entrusted it to her husband, he would dispose of it foolishly, and she was too young to go herself to the cloth-market. Having no one else with whom to discuss the subject, she finally mentioned it to her husband, and as he was anxious to please her, he urged her to let him take it to market and sell it for her. With much hesitation, she put the cloth in his hands, telling him to be sure that he sold it for the market price. Wishing to fortify him against sharpers, she indulged in a little tirade against human beings generally, and ended up by saying, "Now, remember that among all whose nostrils open downward, not one is honest." The husband wished to win his wife's approbation, and as he went, he repeated over and over to himself her last assertion that "among all whose nostrils open downward, not one is honest." To and fro through the market he paced, with the cloth under his arm, but as all the buyers there had nostrils opening downwards, he considered that they came under his wife's ban, and he made no attempt to negotiate with them. But toward nightfall, he saw a gentleman who was reading a proclamation posted high on a wall, and as his nostrils therefore opened upward, the fool pulled at his tunic and said to him, "Sir, I have been looking for you all day. My wife told me that among all whose nostrils opened downward, not one is honest; and as your nostrils open upward, I wish to sell you this piece of cloth for its true market value." The gentleman perceived that he had a fool to deal with, so he took the cloth and said, "Go home and tell your wife that her cloth was bought by Mr. Seven-Eight, who lives in the house beside the wasps' nest, behind a grove of jointless bamboos, and that she can send there tomorrow for the payment." The fool went and gave his wife the message; and as complaint was useless, she set herself to solve the riddle propounded. She concluded that, since seven and eight are fifteen years old; that a wasps' nest, whose inmates go in and out with much noise, was most like a boys' school; and that if a jointless bamboo could be found in the world, it would resemble a gigantic onion-top. She inquired among the old women of the neighborhood whether anyone among their acquaintances had, at the age of fifteen, had a son born to him, and she was told of two such, and learned where these sons lived. She then sent her husband to look at the houses of these two sons, and so gained the information that both had onion beds before them, and that one of them had a boys' school adjoining. To the latter she next day confidently sent her husband to get the payment for the cloth. Mr. Seven-Eight appeared at the door, and when his creditor told him that his wife had sent him, he handed over a fair amount of money and added a covered basket which he told the fool to carry home unopened and to deliver carefully to his wife. The wife received the basket, and did not remove the cover till she was alone. She found in it a lump of dirt beside a pomegranate blossom, and she understood that the donor intended to convey to her the idea that she was a fair flower and her husband a clod. Her fate had seemed hard to her, even when other persons did not allude to it, and this symbol set her to weeping over herself as she had never wept before. Her husband was greatly distressed by her red eyes, and he went off privately to Mr. Seven-Eight and told him that he had paid too little for the cloth, for his wife had been weeping continually about it. Mr. Seven-Eight, being an astute man, not only divined the real cause of the tears, but foresaw that the woman would soon attempt to destroy her own life, and that a deep pool in a creek near her house would be the place where she would go to drown herself. Feeling himself responsible for having impelled her toward suicide, he took a sieve to the pool and began baling it out, tossing the water over the road that lay along its brink. Soon after, he saw a young woman, coming alone, in handsome attire, along the path, and when she turned back on seeing him, he was sure he had monopolized the pool none too soon. She approached again at nightfall, found him still baling, and again retired. At midnight, she came again, but the baling was still going on. She then made up her mind that she would go to the pool next morning, and, if the baling continued, she would say that she wished to pass along that road, complain of its being muddy, and find out how long before the man would stop working there. She accordingly approached near enough to see that the man was baling with a sieve, and she asked him why he was thus spoiling the road by which she wished to journey. He replied that his wife had lately been walking along there, and had lost a needle. He wanted to find it for her, and as he thought it might have dropped into the pool, he was trying to bale the pool dry, to see if the needle was at the bottom.

She said to herself, "Here is a man trying to bale out with a sieve a pool in a running stream in order to find a needle for his wife. I am not the only woman who has a fool for a husband. As this man is much older than my husband, his wife is probably much older than I, and she has not killed herself. If she can endure life with her husband, who is certainly a greater fool than mine, then I ought also to be able to live." Thus reasoning, she turned back homeward, and Mr. Seven-Eight, perceiving that his object was accomplished, also went his way.

The Old Woman
and the Lame Devil

CHUMASH PEOPLE, NORTH AMERICA[125]

The people of Kalawašaq always seemed to have bad luck. A big fiesta was once held at Soxtonokmu as was the custom and the people of other villages were invited to attend. A certain blind old woman lived at Kalawašaq with her daughter and her son-in-law. The husband said, "Wife, let us go to the fiesta at Soxtonokmu. All the ʔalapkalawasaq* are going." But the wife said she couldn't go and leave her mother behind for the old woman was blind. So the man said that they should take the old woman along with them. The three started off and arrived without mishap at Soxtonokmu, and the fiesta began. The husband noticed that his wife was talking to other men and he started getting jealous. They had an argument and he told her, "We'd better go home." So they started off with the wife leading her mother by the hand. When they were close to Kalawašaq but had not yet crossed the river, the husband and wife began to argue again and the man got so mad he started thrashing the wife. The old woman was there by the trail with her bundle, but the couple were so upset that they went off and left her standing there.

It got dark and she was still standing there. The old woman said to herself, "I'll stay here by the trail until they come back for me." She stood right in the middle of the trail holding her walking stick in her hand. Pretty soon she felt a hot wind (she was naked, as was

*ʔalapkalawasaq: inhabitants of the Kalawašaq village (the ʔ denotes a sound not found in English)

193

the custom). She said to herself that something was going to happen to her. It grew warmer. She heard a sound like a man stepping every now and then. She said to herself, "This is not my daughter, it isn't anyone of this world." But she was not an ordinary old woman—she was shrewd—and she stood up and said, "I will remain here!" She took her staff and held it firmly in her hand.

She heard the fall of a single foot coming, and she thought that it must be the lame devil who goes around the world. The creature approached the old woman and stood there. Then he gave her a shove, but she didn't budge. "Get away from here," said the devil. He shoved her again. But she said, "I won't move from here!" He said, "Get off the trail. Don't you see that I have to pass?"

"Why don't you go around?" she asked, and he shoved her again. She grabbed him by the wrist and began to wrestle with him. She was very strong because of her magic.

"Let go!" said the devil at midnight, for they were still wrestling. A little after midnight the devil said, "If you let me go I'll give you plenty of money and lots of food to eat."

But the old woman replied, "No, I won't let go. I'll hold you until sunrise, so that people can see you and make you ashamed of yourself!"

"No!" said the devil. "If you let go you will have many years to live and you will see the world."

"No!" replied the old woman.

The daughter and husband, meanwhile, had discovered that the old woman was missing. "Oh, you ungrateful one!" said the wife. "Where is my mother? She must be frozen to death!" They set out to find the old woman and bring her home. At daylight they came to the top of a hill and saw in the distance the old woman still wrestling with the devil. Before they could reach her they saw her fall. A little cloud of smoke left the spot and entered the hollow of an oak. When they reached the place the old woman was lying there on the ground in a faint, but the son-in-law cured her with his ?atiswɨn.*

*?atiswɨn: talisman, fetish, spirit helper

The Woman with Red Leggings

ARIKARA PEOPLE, NORTH AMERICA[126]

When Heart Village was in the woods in the Missouri River bottomlands, the Arikaras were starving. It was in the winter, and they were starving then.

One time after everyone had gone to bed, someone came to one tipi walking plainly on the snow. Then a woman lifted the door flap of the tipi. Then she lifted the door flap of the tipi. Then she put one foot inside near where the woman and man lay in the lodge. And then the woman said, "I came to borrow your kettle. I want to use your kettle."

And then the woman in the tipi said, "There it is. There it is by the door where you are standing."

Then the people in the tipi saw her leggings. She had red leggings—the kind made of red trade cloth that the old people used to wear.

The woman picked up the kettle. Then she went out. She replaced the door flap. Then she walked off distinctly on the snow, making a crunching sound, going wherever she went.

It was a long while later. Then they heard her again, as she came just before dawn. The woman lifted the door flap.

Then the woman said, "Here is your kettle. I have brought it back."

Then the main woman inside said, "Set it there!"

Then she set the kettle down. Then she went out again. Then the woman inside got up. Then she uncovered it. Then she took the lid off the kettle that the other woman had brought back. And there in boiling water were strips of old leather rawhide. There they were in boiling water.

After they had uncovered the kettle, they said, "Here's a pot full of pieces of old leather."

And then one man said, "Why, she's brought us good fortune!" Then a group of men tracked the woman over the snow where she had gone in the night. And there she lay on a scaffold.* When they looked at her clothing, it was the woman who had entered the tipi the previous night. It was the woman: she had red leggings. She lay there on the scaffold.

When morning came and the men went up onto the hill, there was a herd of buffalo there.

Now that is what happened when the people were starving in Heart Village over there in the woods. That woman was the one who changed their fortune when they were starving. There was a herd of buffalo there.

*scaffold: a burial place

The Old Lady of Littledean

SCOTLAND[127]

The old tower of Littledean, on Tweedside, had long been haunted by the spirit of an old lady, once its mistress, who had been a covetous, grasping woman, and oppressive to the poor. Tradition averred that she had amassed a large sum of money by thrift or extortion, and now could not rest in her grave because of it. In spite of its ghost, however, Littledean Tower was inhabited by a laird and his family, who found no fault with their place of abode, and were not much troubled by thoughts of the supernatural world. One Saturday evening, however, a servant girl who was cleaning shoes in the kitchen by herself suddenly observed an elf-light shining on the floor. While she gazed on it, it disappeared, and in its place stood an old woman wrapped in a brown cloak, who muttered something about being cold, and asked to warm herself at the fire. The girl readily consented, and seeing that her visitor's shoes were wet, and her toes peeping out blue and cold from their tips, she good-naturedly offered to dry and clean the shoes, and did so. The old lady, touched by this attention, confessed herself frankly to be the apparition that haunted the house. "My gold would not let me rest," says she, "but I'll tell ye where it lies; it is beneath the lowest step of the Tower stairs. Take the laird* there, and tell him what I now tell you; then dig up the treasure, and put it in his hands. And tell him to part it in two shares; one share let him keep, for he's master here now; the other share he

*laird: lord

197

must part again, and give half to you, for you are a kind lassie and a true, and half he must give to the poor of Maxton, the old folk and the fatherless bairns,* and those that need it most. Do this and I shall rest in my grave, where I've not rested yet; and never will I trouble the house more till the day of doom." The girl rubbed her eyes, looked again, and behold the old woman was gone!

Next morning, the young servant took her master to the spot which had been indicated to her, and told him what had taken place. The stone was removed, and the treasure discovered, and divided according to the instructions given. The laird, being blessed with a goodly family of sturdy lads and smiling maidens, found no difficulty in disposing of his share. The servant girl, so richly dowered, found a good husband ere the year had passed. The poor of Maxton, for the first time in their lives, blessed the old lady of Littledean; and never was the ancient tower troubled again by ghost or apparition.

*bairns: children

The Milk and Butter Stones

This was another witchcraft story, very typical of what went on in those days, an' this was a very religious woman, a well-living woman, and she said to her dying day that she had this experience. She lived away at Colbastoft, her maiden name was Christian Ganson, and she married a Laurenson man, one of the survivors of the *Diana*, the whaler that was frozen in. It was the means of his death; he died a young man—but that was the woman. And she lived, as I say, at the East House of Colbastoft—that's the north side of Fetlar. And when she was going to get married and be leaving that place—then she went to live at Houbie—an old woman that lived in a small house at Grue, she told her that she had to come and see her before she left. So she came.

And she said, "Well, my jewel, you're leaving," and she says, "you've been a fine neighbour, a fine girl on the place. We'll miss you very much. And you're getting married, but I'm very sorry that I don't have very much to give you. But I have something that's very valuable: it's not money but it may be in a way it's even better than money. And while you keep it, it'll be of great help to you." And she says, "First of all, look at the door that there is nobody coming in, because this is a secret."

She said, "No, there's nobody."

So she went out and she opened up an old sock, and then out of that she loosed a piece of old flannelette and she took two stones. One was a yellow stone and the other was a white stone. "Now," she says, "this is what I'm going to give thee: it's served me well, all these years. But my day is getting done now and it's no farther use to me, but it could be of use to you, for you're a young woman, setting out on life's journey. Now," she says, "that yellow one is a butter stone, the white one is a milk stone. And these were stones specially enchanted by the Pics* (or the trows),† and we . . . they came our way—the peerie folk‡ gave us them because we were pretty chummy with them."

And she looked—she didn't know whether to take them or not—"No, no," she says, "you . . . you take them."

And she says, "Well, what would I do with them?"

"Well," she says, "what you do if you're ever in need of a little milk and your cow is not giving milk—take this white stone and heat him in the fire and dip him in water and pat him three turns with the sun, three turns against the sun, and say—and whoever you want this milk taken from in the township, anybody that has a good cow, just point with the tongs to that house and say,

> 'Taka a fae until aa's teen
> Quhat might blaa dee fae the been.' "§

That's what she had to say. And when she wanted the spell broken again she turned them the opposite way, you see, and pointed to the house, that broke the spell. And the same with the butter— she wanted a good bit of butter from anybody's cow or off their milk, you see, she did the same.

Well, she decided that she would take the stones. So she took them and tied them up in a bit of cloth very, very carefully, and after that, of course, she got married to this man who lived at Houbie. (I could tell you the house they lived in, where Martha Henderson lives. You see as this history's supposed to be true, now they know the houses where the people lived in.) And so she mar-

*Pics: fairies
†trows: trolls
‡peerie folk: fairies
§blaa dee fae the been: may mean "bleed from the bone"

ried, and if she didn't have time, and a young married woman, to bother about these things—but in after years—a few years after, she thinks, "I wonder whether old Maggie's stones—I wonder if I could try it, just for curiosity?—Not that I want the milk or the butter, but just to try it." She said, "Yes. The next time that I churn"—she had a cow that wasn't much worth, you know . . . she was a very indifferent cow—"Yes, well, I'll have a shot at it."

So she minded what old Maggie said to her, what she had to do. You know, when they put the milk in the churn, they had to put a little of warm water in it, you see, to bring out the butter. So she heated the stone in the fire, with the tongs, put him in the water, minded what she had to say—

> *"Taka a fae until aa's teen*
> *Quhat might blaa dee fae the been."*

Pointed to this house in Houbie where there was a woman had a good milking cow. And she hadn't churned very long till she knew that there was something going to happen that she had never seen before, you know, before the butter comes on, you know, that there's a lot of frothy stuff that makes the butter. And this came up, up, till she thought that there was something odd here happening, so she was afraid if anybody came in in the sitting-end. So she got it taken back in the back end so that nobody would come in— if she heard any footsteps she was just going to leave off churning and just go in the other end yonder, like you could in here.*

And she churned away and the butter started to come on and she never saw such a lot of butter in her life. And she got excited. But she calmed herself and she said, "Well, I'll have to go on with it now, but I couldn't continue doing this." And she churned away and all this butter came on. And she kept it out of the way, for nobody could know she was doing this, you know.

---

*The stolen butter is coming directly from the other lady's cow into the young lady's milk churn, and the young lady must hide that she's using magic to steal the butter.

And a day or two after, that woman that she had taken the butter of the cow of, the neighbor, stood on a high part of the township and said, "Now hear what I have to say, you devils that you are! Some of you are taken by your Devil's arts my butter, from my young children that need it. But I'm going to the minister to lay you before the Session and he'll deal with you. And," she says, "I have a good idea who it is. But I'm not speaking about the young, fine young woman that's come in to the township, I'm exempting her, because I know she wouldn't do a thing like that." And so she gave them a proper telling-off.

But next day when everything was quiet, Kirsty took a spade and went to the yard (and I could show you the yard in Houbie yet, mind, the cabbage place) and dug a hole deep, deep, deep, deep and she put the two stones in.

"Now," she says, "no more witchcraft for me with you buggering* things," and digged them down under. And they're there in that yard yet. The two stones are in that yard in Houbie yet.

*buggering: damn, darn

The Inexhaustible Meal-Chest

IRELAND[129]*

One Samhain Eve[†] Peggy Néill of Bun Binne was tidying the house. Niall himself was sitting on a straw seat by the fire with his back against the wall. He was puffing at his pipe and humming because his mind was content. He had pitted his last potato that afternoon and was thinking of the comfort he would have until the first day of spring. There was a pot of water heating on the fire and after Peggy had washed the dishes and set them on the dresser she lifted the lid of the pot and thrust a stick in. She took a cup which was hanging on the closed door and went to a chest in the corner into which the oatmeal was put every year when it was brought back from the mill.

"By my soul, Niall," said Peggy, looking into the chest, "although it was a large store of meal it would be easy to gather up what remains now! There is just about what will make tonight's stirabout."[‡]

"Well, woman dear," said Niall, "it is hard for a store to last when it is often drawn upon."

"That is a true saying, Niall," said Peggy, "but we will miss the meal. Potatoes are good, but a spoonful of stirabout is much tastier for supper."

*Séan Ó hEochaidh, Máire Ní Néill, Séamas Ó Catháin, *Síscéalta Ó Thír Chonaill/Fairy legends from Donegal*, Baile Átha Cliath/Dublin: Comhairle Bhéaloideas Éireann, 1977, pp. 336–43. Published with permission.
†Samhain Eve: Halloween
‡stirabout: porridge

"We won't die of hunger!" said Niall, "if it goes hard on us I will thresh a heap of this harvest's grain and get it ground. It is a small fistful of meal that will make stirabout for a childless old couple like ourselves from now until Patrick's Feast."

Peggy bent over the chest and began to take the meal bit by bit to fill the cup.

"Stop, woman!" said Niall, "surely you are not going to make stirabout of those leavings! There is nothing there but dust, and I would not want it full of straws!"

Peggy emptied the cup back into the chest and said, "Very well, but you will have to get a fistful of potatoes from the barn and I will make a meal of mashed potatoes."

"Aroo," said Niall, "a few baked in the ashes would do fine. There are enough in yon vessel to do us." And he settled himself more comfortably on the seat. The poor man was tired after the day.

"That is very fine," said Peggy, "but the fowl have to be fed and there will be little for them in the morning if we do not boil potatoes for them."

Niall rose reluctantly and said, "Pip on the same hens! Throw me over those boots!"

He put on his boots and took a basket and a lighted stick in his hand. Peggy went on with her household tasks. She began to liven the fire under the pot and stretched out with the tongs to get a sod or two of turf from under the bed. But as she did so her heart stopped when she saw out of the corner of her eye a little old woman standing by the wall. Peggy herself used to say when telling about it afterwards, "She wasn't as big as a broody hen but, o wirra, if you could have seen the bright eyes she had dancing in her head under black bushy eyebrows! She had a worn wrinkled face, a long chin and a nose that would go through the eye of a needle, and she had not a tooth in her head but her eye-teeth.* I can tell you, the life nearly left me!"

When Peggy caught her breath she greeted the apparition and

*eye-teeth: canine teeth in the upper jaw

invited her to sit at the fire and warm herself. She gently declined Peggy's invitation and said, "It is not the cold that sent me in, but a loan I want to ask of you."

She put her hand under her bosom and took out an oak cup and said while she handed it to Peggy, "Fill that with last year's meal, for there is a mouth waiting for it!"

"God's blessing on us and the Cross between us and harm! Who are you?" said Peggy, and at the same time she made the Sign of the Cross.

"I am Maireog the Great, Queen of the Hosts of Binn Bhuí and of Pollán an Raithnigh!"

"Musha, you knocked on our door in an evil hour," said Peggy. "Our meal has run out and the leavings is a poor gift but if it is any good to you, you may have it and welcome since I would like to oblige you."

She took the cup and filled it. The fairy woman took it and drew out a rod that was hanging by a string from her waist, raised it above the chest, and spoke a charm in some language Peggy did not understand. Then she struck the chest lightly and said, "From this day forward this chest will never be without meal, but do not let any living being except yourself put a hand in it: if you do, my charm will be broken and you will be the poorer!"

With this she put her petticoat over her head and went out the door like lightning. When she was gone, Peggy's hands dropped to her sides and she sat down by the fire as if she was going to faint. She was not able to rise when Niall came in with a handful of potatoes. He noticed that Peggy was in a weakness and asked her what was wrong with her. "You would think you had seen a ghost since I went out, you are so white."

"A ghost, indeed," said Peggy, and she told him what I have told you.

Niall burst out laughing.

"God look down on us!" said he. "Some joker played a trick on Peggy Néill tonight! Shake your feathers, old woman, and put a little of this wonderful meal into the pot until I see what kind of a hand the wee folk of Binn Bhuí make of turning the quern-stone!"

"It is not good to meddle with magic!" said Peggy.

"Don't bother me with your pishrogues!"* said Niall. "I will see for myself the power of your lying old woman!" and with that he went towards the chest. But well for Peggy, she got there before he did and lifted the lid of the chest, and great was the surprise of both when they saw the chest well filled with as nice, clean meal as was ever ground.

"God protect us!" said Niall. "This is truly a night of wonders!"

"Don't you know," said Peggy, "that this is Samhain Eve and that the gentry are going about?"

"By my soul, I never thought what night of the year it was!" exclaimed Niall. "Whatever about that, you got a good exchange. I hope that this will be to our advantage."

It was. Peggy was as careful of the chest as if it had been a golden treasure. She put a lock and key on it and for five years no one put a hand in it except herself. During that time the meal in the chest never lessened, and not alone that, but Peggy gave many a good heavy bagful of it to the neighbors. She was so generous and gave away so much meal that the neighbors remarked it. They did not see Niall going to the mill with grain nor coming home with a sack of meal, and the end of it was that some said that Niall and Peggy had the black magic.

Well and good. One gloomy night between Christmas and Little Christmas, Peggy had opened the chest to throw a handful of meal to the hens before they went to roost when a boy from near by came in breathless with news that his mother had been suddenly stricken with illness and was dying. Peggy was always an obliging woman and she did not delay to hear the second word but ran out the door and in her haste she forgot to close the chest.

Niall was in the byre at this time giving fodder to the cattle. He came in with a pail to get a drink of gruel for a young calf. He did not find Peggy in the house and without thinking he put his hand

*pishrogue: aphorism, adage

in the chest and took a fistful of meal for the pail. He went out then about his work.

Peggy came back with the news that Séamas of Pollán's wife was dead. Niall said a prayer for her soul, and the pair of them sat for a while talking about the dead woman. They noticed nothing until Peggy rose to make a cup of tea and then she saw the open chest. She raced over to close it and when she looked inside there was nothing in it but dusty leavings just as on the night when the fairy of Binn Bhuí had come to visit her.

"It is not possible, Niall," said Peggy, "that you put your hand in the chest?"

"O, may I not see God's dwelling if I didn't take a bit of it for the calf!"

"It cannot be helped!" said Peggy. "There is no mending it now!"

From that day until the day they died there was no luck with the chest.

Unhistoric Acts

A friend of my husband's had come for a visit and I was packing a snack for him as he left to continue his trip. There were no plastic sandwich bags, not even any plastic wrap in the house. I always used reusable containers because they are better for the environment. As I desperately searched for something to wrap his sandwich in, he said with withering sarcasm, "You think you matter?" Although he never meant it as a question, I wondered about my answer, would it be yes or no?

Where, after all, do universal human rights begin? In small places, close to home—so close and so small that they cannot be seen on any maps of the world. Yet they are the world of the individual person; the neighborhood he lives in; the school or college he attends; the factory, farm, or office where he works. Such are the places where every man, woman, and child seeks equal justice, equal opportunity, equal dignity without discrimination. Unless these rights have meaning there, they have little meaning anywhere. Without concerned citizen action to uphold them close to home, we shall look in vain for progress in the larger world.

—Eleanor Roosevelt[130]

Folktales are champions of the small act which has huge ramifications— sharing a crust of bread wins the throne, a song or stubbornness defeats a monster. Folktales champion ordinary people—the stupid third son or the cast-off daughter. The one action of an ordinary person, be it telling the truth, telling a lie, or inviting our enemies to a feast, can change the world. Folktales live in small places, close to home.

In folktales we defeat ogres by pounding on pots and pans. We shame a devil into submission, we lend a stranger a kettle, clean someone's shoes; we share our food or we simply refuse to take advantage of others. It's not an action that makes it to the history books or headlines, and tomorrow we may have to do it all over again—hand back money when a sales clerk has miscounted, respond to anger with empathy, travel to another continent and spend a year or five teaching, learning, or building houses.

"Your mom is always so happy," a local shopkeeper said to my girls. They might beg to differ, but it's true, I smile a lot. I smile at the shops and at the girls' school and on the street. I try to insist that our lives be made of moments like these: noticing the little hands so soft they have dimples instead of knuckles, the first kiss with my life partner, an all-enveloping hug from my mom, a laugh that makes me roll in the aisles. Is it great or insignificant, true or false, yes or no? Our minds are tempted by simple dichotomies, yet our lives are rainbows. The enemy is really a friend or can be turned into an ally, or is hungry and we can feed them. Folktales reminded me to include the laughter when I thought about fear, to include the actions of ordinary people as well as the famous ones.

> *For the growing good of the world is partly dependent on unhistoric acts; and that things are not so ill with you and me as they might have been, is half owing to the number who lived faithfully a hidden life, and rest in unvisited tombs.*
>
> —George Eliot[131]

And so, after fearing, I laughed, I kissed my daughter and made dinner and wrote this book, as though I could change the outcome, bend it to a better solution.

The Long Haired Girl

CHINA[132]

Halfway up a high mountain is a long waterfall, which looks just like a young girl lying on the cliff with her long white hair hanging down the mountainside. The local people call it the White Hair Fall, and there is a popular story told about it—the story of the Long Haired Girl.

Long, long ago, there was no water near this high mountain. People had to collect rainwater for drinking and irrigation. If it did not rain, then they had to walk over two miles to draw water in buckets from a stream. Water was prized as highly as oil.

In a village near the high mountain lived a girl with long raven black hair which reached her heels. Everyone called her the Long Haired Girl. She lived with her bedridden mother and raised pigs to support them both. Every day she fetched water from the stream over two miles away and then went up the mountain to gather wild herbs for her pigs. She toiled from morning till night.

One day she went up the mountain as usual with a basket on her back to gather wild herbs. When she was halfway, she scrambled up a cliff and saw a turnip growing on the rockface. Its leaves were luxuriant and green. "I bet that would make a delicious dish," she thought to herself, "if I took it home and cooked it."

She tugged with both hands and pulled out the turnip, which was red and round and as big as a teacup. It left a hole in the rock, from which a stream of clear spring water began to flow. After a short while, the turnip jumped out of her hands with a whoosh! and landed back in the hole again, blocking the flow of the water.

The Long Haired Girl was thirsty and wanted very much to have a drink. She pulled out the turnip again to let the water flow from the hole, put her mouth to the hole and drank her fill. The water was cool and as sweet as pear juice. But as soon as her mouth left the hole, the turnip jumped out of her hand with a whoosh! It landed in the hole again and the water ceased flowing.

She was standing there gazing at the cliff in amazement when all of a sudden a gust of wind whisked her away to a cave. There, on a block of stone, sat a man whose body was entirely covered with brown hair. He said to her in a fierce voice, "Now that you know the secret of my spring, you must not tell it to a soul! If you do and others come here to take my water, I will kill you. Mark well my words! I am the god of the mountain!"

Another gust of wind carried her down to the foot of the mountain. She made her way home silently and did not mention the spring to her mother, let alone the other villagers. She saw how parched the fields were and how hard all the villagers had to work. Men and women, young and old alike, panted and sweated as they carried buckets of water from the stream more than two miles away. If only she could tell them about the spring on the mountain! If only they could pull out the turnip, cut it into pieces and widen the hole with chisels, then the water would flow gurgling down the mountain! But she remembered the fierce hairy man and decided she had best keep all this to herself.

She underwent great agony of mind, lost her appetite completely and could not sleep at night. She became more and more like a mute or a simpleton. Her eyes lost their lustre and appeared glazed and lifeless; her cheeks lost their very glow and became sallow, and her shining black hair became dry and brittle. Her mother grasped her by her emaciated hands and asked her, "What is wrong with you, my child?"

But the Long Haired Girl just bit her lip and did not say a word.

Day followed day, month followed month. With time her raven hair turned snow white. She had no inclination to comb or dress it, but let it hang loose on her shoulders. Behind her back the villagers gossiped, saying, "How strange that such a young girl's hair should turn as white as snow!"

But she just leaned against the gate and stared blankly at the passersby, murmuring to herself, "On the high mountain there is a . . ."

She would never complete the sentence but bit her lip till it was flecked with blood.

One day, from where she stood at the gate, she saw an old man with a white beard tottering along the road. He was carrying water from the stream more than two miles away. He slipped, stumbled on a rock and fell to the ground. The buckets broke and the water spilled. He had a nasty wound and blood began to stream down his leg.

The Long Haired Girl ran over to help the old man up. She tore a piece of cloth from the hem of her dress and, crouching on the ground, bound up his wound. All the while she listened to his groans, looked at his closed eyes and the wrinkles on his face that contracted as he winced with pain.

"What a coward I am!" The Long Haired Girl rebuked herself. "It is my fear of death that has made the fields so dry and the crops so withered! My fear has left the villagers sweating and panting! My fear has caused this old man's leg to be broken! Coward! Coward!"

She could bear it no longer. Suddenly she blurted out to the old man, "Grandpa, there is a spring on the high mountain. If you pull out the turnip, cut it to pieces and widen the hole with chisels, the water will rush down the mountain. It's the truth! I have seen it with my own eyes!"

She stood up before the old man had time to say anything and, with her long white hair trailing down her back, ran back and forth in the village, shouting, "Come along, everyone! There's a spring up on the mountain!"

Then she told them how she had found the spring, without mentioning the mountain god's warning. The villagers had always regarded her as a good-hearted girl and they believed what she said. They took their knives and chisels and followed her up the high mountain and over the cliff. There she pulled out the turnip with her hands and threw it down onto the stone, saying, "Be quick! Cut it to pieces! Be quick!"

Several knives chopped the turnip into pieces. Meanwhile, the water was whooshing out of the hole. But the hole was still only as big as a teacup.

"Quick!" cried the Long Haired Girl. "Take your chisels and make the hole wider. Quick now! As quick as you can!"

They went at it. They chiseled and chiseled and soon the hole was as wide as a bowl. After another while, it grew as big as a bucket. And finally, it was the size of a vat. The water ran gurgling down the mountain, and the villagers laughed and cheered.

Just at this moment, a fierce wind blew up and the Long Haired Girl vanished from sight. But the villagers were too busy gazing at the spring to notice anything. Later, one of them asked, "Where is the Long Haired Girl?"

"She has probably gone home ahead of us," replied another, "to tell her sick mother the good news."

In high spirits they all climbed back over the cliff and went down the mountain.

In fact, the Long Haired Girl had not gone home. She had been carried off by the god of the mountain.

"I warned you not to tell a soul!" he snarled at her. "But you led all those people up there, and now they have chopped up the turnip and widened the hole! I shall kill you for this!"

With her white hair hanging loose on her shoulders, the Long Haired Girl replied calmly, "I would gladly die for their sake!"

"I shall not let you die easily," said the god of the mountain, grinding his teeth. "I shall make you lie on the cliff and let the spring water fall on your body from the high mountain. This will be your punishment—a long and painful one."

"For their sake I will gladly lie beneath the water," said the Long Haired Girl in the same calm tone of voice. "But will you please allow me to go home first to find someone to take care of my sick mother and my little pigs."

"Very well, you can go," said the god of the mountain after a moment's thought. "But if you do not return, I shall stop up the hole and kill all the villagers. When you return, just go and lie down on the cliff yourself. Don't bother me again!"

The Long Haired Girl nodded. A gust of wind blew her down from the cave to the foot of the mountain. There, when she saw the water gurgling down from the mountain through the fields, lush with green crops, she laughed for joy.

When she got home, she did not have the heart to tell her mother the truth. She just said, "Mother, now we have water flowing down from the mountain. We will never need to worry about water again."

Then she added, "Some girls in the next village have invited me to stay and play with them for a few days. I've asked Auntie next door to take care of you and to look after the pigs."

"Very well," said her mother with a smile.

The Long Haired Girl went and entrusted her affairs to the lady next door. She then came back and said to her mother, "Mother, I may stay there at least a fortnight. I hope you'll—"

"Just go ahead and enjoy yourself," said her mother. "The lady next door is very kind. She will take good care of me."

The Long Haired Girl stroked her mother's hands and face and tears rolled down her cheeks. She went to the pigsty and when she stroked her little pigs on their heads and tails, tears streamed down her face again.

From the doorway, she said to her mother, "Mother, I am going now."

Before her mother could say anything in reply, she walked out towards the high mountain, her long white hair swinging from side to side.

Halfway to the mountain stood a big banyan tree with long branches and thick leaves growing by the side of the road. As she passed the tree, the Long Haired Girl touched its trunk, saying, "Big banyan, from now on I shall no longer be able to come and cool myself in your shade."

Suddenly an old man walked out from behind the tree. He had green hair, a green beard and was clothed in green.

"Where are you going, Long Haired Girl?" he asked her.

She sighed and bowed her head in silence.

"I know of all your troubles," said the old man. "You are a kind-hearted person, and I have it in my mind to save you. I have carved a girl of stone, which is an exact likeness of you. Come behind the tree and have a look."

The Long Haired Girl went behind the tree and saw the stone figure of a girl, which was like herself in every respect except that it had no hair. She was amazed at the sight.

"The god of the mountain wants you to lie on the cliff beneath the water," said the old man. "You would never be able to survive such an ordeal. I shall carry the stone figure to the cliff and it will lie there in your stead. But it does not have long white hair like yours. You will have to bear pain for a little while. I am going to tear out your white hair and put it on the stone girl's head so that the god of the mountain will not suspect."

Before the Long Haired Girl could say a word, the old man held down her head and tore out her hair. Then he put the hair on the head of the stone figure. Amazingly enough, it began to take root as soon as it touched the stone head. The Long Haired Girl was hairless, while her long white hair continued to grow as healthily as ever on the head of the stone figure.

"Young girl," said the old man with a kindly smile, "you may go home now. There will be plenty of water for the fields. Just work hard, you and the villagers, and life in the village will gradually improve."

As soon as he finished speaking, he put the stone figure on his shoulders and hurried to the high mountain. He placed it on the cliff so that the torrent of water would run over it. The water fell down onto the stone girl's body and mingling with the long white hair, flowed on down the mountainside.

As the Long Haired Girl stood leaning against the banyan tree silently watching, she felt her head beginning to itch. She touched her scalp and could feel that hair was beginning to grow again. It grew and grew until it touched the ground once more. She held it out in front of her and saw that it was raven black again. She began to dance for joy.

She waited for a long time under the tree, but the old man in green did not appear again. Suddenly the leaves and branches of the tree trembled in the breeze, and in their rustling sound she heard the words, "Long Haired Girl! We have tricked the god of the mountain! You can go home now!"

The Long Haired Girl looked at the long stream of water flowing down the steep mountain, the green crops at the foot of the mountain, the joyous people at the ends of the fields and the verdant giant banyan tree. Swinging her long, shiny raven hair, she skipped back home.

The Good Lie

T he king was angry with the foreign captive who had been thrown down before him. "Put him to death!" he ordered.

The captive had been expecting it. He had up to now been silent but, now that death was certain, he gave up all hope and cursed the king, using the foulest words in his native tongue. He was like a cat, spitting and screeching at dogs who are at its throat.

The king, not knowing the language, did not understand what the captive was screaming but he knew that one or two of his viziers* were familiar with the tongue.

"What is he saying?" he asked them.

The viziers looked at each other. Then, one, who was good-natured, replied, "My lord, he is quoting from the sacred Koran."

"Indeed?" said the king. "From which verse?"

The vizier went on, "From the verse which speaks of the Paradise which awaits those who control their anger and forgive, for God loves men of goodwill."

"I see," said the king, thoughtfully. He turned to the now silent captive.

"You have done well to remind me of that," he said. "I will control my anger. And I will forgive you. You can go free."

"That was disgraceful!" muttered another vizier, an enemy and rival of the one who had replied to the king's question. "People of our rank should speak nothing but the truth, particularly before the king."

*vizier: a minister or councillor of state

The king overheard. "What was that?" he asked.

"My lord!" protested the second vizier, "I am sorry, but you were told a lie by that vizier! The captive was certainly not quoting from the Koran. The truth is that he was pouring foul abuse and the filthiest of insults upon you!"

The king frowned at this. "Then I prefer his lie to your truth!" he said. "I think that your truth came from a heart bent upon mischief. His lie came from a good heart, and good has come of it, as you have seen."

Ayak and Her Lost Bridegroom

DINKA PEOPLE, SUDAN [134]

This is an ancient event.

Ajiech was so handsome, so very handsome. He was about the most handsome of all men.

Ajiech married a girl called Ayak. He brought the cattle for the marriage with his age-mates. Among his age-mates was a lion. But no one knew he was a lion. They drove the cattle to Ayak's family.

A very great feast was held by Ayak's family. People ate and ate. One night during the celebration, while Ajiech was in a deep sleep, the lion came and gave him some medicine so that he would not wake up from his sleep. Then he took him away to his home. He broke his neck and seated him in the hut with his back resting against the wall. Then he left the body under the care of his wife.

Meanwhile, Ayak was shaken with sudden grief. She cried and cried and cried, and wandered away from her house. She just walked and walked in the wilderness, not knowing or caring where she was going. She did not care whether she lived or died.

On the way, she met a group of foxes and sang as they approached:

> *"My man Ajiech,*
> *My man, Ajiech, the Shining One,*
> *He courted me with tenderness,*
> *He courted me with the sweet words of youth,*
> *The sweet words of age-mateship,*
> *And when he married me,*

He paid a hundred cows which I could not count,
O, Ajiech, my shining husband."

The foxes asked her, "Lady, what is the matter? Why are you crying?"

She answered, "I have lost a man. He had just brought his cattle for marriage, but had not yet completed the marriage, when someone came and took him away; I do not know where he has been taken."

The foxes then consoled her and said that they had seen a person passing by, carrying something on his shoulders. "Hurry, you may never catch up with him; he is really a long way away."

She threw herself down crying. Then she got up and ran on. She ran and ran, until she met a group of lions. She sang the same song to them as they approached. They asked her what was troubling her. When she explained to them, they said, "We met a man on the way, carrying something on his shoulders, but if he is the one, he is too far; you can never catch up with him."

She said to them, "Please do not kill my hope. Why do you put it in that way? I must catch up with him."

And she ran and ran and ran. Then she met a group of hyenas and sang to them. She went on running and meeting all sorts of animals until she met a herd of elephants. They told her they had seen a man enter a village. One bull took pity on her and offered to carry her there. They ran and ran until they could see houses in the distance. When the elephant pointed out the huts, she pretended she did not see them. She wanted the elephant to take her right into the village.

Only when they were nearly there did she agree she saw the huts. The elephant then put her down to enter the village by herself. But the elephant gave her some medicine and said, "This will be your weapon against the lion. If he attacks you, throw some into his face and he will fall dead. But then put this other medicine in his nostrils and he will come back to life. When he comes back to life, have him remake your husband exactly as he used to be. Make sure the lion makes him so well that he can run with the wind. When he has made him perfect, he will probably want to kill him again. At that point, throw the medicine in the lion's face. He will die. But then bring him back to life again so that he may bless you in his last words."

She went and sat near the cooking-place in front of a hut and sang. She sang until the wife of the lion came and asked her what she wanted.

"My husband is inside that hut," she said. "I want him."

"You will never have him," said the lioness.

"I have an idea," said Ayak. "You are a woman and I am a woman. Why don't you create him, make him come back to life as complete as he used to be, and then we will fight in competition for him. I dare you!"

The lioness got angry and said, "Very well, he will be created this evening."

That night, the lioness asked Ayak to kindle the fire so that she might have light to work with. As she kindled the fire, Ayak sang:

> "Fire, fire, come, light up,
> Our word is a word of honor,
> Fire, fire, come, light up,
> Our word is a word of honor."

When the fire died down, Ayak threw more grass into it and sang.

The lioness worked until Ajiech was re-created. But one eye was pulled in. So Ayak said, "My dear woman, did you not see that his eyes were perfect? Go on, make them what they used to be!"

So the lioness worked on his eyes. Then Ayak said, "He used to outrun the wind; so bring back his speed. He was also a very strong man, who could pull down a big tree. That husband of mine was not an ordinary man."

The lioness worked on him again. But when he raced with the wind, he was outrun. Ayak insisted that she work on him some more. She worked on him until he was perfect in every way.

Then the lioness said, "It is now time for us to fight for him. I cannot leave him to you!"

So they fought. After wrestling for some time, the lioness began to turn wild in order to eat her, but Ayak threw the medicine into her face. The lioness died. So Ayak put the medicine of life into her nostrils and she came back to life.

Then the lioness said, "My dear woman, I will no longer stand between you and your husband. Go with him. You will have seven children, but on the birth of your seventh child, you will both die together the same day."

Ayak said, "Increase the number of children we shall have."

"Very well," said the lioness. "You will have eight children and they will all grow up to be big. But you will both die the day you bear your eighth child."

"Very well," said Ayak. "Our children will continue our life if we die."

Bluejay Brings the Chinook Wind

FLATHEAD-KALISPEL PEOPLE, NORTH AMERICA[135]

W hen the world was very young, Amotken, the Creative High Mystery, gave a little part of the Salish country to Thunderbird. This was the North Crow Creek Canyon of the Mission Range. Thunderbird was happy to have an area of her own and to know that her long-time enemy, Coyote, could not enter it. There had been much jealousy between the two. Now she was free to lay her eggs and to hatch her young without being troubled. There in North Crow Creek Canyon she gave birth to her three daughters: Bluejay, Crow, and Magpie.

Thunderbird was kind to people when they came from the valley of the Bitterroot to hunt, to fish, and to gather huckleberries in her canyon. If a storm was coming through the East Pass, she would warn the people to leave. Her deep thunder noises were her warning to them.

All went well for a long time. Then a careless hunter failed to put out his campfire, and a great fire spread through Thunderbird's canyon. The forest on the canyon floor was destroyed; the flowers and the berries were burned; the deer, elk, and birds left the canyon. Worst of all, the creek became smaller and smaller, and then dried up.

Thunderbird was much annoyed by the destruction of her canyon country. Angrily she beat her huge wings against her breast and thundered out punishment against the people of the valley.

To the cold Northeast Wind she said, "Stand in the pass. Blow hard. Blow your chill breath down my canyon and out on the valley. Drive away the people who have destroyed my country."

So at each darkness, Northeast Wind came and blew his cold breath into the valley. Soon the grasses and the plants died, and ice came upon the big lake in the Salish country, the one now called Flathead Lake. Shivering with the cold, the people went into the Bitterroot country. Animals and birds took refuge there also, as did Bluejay, Crow, and Magpie, the daughters of Thunderbird. Nothing with life remained in the valley.

After many snows had passed, Thunderbird's anger softened. Then she became lonely, and she longed to see her daughters, the Indians, the animals, and the little birds. Again she spoke to Northeast Wind. "Cease blowing your icy breath, and go. Too long you have punished the valley. If you will go, perhaps my daughters, at least, will come to see me."

Almost at once a great stillness came over the land. A scout felt the silence and reported to the Salish chief living at the place where the warm waters flow.

"The icy wind blows no longer in the valley," the scout told his chief. "And Thunderbird in the canyon is making a noise like sobbing."

Then the head chief said to his people, "When the land becomes warm again, we shall go back to our old homes in the valley. Will Coyote tell us how we can please Thunderbird so that she will hasten the warming of our country?"

But Coyote, not liking Thunderbird, replied, "Let the big bird with the big noise sit forever in the region she has made desolate. I shall not help."

Then Bluejay, who loved the Salish people, offered her help. "Coyote is old and lazy," she said. "He thinks of nothing but of filling his stomach with salmon. So he has become a deceitful boaster like my sisters, Crow and Magpie. I myself will help the Salish and make glad the heart of my mother, Thunderbird."

So at the right time, Bluejay flew west to ask Chinook Wind to warm the valley and help her friends. Chinook Wind's heart was warm and kind.

"Gay and good little bird," he said to Bluejay, "I will hasten to the relief of your friends if you will show me the way."

So Bluejay flew before the Chinook Wind until they came to the valley below the Mission Range. There Chinook Wind blew his warm, moist breath a long, long time across the land. The ice melted, grass and flowers grew, trees came to the Mission Range, deer and elk returned to the canyon.

Thunderbird was happy. "How can I repay you, little daughter?" she asked.

Bluejay answered, "Keep your temper down, my mother, so that the innocent will not suffer with the careless ones."

The Lions of Vancouver

SALISH PEOPLE, NORTH AMERICA[136]

Spring had come with its gentle winds, with opening leaf and frond of fern. Back to the north country the birds were winging. The swollen rivers teemed with the first great run of salmon. The slumbering land was quickening into life, and all the world moved in rhythm with the heartbeat of the universe.

From many leagues away the nations of the north were coming to the Salish village. From far up the coast came the high-bowed canoes. From distant points where the snow still lingered. From the inland plains where the caribou roamed, from the islands and from the mountains they traveled.

With the coming of spring, the two daughters of the Salish chief had grown to womanhood. Because of this there would be long days of feasting and rejoicing. For when a girl-child responds to that rhythmic pulsation of life, she is honored above all others. A girl-child brings gifts to her people—men-children to lead and protect; girl-children to become the mothers of warriors; sons and daughters to have sons and daughters of their own. A girl-child is a part of that strange rhythm of nature. A man-child is like the sun and the rain, but a man-child brings no gifts. A man-child is only himself.

Now had these maidens left childhood behind them. And because their father was a great chief, the festival was to be the most lavish of all. There was only one shadow to mar the occasion.

Between these people and a tribe from the upper coast, a quarrel was raging. For many moons there had been fighting and bloodshed. The long canoes of war were even now upon the water and the insulting taunts of the paddlers were borne upon the wind.

For the week of feasting and dancing, and for the period of getting ready, the chief of the Salish had turned his back upon the fighting. His ears were deaf to the war cries of the enemy. His eyes were blind to the hovering canoes within his own waters. He accepted no challenge, he made no threat, for to him the traditional feast for his daughters was of greater importance. When once it was ended, the war could begin anew. The enemy, too, must bide their time, for so many nations were gathered within the Salish village that an attack would mean only disaster.

And so the elaborate preparations went on. When but a few days from completion the daughters of the chief asked of him a favor. Asked of him that the Hostile Ones be invited to their feast—the feast of friendship in honor of women. Such was the law of the tribe, that a maiden who asked a favor at the time of this sacred ritual must have that favor granted, and their father could not deny them.

Upon the headlands of the coast great fires of welcome were lighted. The word went forth and those who had come in anger hurried to take part in the ceremonies. They came, bringing their women and children. Their weapons of war became weapons of the hunt, and the gifts they brought were gifts of game and of fish, of thick fur pelts, and of blankets woven from the hair of the mountain goat. In all the days before and that came after, there was never a Feast of the Maidens to equal this. For two tribes that had hated for years without number were now friends and between them a lasting peace was founded.

Somewhere, the Great Spirit heard of the feast, for whether a deed be great or small, good or evil, always He knows and is glad or is sorry.

"Forever these maidens shall dwell in a high place," said the Great One. "Forever they shall be looked up to with reverence. Into the land they have brought peace and friendship, and while they stand watchful this peace shall never be broken."

High on the mountain crests abide the two sisters, enduring, eternal. They are loved by the ones who live in their shadow, for the gifts that they brought to the nations of the north have remained through the ages.

Sunrise Never Failed Us Yet

We had moved continents, from France to Australia. We had changed languages, from French to English. As fast as she could, with all the intensity and concentration an eight-year-old could muster, my little girl was learning English. However, no one, neither her teacher, nor her friends, nor the other pupils could understand the earth shaking beneath her feet as she tried to survive in this new world, with a new language and new rules. And so my little girl was having trouble. Her days were constant battles and her nights were replete with nightmares. To comfort her, I explained, I reasoned with her, I held her, I told her stories. One night I began, "Once upon a time . . ."

"Don't tell me that!" Colleen cut me off. "It's just a fairy tale. They're not hard!"

"You think fairy tales are easy? You think fighting an ogre and carrying his head for seven years and keeping away ghosts and fire is easy!" I protested.

Colleen sighed and I didn't make her listen, but I eventually understood what she meant. Fairy tales guarantee us the happy ending. No matter what monsters we fight, what revelations we uncover, we know it will all be okay in the end. It all can seem so easy. However, what happens when we lose that context of hope, the context of life that encourages us to face challenges with the belief that things will work out? In our modern rush to reality, have we lost the ability to choose the shape of our future? Are we convinced that reality is so set in stone that we cannot see the alternative paths we might chart in future seas? Human culture, folktales, science give us maps on which we can locate mountains and seas and stars. The reality of our future is not something already written on those maps. It is the reality we build in our hearts and minds. It is the course we chart across those seas and skies. Our future is the ability to choose our future and maybe even to base that future more on hope and less on fear.

People all over the world are striving to find a way to have a world at peace. People all over the world are coming to the conclusion that humans have reached the point where we will all live together, or we shall die together. Our job now is not only to live with fear, but also to envision and hope for the future.

The philosopher Ernst Bloch wrote that in folktales "the power of the giant is painted as power with a hole in it through which the weak individual can crawl triumphantly."[137] I read folktale after folktale and found that the giant had many holes. I crawled through every one and found I was crawling through myself. I listened with horror and approval as I roasted the spook on the spit. I sighed gratefully when the wicked ghost helped save my sister's life. I remembered courage and that there are many different kinds of monsters. I remembered to laugh. I remembered hope, that our children may live, and that we will somehow find a way.

NOTES

1. For an interesting summary of this kind of processing of fear, see Daniel Goleman, *Emotional Intelligence: Why It Can Matter More Than IQ* (London: Bloomsbury Publishing, 1996), pp. 207–14.

2. See Kathleen Ragan, *Fearless Girls, Wise Women, and Beloved Sisters: Heroines in Folktales from Around the World* (New York and London: W. W. Norton, 1998).

3. " 'What Are You the Most Scared Of?'": Fanny Hagin Mayer, *Ancient Tales in Modern Japan* (Bloomington: Indiana University Press, 1984), pp. 173–74.

    The tale was told by Iwakura Ichirō in Okinoshima, Shimane.

    While living in Japan, I was told that the monster in this story, the *tengu*, represented Western foreigners, who were perceived to have big noses.

    The Japanese language resembles Korean in grammatical structure. Japanese has three major alphabets. Kanji, Chinese pictographs, are used for major nouns, verbs, and adjectives. The kanji are supplemented by hiragana and katakana, two alphabets representing an identical group of about fifty-five syllables. Hiragana, with its flowing characters, is used mostly for suffixes, particles, and conjunctions, while katakana, with its more angular characters, is used mostly for foreign words.

4. "The Robbers and the Auld Woman": Peter Buchan, collector, John A. Fairley, ed., *Ancient Scottish Tales* (Peterhead, Scotland: 1908), pp. 57–59.

5. "Cauth Morrisy Looking for Service": Patrick Kennedy, *Legendary Fictions of the Irish Celts* (London and New York: Macmillan, 1891), pp. 158–63.

6. "Death and the Old Woman": Gyula Ortutay, *Hungarian Folk Tales* (Budapest: Kossuth Printing House, 1962), pp. 462–65.

7. "The Story of the Caterpillar and the Wild Animals": A. C. Hollis, *The Masai: Their Language and Folklore* (Oxford: Clarendon Press, 1905), pp. 184–85.

The Masai are nomadic herdsmen living in Kenya and Tanzania. The Masai live almost entirely off the meat, blood, and milk of their herds. Masai warriors are known for their strength, courage, and endurance. Masai is essentially a linguistic term referring to speakers of this Nilo-Saharan language.

8. See "'What Are You the Most Scared Of?,'" p. 6.

9. See Jack Zipes, *Breaking the Magic Spell: Radical Theories of Folk and Fairy Tales* (New York: Routledge, 1979), pp. 138–41. See also Jack Zipes, "Marxists and the Illumination of Folk and Fairy Tales," in *Fairy Tales and Society*, ed. Ruth Bottigheimer (Philadelphia: University of Pennsylvania Press, 1986). See also Bruno Bettelheim, *The Uses of Enchantment: The Meaning and Importance of Fairy Tales* (New York: Vintage Books, 1975), pp. 4–10.

10. This description is of a remarkable photograph in *The Family of Man*, Edward Steichen (New York: Museum of Modern Art, 1953), p. 120.

11. "Magic to Overcome Anxiety: Turtledove Cannot Change Its Nature: What Turtledove Says": Melville J. Herskovits and Frances S. Herskovits, *Dahomean Narrative: A Cross-Cultural Analysis* (Evanston, Ill.: Northwestern University Press, 1958), pp. 415–16.

Recorded in 1931 in Dahomey, West Africa.

The Dahomey kingdom of western Africa during the eighteenth and nineteenth centuries was in the region which is now southern Benin. Dahomey was an absolute monarchy with a centralized bureaucracy staffed by commoners who could not challenge the power of the king. Dahomey had a contingent of female warriors who served as the king's bodyguards when they were not in combat and whom the Europeans called Amazons, after the Amazons of Greek mythology.

In their introduction, the Herskovitses explain that all of the narrators who contributed to their book were male. The Herskovitses were interested to find out if the focus on women's shortcomings in the men's tales was paralleled by a focus on men's shortcomings in the women's tales. They finally found one woman who agreed to tell them some of the women's stories. However, her husband, when he heard of the enterprise, forbade her to tell them the stories and threatened to divorce her if she disobeyed.

Another description of forces eliminating women's tales from the written record is found in Z. Pallo Jordan, *Tales from Southern Africa* (Berkeley: University of California Press, 1973), pp. xx–xxi.

12. "How Thomas Connolly Met the Banshee": William Butler Yeats, *Fairy and Folk Tales of the Irish Peasantry* (1888), in *A Treasury of Irish Myth, Legend and Folklore* (New York: Avenel Books, 1986), pp. 108–12.

Yeats cites J. Todhunter as the storyteller.

Yeats had a wonderful knack for writing down the Irish as he heard it, and because I am used to reading stories written like this, I enjoy the transcription. However, in consideration for readers less accustomed to the accent, I have normalized a little of the spelling. I have changed the long Irish *a* to the modern spelling using *e*, the Irish *th* to *t*, the Irish *dh* to *d*, and the Irish *ou* and *ow* to *o*. For example, "sthrames" I have normalized to "streams" and "dacent" to "decent" and "cowld" to "cold." In addition, I have spelled "wid" as "with," "brudge" as "bridge," and "sez" as "says." If you would like to tell the story with an Irish accent and you're not Irish, I heartily recommend that you find a copy of the Yeats original and practice reading it out loud exactly as written.

13. "The Frightened Fox": Arthur Scholey, *The Discontented Dervishes and Other Persian Tales* (London: Andre Deutsch, 1977), p. 96.

   Scholey notes that the tales in his book come from *The Fruit Garden* and *The Rose Garden*, two books by the well-known poet Sa'di (d. 1292). Sa'di was born poor but managed to get an education and then traveled extensively, gathering experience, wisdom, and tales. He became royal poet to the Persian king Sad Atabak.

   Persia has been used by Westerners to designate first part and then all of Iran. The people of Iran know their country as Iran, the Land of the Aryans. Shi'ite Islam is modern Iran's official religion. The Persians as a people make up about 45 percent of the population of Iran. The Persians established a vast empire in the Middle East in 550 B.C. which ended with the invasion of Alexander the Great. Another famous Persian poet is Omar Khayyám.

14. See "The Frightened Fox," p. 29.

15. See Jared Diamond, *Guns, Germs and Steel: A Short History of Everybody for the Last 13,000 Years* (London: Jonathan Cape, 1997), and William H. McNeill, *Plagues and Peoples* (New York and London: Anchor Books, Doubleday, 1977), for interesting perspectives on the relationship between people and microbes.

16. See Daniel C. Dennett, *Darwin's Dangerous Idea: Evolution and the Meanings of Life* (London and New York: Allen Lane, Penguin Press, 1995), for a thoughtful and thorough explanation of Darwinism.

17. See "How Thomas Connolly Met the Banshee," p. 25.

18. See "Magic to Overcome Anxiety," p. 23.

19. "There Is Nothing Anywhere (That We Fear)": R. Sutherland Rattray, *Akan-Ashanti Folk-Tales* (Oxford: Clarendon Press, 1930), pp. 267–68.

   Rattray notes that he collected these tales "in the remoter villages, as told at night by the old folk, under the stars." The translation is as nearly literal as possible.

   The Akan are an ethnic group of peoples who speak Akan languages and live on the Guinea coast. The Ashanti are a section of the Akan peo-

ple who live in south-central Ghana. Akan tribes are grouped into matrilineal clans. Matrilineal descent based on descent from a common ances-
tress governs inheritance, succession, and land tenure. Paternal descent
is also recognized and determines membership in special groups called
ntoro. Men are involved in politics, religion, and the military.

20. "The Boy Who Went in Search of Fear": Brothers Grimm, *Kinder und
    Hausmärchen*, second edition, 1812. Translated by Kathleen Ragan.

21. "The Fearless Captain": Im Bang and Yi Ryuk, *Korean Folk Tales: Imps, Ghosts
    and Fairies*, trans. James S. Gale (New York: J. M. Dent & Sons, 1913),
    pp. 162–64.

    Im Bang says that men have been killed by goblins. This is not so much
    because goblins are wicked as because men are afraid of them. Many died
    in North Ham-kyong, but those who were brave, and cleaved them with
    a knife, or struck them down, lived. If they had been afraid, they too
    would have died.

    The grammatical structure of Korean is most similar to Japanese.
    More than half the vocabulary is of Chinese origin, and Korean has used
    Chinese characters along with the Korean alphabet for centuries. As with
    Japanese, this is probably not only due to Chinese cultural influence, but
    also because there are many Korean words that are homonyms, and the
    Chinese characters that represent concepts serve to clarify the meaning.

22. See "The Fearless Captain," p. 44.

23. See "The Boy Who Went in Search of Fear," p. 34.

24. See ibid.

25. See H. H. Munroe, *The Complete Works of Saki* (Garden City, N.Y.:
    Doubleday, 1976). My personal favorite is "The Open Window," pp.
    259–62.

26. See Vera Brittain, *Testament of Youth: An Autobiographical Study of the Years
    1900–1925* (New York: Penguin Books, 1994).

27. Wilfred Owen, "Dulce et Decorum Est."

28. "Girl Learns to Write by Practising on Frozen Pond": Magnùs Einarsson,
    Icelandic-Canadian Oral Narratives (Canadian Centre for Folk Culture
    Studies, Mercury Series Paper no. 63, Canadian Museum of Civilization,
    1991), pp. 169–70.

    The storyteller was Mrs. Steinunn Inge.

    The stories in this book were recorded from oral sources during 1966,
    1967, and 1969 in the Icelandic communities in North America: all of
    the western provinces of Canada and three of the American border states,
    Wisconsin, North Dakota, and Washington. Large-scale emigration from
    Iceland began in the 1870s and continued for about forty years and rep-
    resented about one-seventh of the total Icelandic population.

29. "The Cakes of Oatmeal and Blood": Sean O'Sullivan, *Folktales of Ireland* (Chicago: University of Chicago Press, 1966), pp. 105–9.

30. "The Neckbone on the Knife": Jacqueline Simpson, *Icelandic Folktales and Legends* (Berkeley: University of California Press, 1979), p. 153.

31. "The Death 'Bree'": W. W. Gibbings, *Folk-Lore and Legends: Scotland* (London: 1889), p. 189.

32. Everywhere in the world, high death rates are associated with women's early marriage and childbearing, and with low levels of education for women. See Joni Seager and Ann Olson, *Women in the World Atlas* (New York: Touchstone, Simon & Schuster, 1986), map 2 and pp. 101–2, map 10 and p. 106. For information on the female-male education gap, see Seager and Olson, *Women in the World Atlas*, map 22 and pp. 112–13, map 24 and pp. 111–13.

33. George Eliot, *Middlemarch*.

34. Even before this particular section, there have been examples of daily courage in this anthology such as " 'What Are You the Most Scared Of?,' " p. 6 (answering the door and finding a stranger), "The Robbers and the Old Woman," p. 8 (being old and living alone), and "How Thomas Connolly Met the Banshee," p. 25 (walking home at night).

35. See Carl Lindahl, "Jacks: The Name, the Tale, the American Traditions," in *Jack in Two Worlds*, ed. William McCarthy (Chapel Hill: University of North Carolina Press, 1994), p. xvii.

36. For the idea that "once upon a time" is not a past designation, see Jack Zipes, *When Dreams Came True* (New York and London: Routledge, 1999), p. 4, and Jack Zipes, *Spells of Enchantment: The Wondrous Fairy Tales of Western Culture* (New York and London: Penguin Books, 1991), p. xiii.

37. See Jack Zipes, *The Great Fairy Tale Tradition* (New York and London: W. W. Norton, 2001), pp. 845–47. See also William Kelly Simpson, ed., *The Literature of Ancient Egypt* (New Haven and London: Yale University Press, 1973). For folktales from preagricultural societies, see "The Story of the Caterpillar and the Wild Animals," p. 19, and "The Oyster and the Shark," p. 156, and others in this volume.

38. A child narrator was included in the book *Folktales of Egypt*, ed. Hasan M. El-Shamy (Chicago and London: University of Chicago Press, 1980). Women told all of the stories in Monia Hejaiej, *Behind Closed Doors: Women's Oral Narratives in Tunis* (New Brunswick, N.J.: Rutgers University Press, 1996). As noted on p. 232, note 11, men told all the stories in Melville J. Herskovits and Frances S. Herskovits, *Dahomean Narrative: A Cross-Cultural Analysis* (Evanston, Ill.: Northwestern University Press, 1958). See also Zipes, *The Great Fairy Tale Tradition*, p. 850.

For an interesting analysis of the differences between male and female narrators, see Margaret R. Yocom, "Woman to Woman: Fieldwork and the Private Sphere," in *Women's Folklore, Women's Culture*, ed. Rosan A. Jordan and Susan J. Kalčik (Philadelphia: University of Pennsylvania Press, 1985), pp. 46–53. See also Ibrahim Muhawi and Sharif Kanaana, *Speak, Bird, Speak Again: Palestinian Arab Folktales* (Berkeley: University of California Press, 1989), pp. 2–3.

39. For a wonderful account of audience participation in folktales, see Z. Pallo Jordan, *Tales from Southern Africa* (Berkeley: University of California Press, 1973), pp. xvi–xvii. Regarding a story being adapted for specific audiences, see Jack Zipes, ed., *The Trials and Tribulations of Little Red Riding Hood* (New York and London: Routledge, 1993). See also Muhawi and Kanaana, *Speak, Bird, Speak Again*, pp. 2–3.

40. See "Girl Learns to Write by Practising on Frozen Pond," p. 49.

41. See "The Neckbone on the Knife," p. 55.

42. Regarding the uses of the happy ending, see Bruno Bettelheim, *The Uses of Enchantment* (New York: Vintage Books, 1977), pp. 10–11, 32, and 143–44. The general impression we have is that tales end happily ever after, and in many tales the heroes and heroines do get to live happily ever after, but some tales don't have happy endings. See Maria Tatar, *The Hard Facts of the Grimms' Fairy Tales* (Princeton, N.J.: Princeton University Press, 1987), pp. 179–80.

43. "The Snail": Zora Neale Hurston, *Every Tongue Got to Confess: Negro Folk-Tales from the Gulf States*, ed. Carla Kaplan (New York: HarperCollins Publishers, 2001), p. 251.

    Possibly narrated by Kossula or Cudjo Lewis, one of the last surviving slaves of the ship *Chlotilde*.

    Zora Neale Hurston (1903–1960) an African-American woman, the daughter of Alabama tenant farmers, was a major figure in the Harlem Renaissance of the 1920s and 1930s. She studied anthropology at Barnard College, graduated in 1928, and for the next five years collected folktales throughout the American South and the Caribbean. She then wrote fiction and a wonderful autobiography entitled *Dust Tracks on a Road* in which she recounts how her mother told her to "jump at the sun"—she might not land on it, but at least she would get off the ground.

44. "Different Times Have Different 'Adans'": Helen Mitchnik, *Egyptian and Sudanese Folk-Tales* (Oxford, New York, and Toronto: Oxford University Press, 1978), pp. 21–22.

45. "The Story of the King and the Four Girls": Charles Swynnerton, *Indian Nights' Entertainments; or, Folk-Tales from the Upper Indus* (London: E. Stock, 1892), pp. 56–62.

46. "The Story of the Demon Who Ate People, and the Child": A. C. Hollis,

The Masai: Their Language and Folklore (Oxford: Clarendon Press, 1905), pp. 221–23.

47. "De White Man's Prayer": Hurston, *Every Tongue Got to Confess*, p. 251.

Narrated by James Presley, a musician and sawmill hand, about forty years old, born in Georgia.

48. For one of the most insightful descriptions of learning a new language and being without your own language, see Gerda Lerner, *Why History Matters: Life and Thought* (New York and Oxford: Oxford University Press, 1997), pp. 31–38.

49. See "De White Man's Prayer," p. 75.

50. See "The Snail," p. 62.

51. See "The Story of the Demon Who Ate People, and the Child," p. 72.

52. "The Ghost of Farnell": R. Macdonald Robertson, *Selected Highland Folk Tales & More Selected Highland Folk Tales* (United Kingdom: Pearson Education), p. 41.

53. "The Fox and Her Children and Nekhailo the Loafer": Irina Zheleznova, trans., *Ukrainian Folk Tales* (Kiev: Dnipro Publishers, 1986), pp. 39–40.

I almost didn't include a note about Ukraine in this volume. It seemed much less necessary than a note about unusual tribal cultures. However, to get permission to reprint these stories, I had to find a Ukrainian woman to call Kiev for me. Before and after the phone call, she lectured me about the current difficulties in Ukraine. I promised her I would write a bit about it. Life expectancy in Ukraine now is less than it was in 1980. Ukraine fertility rates are below replacement levels and more people leave the country than come in. Mortality rates are increasing due to epidemics of AIDS and tuberculosis. In 2001 Ukraine had the highest number of AIDS deaths in central and eastern Europe. There is high unemployment. My translator wished that when people were looking for charities, they would think of Ukraine as a place that could use help.

54. "The Lion Who Drowned in a Well": Zheleznova, trans., *Ukrainian Folk Tales*, pp. 67–70.

55. "The Tiger, the Brahman, and the Jackal": Flora Annie Steel, *Tales of the Punjab, Told by the People* (London: Macmillan, 1894), pp. 107–10.

When the British Empire had holdings all over the world, many British women took an interest in collecting folktales. Thanks to these women, we have collections from the turn of the last century from such faraway lands as New Zealand, Australia, China, and India.

56. Regarding the uses of the happy ending, see Bruno Bettelheim, *The Uses of Enchantment: The Meaning and Importance of Fairy Tales* (New York: Vintage Books, 1977), pp. 10–11, 32, and 143–44. The general impression we have is that tales end happily ever after, and in many tales the heroes and

heroines do get to live happily ever after, but some tales don't have happy endings. See Maria Tatar, *The Hard Facts of the Grimms' Fairy Tales* (Princeton, N.J.: Princeton University Press, 1987), pp. 179–80.

57. Kay Stone, *Burning Brightly: New Light on Old Tales Told Today* (Peterborough, Ontario, and Orchard Park, N.Y.: Broadview Press, 1985), p. 243.

58. See "The Fox and Her Children and Nekhailo the Loafer," p. 80.

59. See "The Tiger, the Brahman, and the Jackal," p. 86.

60. See " 'What Are You the Most Scared Of?,' " p. 6.

61. Regarding the variable characteristics of heroines and heroes in folktales, see Tatar, *The Hard Facts of the Grimms' Fairy Tales*, pp. 5 and 164.

62. See "The Ghost of Farnell," p. 78.

63. "The Bee and the Ásya," H. R. Voth, "Traditions of the Hopi," *Field Columbian Museum Publications: Anthropology*, vol. 8, March 1905, pp. 235–36.

The Hopitu-shinumu, the complete name of this Native American people, means "peaceful people." Hopi belongs to the Uto-Aztecan branch of the Amerind language family. The Hopi lived in pueblos in northeastern Arizona and defended themselves against the Spanish a number of times, but lived far enough away from the center of Spanish power to be largely ignored. The Hopi were able to grow corn even in their desert soil. However, when crops failed, the Hopi broke into smaller foraging groups able to live off naturally available food. Descent was traced through the women. Hopi women owned the homes and built them for the most part. Women owned the cornfields and preserved the sacred objects of the clans. The Hopi women made pottery and baskets. The Hopi men did the weaving and hunting and worked in the cornfields. The men dominated religion and politics.

64. "The Broken Friendship": Cecil Henry Bompas, *Folklore of the Santal Parganas* (London: David Nutt, 1909), pp. 142–44.

The Santal are a patrilineal, Munda, tribal people who live in the area where Bangladesh, West Bengal, and Bihar intersect. When these stories were collected, the Santal Parganas was a district lying about 150 miles north of Calcutta. The tales were originally written out in Santali, and Bompas asserts that his translation is very literal. He describes the Santals as great storytellers, with tales told when old folk gather the young folk around them in the evening or when the men watch the crops on the threshing floor and stay up all night.

65. "The Lady and the Unjust Judge": Allan Ramsay and Francis McCullagh, *Tales from Turkey* (London: Simpkin, Marshall, Hamilton, Kent, 1914); also in Milton Rugoff, *The Penguin Book of World Folk Tales* (Harmondsworth, England: Penguin, 1949), pp. 165–67.

Turkey is a melting pot of ethnically and culturally distinct groups

including the Turkic people, Kurds, and Arabs. The main religion is the
Sunnite sect of Islam; however, the government is a secular, democratic,
parliamentary system of government. Ancient Turkey—Anatolia—was
home to the Hittites, who produced iron and established a large empire
(1500–1190 B.C.). In the eleventh century A.D. there was a large incur-
sion of Turkic people from the east, and in the twelfth century one of
these Turkic people established the Ottoman dynasty. At its height, the
Ottoman Empire included most of the Balkans, much of Hungary, and
most of the Middle East and North Africa. After the reign of Sultan
Suleyman the Magnificent (1494–1566), the Ottoman Empire began to
decline. Turkey sided with Germany in World War I, and its present
boundaries were drawn in 1923. Its first president, Atatürk, secularized
Turkish society and replaced the Arabic alphabet with the Latin alphabet
for writing Turkish.

66. "Today Me, Tomorrow Thee": Jessie Alford Nunn, *African Folk Tales*, illus.
Ernest Crichlow (New York: Funk and Wagnalls, 1969), pp. 21–25.

The Kikuyu are agriculturalists who live in the highlands of Kenya.
The Kikuyu spearheaded Kenya's drive for independence, and Jomo
Kenyatta, a Kikuyu, was Kenya's first president (1964). Kikuyu is in the
Bantu language family. Bantu speakers are spread out over most of mid-
dle and southern Africa.

67. "Ole Sis Goose": Mody C. Boatright, Wilson M. Hudson, and Allen
Maxwell, eds., *The Best of Texas Folk and Folklore, 1916–1954*, Texas
Folklore Society no. 26. (Denton: University of North Texas Press,
1998), p. 50.

68. See "Today Me, Tomorrow Thee," p. 100.

69. See "Ole Sis Goose," p. 104.

70. See "The Broken Friendship," p. 94.

71. "The Tale of the Emir's Sword": John Charles Edward Bowen, *Plain Tales
of the Afghan Border* (London: Springwood Books, 1982), pp. 42–46.

Bowen recounts how on an official tour he met Mohammad Zarif
Khan, an Afridi who had entered the British Provincial Civil Service.
During the course of many visits, Bowen recorded many stories told to
him by Zarif, a born storyteller.

Afghanistan lies at a strategic crossroads and has been coveted by a
number of great empires. It became part of the Persian Empire of Cyrus
the Great in the sixth century B.C., was invaded by Alexander the Great
in the fourth century B.C. and by Ghengis Khan in 1219. Later
Afghanistan was split between the Indian Mughal Empire and the Persian
Safavid Empire. In the early 1700s Afghanistan was united as one country. The British tried to establish control over Afghanistan in a series of
wars in the 1800s and in 1919, and the Soviets invaded in 1979.

72. "The Revolution": Robert Laughlin, collector and trans., Carol Karasik, ed., *Mayan Tales from Zinacantán: Dreams and Stories from the People of the Bat* (Washington, D.C., and London: Smithsonian Institution Press, 1988), pp. 168–71.

Narrator Tonik Nibak was a woman sixty-two years old, but some of her narratives cast doubt on her reckoning of her age. She had graying hair, a bright smile, and a twinkle in her eye. Laughlin describes her as an independent woman, a "strong-hearted woman" with a sharp wit. Orphaned at age seven, she nonetheless learned to read and write, a special accomplishment considering her situation and the fact that not many people around her were literate.

Zinacantán is a small Mayan community of about 12,000 in Chiapas, the southernmost state in Mexico. At the end of the Classic Mayan period, Zinacantán became a thriving market and had a trade network extending from Guatemala north to the Aztec Empire. In 1524 Zinacantán surrendered to a handful of Spaniards. For three centuries the people of Zinacantán suffered under epidemics, famines, and extremely high taxes. The year 1712 marked the Tzeltal Rebellion, which was brutally crushed, and the memory of it kept the Indians subdued until the War of the Castes in 1869, which was also brutally crushed. Even in 1910, the Chiapas Indians' plight was one of the worst in all of Mexico. However, since 1950 conditions have been improving.

Zinacantán tales range from myth and legends to personal historical accounts and even gossip. There is a scarcity of public storytelling, but tales are valued because they tell of the people's past in a place where few can read or write.

73. "The Stone Coat Woman": Joseph Bruchac, *Heroes and Heroines, Monsters and Magic: Iroquois Stories* (Berkeley, Calif.: Crossing Press, 1985), pp. 135–44.

The Iroquois were a confederation of five nations, originally the Mohawk, Oneida, Onondaga, Cayuga, and Seneca, and in 1717 the Tuscarora joined as well. At the height of their power, they controlled most of New York, Pennsylvania, and Ohio. The name Iroquois means "real adders" and was coined by their enemies, the Algonquin. The Iroquois referred to themselves as "We Who Are of the Extended Lodge." Traditionally, the Iroquois lived in longhouses, which averaged fifty to one hundred feet in length. Each longhouse was headed by a clan mother. Women owned the family's property and arranged the marriages. Children inherited clan membership through their mothers. When a man married, he went to live with his wife's clan, but he never became a part of her clan. The Iroquois were a democratic society, and although men were chiefs, the women controlled the nomination process.

74. See "The Stone Coat Woman," p. 116.

75. See "The Tale of the Emir's Sword," p. 107.

76. See "The Revolution," p. 112.

77. This description is of a remarkable photograph taken by Emile Fréchon around 1900 in Marina Warner, *From the Beast to the Blonde: On Fairy Tales and Their Tellers* (New York: Noonday Press, Farrar, Straus and Giroux, 1996), p. 20.

78. See Jack Zipes, "Cross-Cultural Connections and the Contamination of the Classical Fairy Tale," in *The Great Fairy Tale Tradition* (New York and London: W. W. Norton, 2001). See also R. Sutherland Rattray, *Akan-Ashanti Folk-Tales* (Oxford: Clarendon Press, 1930), p. viii.

79. "The Devil's Little Joke": Dagobert C. Runes, *Lost Legends of Israel* (New York: Philosophical Library, 1961), pp. 71–72.

    Runes notes that the tales in his book come from his grandfather and many other people on three continents and that some are just daydreams.

80. According to Jewish legend, Lilith was created concurrently with Adam and was his equal, unlike Eve. Lilith refused to be subservient to Adam. Lilith then tricked Jehovah into revealing his secret name of power and demanded wings. She flew to the desert and consorted with elemental spirits and sand demons and had many demon children. She was sometimes accepted by God as his consort, supplanting the good wife, Matronit, and those were Israel's hardest times. Originally Lilith was credited with helping pregnant women and newborns, but then was blamed with causing stillbirths and became known as a stealer of babies. She has been classified as a vampire, child-eater, and man-killer.

81. "Solomon and the Vulture": Warren S. Walker and Ahmet Uysal, *Tales Alive in Turkey* (Cambridge, Mass.: Harvard University Press, 1966), pp. 181–83.

    Narrator Hasan Hazir. Recorded in Chamalan village of the caza of Tarsus of the province of Ichel in February 1962.

    Walker notes that the tales in this book are in the oral tradition of Turkey today, and are told in the Turkic language. Turkey is still dominated by its oral tradition, and many of these tales were collected in coffeehouses where men and boys gather, and are drawn from more than two hundred cities, towns, and villages. The translation is literal.

82. Azrail is the Angel of Death in Islamic mythology. He is comparable to the Grim Reaper in the Western tradition. Frequently he is pictured as an old man carrying a scythe.

83. "The Landlord and His Son": Dov Noy, *Folktales of Israel*, Gene Baharav, trans., Folktales of the World Series, ed. Richard Dorson (Chicago: University of Chicago Press, 1963), pp. 40–41.

    Recorded by M. Glass from his Lithuanian-born grandmother, 1913.

84. "Old Man and Old Woman": Ella E. Clark, *Indian Legends from the North*

Rockies (Norman, Okla.: University of Oklahoma Press, 1966), pp. 257–59.

Narrated by Chewing Blackbones, an old grandfather in 1953, who told it in the old language of the Blackfeet.

The Blackfeet, of Siksika, are western members of the Algonquian linguistic family and were one of the largest of the Algonquian tribes and the most powerful on the northwestern plains. They once held territory from the North Saskatchewan River, Canada, to the southern headstreams of the Missouri and Yellowstone Rivers, and from the Rocky Mountains to the state of Minnesota. The Blackfeet are a confederacy of three subtribes, the Siksika, the Blood, and the Piegan. Each of these had its independent organization. The Blackfeet were nomadic hunters. The men killed game for the fur trade, but women tanned the skin. Since more work went into processing the fur, the Blackfeet "big men" needed multiple wives to process the proceeds of the hunt. The Blackfeet were aggressive warriors and were hostile to whites. Measles, smallpox, alcohol, and the extermination of the buffalo ended their way of life.

85. "The Moon Goddess": Morag Loh, *People and Stories from Indo-China* (Melbourne: Indo-China Refugee Association of Victoria, 1982), pp. 120–22.

Narrated by Miss Lam, who was born and lived in Cholon, the Chinese section of Saigon, where everyone, including her, spoke Chinese and followed Chinese traditions and thought of themselves as Chinese. She learned Cantonese at home, Mandarin at primary school, and Vietnamese and English in secondary school. The Chinese school was very strict, and between classes the students were allowed to put their heads on their desks and rest a little. During one of these times, the teacher told the story of the Moon Goddess. Tradition has it that the Moon Goddess flew into the moon on the fifteenth of August, and for the Chinese it is a time when they stress the importance of having compassion for others, respecting others, and earning respect. Miss Lam's family immigrated to Australia, where this tale was recorded.

86. "Xueda and Yinlin": Shujiang Li and Karl W. Luckert, *Mythology and Folklore of the Hui, a Muslim Chinese People*, trans. Fenglan Yu, Zhilin Hou, and Ganhui Wang (Albany: State University of New York Press, 1994), pp. 143–47.

Collected in Miquan County, Xinjiang, narrated by Wang Juenquing (Hui), recorded by Liu Yan, Xiaoping, 1984.

The designation Hui denotes a grouping of diverse Chinese people who are adherents of Islam and speak Mandarin Chinese.

87. See "Solomon and the Vulture," p. 127.

88. See "The Landlord and His Son," p. 130.

89. See "The Moon Goddess," p. 134.

90. See Michelle Scalise Sugiyama, "Food, Foragers, and Folklore: The Role of Narrative in Human Subsistence," in *Evolution and Human Behavior* 22 (2001): 221–40. See also Leda Cosmides and John Tooby, "Consider the Source: The Evolution of Adaptations for Decoupling and Metarepresentation," at www.psych.ucsb.edu/research/cep/metarep.html.

91. "Im 'Awwād and the Ghouleh": Ibrahim Muhawi and Sharif Kanaana, *Speak, Bird, Speak Again: Palestinian Arab Folktales* (Berkeley: University of California Press, 1989), pp. 253–54.

    Ibrahim Muhawi was born in 1937 in Ramallah, Palestine. Sharif Kanaana was born in Galilee, Palestine, in 1935. The tales in their book represent the distinctive culture of the Arabs who live in Palestine. The tales were selected on the basis of their popularity and the excellence of their narration. They were collected between 1978 and 1980 in various parts of Palestine, the Galilee (now part of Israel), the West Bank, and Gaza. Of the seventeen tellers included in the book, only three were men, as telling folktales is considered by that society to be a woman's art form. Men prefer the epic stories or stories about raids and adventure which appear more realistic, although it is thought not that they actually happened, but that they could happen. Another difference between tales (told by women) and stories (told by men) is that the women use few gestures and movements and the performance aspect is minimized. The tellers rely on their voices and the power of the language to evoke a response. Therefore, the tales offer more opportunity for linguistic expression, while epic stories are told in the measured language of poetry which must be recited, sometimes even with the aid of a printed text.

92. "An Evil Being Appears at an Appointment Instead of the Right Person": Gunnar Landtman, *The Folk-Tales of the Kiwai Papuans, Acta Societatis Scientiarum Fennicae* 47 (Helsinki: Finnish Society of Literature, 1917), pp. 251–53.

    Landtman spent two years in New Guinea from April 1910 to April 1912, and it was during this time that the tales were told to him. All the narrators were men.

    In order to facilitate understanding, I have slightly normalized the grammar in this selection. I have clarified some tenses. Thus "been go finish" in the original has become "will be finished." In some cases I have made the pronouns agree with their subjects. Thus "You catch him plenty fish, throw him on shore" became "You catch plenty of fish, throw them on shore."

    In New Guinea approximately 20 percent of the world total of languages are spoken. New Guinea has a great concentration and diversity of languages. Imagine if Britain, which is one-third the size of New

Guinea, had two hundred languages separated by distances of only twenty miles. Along large portions of the coastline, Austronesian (formerly Malayo-Polynesian) languages are spoken. The Indo-Pacific (Papuan) languages are relegated mostly to the interior. More than seven hundred distinct Indo-Pacific languages are spoken in New Guinea. New Guinea has some tribes with cultures resembling those of the Stone Age, and because of its difficult terrain, isolated tribes have only recently been discovered.

93. "The Outwitted Ghost of the Forest": Koch-Grunberg, "Indianischermärchen aus Südamerika" (1920), in Felix Karlinger and Elisabeth Zacherl, *Südamerikanische Indianermärchen* (Munich: Eugen Diederichs Verlag, 1976), pp. 98–99. Translated by Kathleen Ragan.

The Arawak live in the northern and western areas of the Amazon Basin. They are sedentary farmers who also hunt and fish. They have a dispersed settlement pattern and little hierarchical organization.

94. See Michelle Scalise Sugiyama, "Narrative Theory and Function: Why Evolution Matters," in *Philosophy and Literature* 25:2 (2001): 233–50.

95. See Leda Cosmides and John Tooby, "Evolutionary Psychology: A Primer," at www.psych.ucsb.edu/research/cep/primer.html.

96. See Bruno Bettelheim, *The Uses of Enchantment: The Meaning and Importance of Fairy Tales* (New York: Vintage Books, 1975). See also Alan Dundes, ed., *Little Red Riding Hood: A Casebook* (Madison: University of Wisconsin Press, 1989), and Maria Tatar, *Off with Their Heads!: Fairy Tales and the Culture of Childhood* (Princeton, N.J.: Princeton University Press, 1992), pp. 120–39.

97. See Sugiyama, "Narrative Theory and Function."

98. "Still Another Spook": Robert Laughlin, collector and trans., Carol Karasik, ed., *Mayan Tales from Zinacantán: Dreams and Stories from the People of the Bat* (Washington, D.C., and London: Smithsonian Institution Press, 1988), pp. 195–97.

Narrator Tonik Nibak. See p. 240, note 72, for further details about the narrator and Zinacantán.

For the interpretation of the Spook as being the legendary Mayan bat demon, see Sarah Blaffer, *The Black-man of Zinacantán: A Central American Legend* (Austin and London: University of Texas Press, 1972). Laughlin also writes that the Spook may represent African slaves and escaped slaves.

99. "The Oyster and the Shark": Ursula McConnel, *Myths of the Muŋkan* (Australia: Melbourne University Press, 1957), pp. 34–35.

The last words of Min Wára the oyster as he goes down into his *auwa* strike the note of self-dedication which underlies all these stories and religious cults. The oyster has a hard shell and is white because Min Wára was hit with ashes by the shark. His shell is flat because the shark hit Min Wára in the face with his spear-thrower, and the shell opens wide from the heat of the ashes, as Min Wára's mouth did when the shark threw hot ashes in his face. The shark's eyes are small, and he can't see far because of the sand thrown in his eyes by the oyster; and the boomerang still sticks up out of his back: it is the shark's fin one sees above water as he hunts up and down for food.

The place of this story is some miles south of the mouth of the Archer River. The narrator was Stephen, to whose people, the Wika-tinda, this ground belonged. The Muŋkan live on the western side of Cape York Peninsula on the Gulf of Carpentaria.

Ursula McConnel (1888–1957) was one of Australia's first women anthropologists and one of the founders of modern anthropology in Australia. She defied the norms of the day and insisted on studying Aboriginal women, their symbolism, ceremonial ornaments, and body decorations, as well as Aboriginal men. Rejected by mainstream Australian anthropology, McConnel's contribution is only now coming to be recognized.

100. "Mr. Fox": Joseph Jacobs, *English Fairy Tales* (New York: G. P. Putnam's Sons; London: D. Nutt, 1891), pp. 146–51.

101. "Mereaira and Kape Tautini": Bradford Haami, *Traditional Māori Love Stories*, illus. Jamie Boynton (New Zealand: HarperCollins Publishers New Zealand, 1997), pp. 32–37.

The Māori people were Polynesians who settled in New Zealand around 800 A.D. They believed in a spiritual "essence" and their deities were rarely represented by images. They were remarkable craftsmen of elaborately carved dugout canoes, which when paddled at full speed could overtake European sailing ships. The Māori were well-known warriors.

102. See the poem "Conscientious Objector" by Edna St. Vincent Millay: "I shall die, but that is all that I shall do for Death;/I am not on his pay-roll . . ."

103. See Kathleen Ragan, *Fearless Girls, Wise Women, and Beloved Sisters: Heroines in Folktales from Around the World* (New York and London: W. W. Norton, 1998).

104. Hermann Kinder and Werner Hilgemann, Ernest A. Menze, trans., *The Anchor Atlas World History*, vol 2 (Garden City, N.Y.: Anchor Press, Doubleday, 1978), p. 218.

105. Ibid., p. 126.

106. www.vietnamwar.com includes the number of U.S. soldiers, Australian soldiers, Vietnamese, Laotians, and Cambodians killed in the conflict.

107. Bonnie S. Anderson and Judith P. Zinsser, *A History of Their Own: Women in*

Europe from Prehistory to the Present, vol. 1 (New York: Harper and Row, 1988), p. 167. This is a brilliant history of Europe with a focus on women.

108. James W. Loewen, *Lies My Teacher Told Me: Everything Your American History Textbook Got Wrong* (New York: New Press, 1995), pp. 54–55.

109. "The Poles of the House": Fay-Cooper Cole, *Traditions of the Tinguian: A Study in Philippine Folk-Lore* (Chicago: Field Museum of Natural History, Publication 180, Anthropological Series, vol. 14, no. 1, 1915), p. 176.

    Cole collected these tales in 1907–8 during a stay of sixteen months with the Tinguian, a tribe of northwestern Luzon in the Philippines. The Philippine archipelago of over seven thousand islands has been a cross-roads of folk migration for centuries. It has been dominated or occupied by Malayans, Hindus, Chinese, Japanese, Spaniards, and Americans. In the fifteenth century, Islam spread to the southern Philippines from the Malaccan empire of Malaya, Sumatra, and Java. Islam's spread was halted in the sixteenth century by Spain, which methodically conquered and converted many of the island people to Christianity.

110. "The Dead Moon": Mrs. Balfour, "Legends of the Cars," *Folk-Lore* 11 (1891).

111. "Legend of Sway-Uock": Emerson N. Matson, *Legends of the Great Chiefs* (Nashville and New York: Thomas Nelson, 1972), pp. 86–90.

    This story is from the family of Chief William Shelton, the last hereditary chief of the Snohomish People, who lived in Washington State north of Seattle. Only remnants of the original tribes still exist.

    For years there was no traceable connection between many Amerindian languages. However, in 1987, Joseph Greenberg presented a new classification system with a broad-based overview of all the languages of the world. In this classification system, all the American Indian languages are grouped into three large groups. In the Greenberg classification system, the Eskimo-Aleut group has only about ten languages and ranges along the northern perimeter of North America from Alaska to Canada to Greenland. The Na-Dene has speakers living in central Alaska and the panhandle as well as the western part of Canada. The final and largest group is the Amerind, which stretches from northern Canada to the tip of South America and includes everything from Salish and Sahaptin to Iroquoian to Aztecan. See Merrit Ruhlen, *The Origin of Language* (New York: John Wiley & Sons, 1994).

112. "How the Young Maidens Saved Guam Island": Eve Grey, *Legends of Micronesia*, Micronesian Reader Series (High Commissioner Trust Territories of the Pacific Islands: Department of Education, 1951), pp. 124–27.

    Close to 40 percent of the world's languages are spoken on islands in the Pacific and Indian Oceans. Almost all of these languages belong to one of three families: Indo-Pacific (concentrated in New Guinea), the Australian family, and the Austronesian family. Austronesian (formerly Malayo-Polynesian) is the most widespread—its languages are spoken on practically every island from Madagascar to Easter Island and from Hawaii to New Zealand.

113. This story is composed from quotes taken from: Mary Harris Jones, *The Autobiography of Mother Jones* (Chicago: Charles H. Kerr Publishing, 1996), pp. 145–47, and *Final Report and Testimony to Congress by the Commission on Industrial Relations*, vol. 11, 64th Congress, 1st Session, U.S. Senate, Document No. 415 (Washington, D.C.: Government Printing Office, 1916), p. 10627.

114. See "How the Maidens Saved Guam Island," p. 176, and " Legend of Sway-Uock," p. 172.

115. The Declaration of Independence.

116. "The Meatballs' Leader": Amina Shah, *Tales of Afghanistan* (London: Octagon Press, 1982), pp. 114–15.

117. "The Maiden Who Lived with the Wolves": Emerson N. Matson, *Legends of the Great Chiefs* (Nashville and New York: Thomas Nelson, 1972), pp. 51–52.

   Told by Frank White Buffalo Man, one of Sitting Bull's grandsons.

   The Sioux Nation is made up of the Lakota, the Dakota, and the Nakota. The Lakota are the hard-riding, buffalo-hunting Plains Indians who had the famous chiefs Red Cloud, Sitting Bull, and Crazy Horse. However, a better way to understand their culture might be by describing them as nomadic pastoralists, traveling with their herds. Although history now records their great chiefs, for the most part the native people of North America originally had social systems which induced people to redistribute wealth, thus reaping status. Authority relied upon generosity. The Sioux worship Wakan Tanka and go on vision quests involving a four-day fast. They defeated Custer at the battle of the Little Bighorn and lost their last battle at Wounded Knee in 1890.

   Emerson Matson has published another book, *Long House Legends*, and his son William Matson is continuing the family tradition, having made a CD of the Crazy Horse family.

118. "The Tale of Nung-kua-ma": Wolfram Eberhard, *Folktales of China*, trans. Desmond Parsons, Folktales of the World Series, ed. Richard Dorson (Chicago: University of Chicago Press, 1965), pp. 143–46.

119. Goldman, William, *Four Screenplays with Essays* (New York: Applause Books, 1997), pp. 302–4.

120. See " 'What Are You the Most Scared Of?,' " p. 6.

121. See "The Snail," p. 62.

122. See "The Moon Goddess," p. 134.

123. See "The Tale of Nung-kua-ma," p. 184.

124. "Baling with a Sieve": Adele M. Fielde, *Chinese Nights' Entertainment* (New York, London: G. P. Putnam's Sons, 1893), pp. 87–91.

Fielde (1839–1916) worked as a missionary for fifteen years in Shantou in southwest China. In 1883 she returned to the United States and studied evolution at the Academy of Natural Sciences in Philadelphia. She researched the Chinese language and literature and women in China. In 1885 she returned to China for seven years, then went back to the United States where she taught.

The collector, Fielde, notes that this tale was told in Swatow vernacular, a Chinese dialect, in the eastern corner of Kwangtung province in southern China. Chinese is spoken by more people than any other language in the world. It is spoken not only in China but also by over a million in each of the following countries—Taiwan, Hong Kong, Thailand, Malaysia, Singapore, and Vietnam—and in lesser numbers in other countries. It is, however, spoken by few people not of Chinese origin. Chinese is a tonal language. Different tones or intonations distinguish words which are otherwise pronounced identically. Chinese is written with ideographs that represent objects as well as abstract concepts without relation to the sound of the word. This makes written communication possible between people speaking the many different languages and dialects in China. Words in different languages would be pronounced differently but written the same. One must learn about five thousand characters to read a newspaper or novel.

125. "The Old Woman and the Lame Devil": Thomas C. Blackburn, *December's Child: A Book of Chumash Oral Narratives* (Berkeley, Los Angeles, and London: University of California Press, 1975), pp. 255–57.

Narrated by Maria Solares.

The Chumash were a foraging people who lived in the neighborhood of today's Santa Barbara, California. A Chumash shaman got his power from a guardian spirit that might appear during a dream or a trance. The Spanish gathered the Native Americans into missions, sometimes by kidnapping them. Once the Indians were at the missions and baptized, they were not allowed to leave. As a result of the concentration of people, the Chumash population was reduced from tens of thousands to a few hundred by disease.

126. "The Woman with Red Leggings": Douglas R. Parks, *Traditional Narratives of the Arikara Indians*, vol. 4 (Lincoln, Neb., and London: University of Nebraska Press, 1991), pp. 630–31.

Narrated by Ella P. Waters, who was born on the Fort Berthold Reservation in 1889 and died in 1984. She was an Arikara doctor. She had a lifelong interest in learning and preserving the Arikara traditions and language.

The woman's spirit saved this Arikara community when the people were living in Heart Village, a winter camp said by the narrator to have been located "in a nice opening among the trees" midway between Like-a-Fishhook Village and Elbowoods. The narrator commented that the woman apparently was not Arikara since the Arikara buried their dead rather than scaffolding them, as the neighboring Mandan, Hidatsa, and Sioux did.

The Arikara People have lived in what is now the Dakotas for over two centuries and are of the Caddoan language family and linguistically close to the Pawnee. The women planted gardens of corn, squash, beans, and sunflowers, thus enabling a more sedentary lifestyle. The corn plant was so important it was personified and deified as Mother Corn, who bestowed culture and protected the people. In fact, in the plains sign language, the Arikara were designated as "corn shellers." The Arikara also hunted buffalo. Village chief was a hereditary position passed through the male line. The leading priest also tended to be a hereditary position. Other men could become chiefs and leaders in political and social affairs through achievements in war, but these positions were not hereditary. Doctors could be men or women and most of the medicine societies had one female member. Band membership passed through the female line.

127. "The Old Lady of Littledean": William Henderson, *Folk-Lore of the Northern Counties* (London: Folk-Lore Society, 1879).

128. "The Milk and Butter Stones": Rewritten into standard English by Kathleen Ragan, based on the story of the same title recorded from Jamie Laurenson by Dr. Alan Bruford and included in Alan Bruford, ed., *The Green Man of Knowledge and Other Scots Traditional Tales* (Aberdeen: Aberdeen University Press, 1982), pp. 87–90.

Narrated by Jamesie Laurenson, who was born in Fetlar, the Shetland Islands, in 1899 and lived there all his life except for naval service in World War I. He was a crofter, parish registrar, and local antiquary who contributed in writing to Shetland papers and magazines and to the collections of the National Museum of Antiquities in Edinburgh, as well as recording his very lively and characteristic storytelling and some old ballads for the School of Scottish Studies. He heard this story from his grandmother. The story was recorded by Alan Bruford, SA 1970/246 A2-B1. First published in *Tocher* 19 (1975).

When a folklorist or anthropologist collects tales, the collector makes many decisions. One of those decisions is whether to write a literal transcription of the story as it was told, or to normalize the language and how much to normalize the language. At the turn of the last century, simply writing down the tales as the storyteller spoke them was often considered unliterary and often the collector rewrote the tales in a more complicated, literary fashion. Yeats was an exception to this pattern, and his collection, *Fairy and Folk Tales of the Irish Peasantry*, is a remarkable rendition not only of the tales but also of the speech patterns and accents. See "How Thomas Connolly Met the Banshee," p. 25. Recently, collectors have focused on taking down the tales exactly as the storytellers tell them.

Dr. Alan Bruford gave respect to the speech of his sources. Dr. Bruford took down the stories with great attention to spelling the words as they were pronounced, thus preserving the accents of the storytellers as well as their stories. For example, in his story "The Milk and Butter Stones," "one" was spelled "wän," "stone" was spelled "ston," "us" was spelled "wis," and "she" was sometimes spelled "shö." Dr. Margaret Mackay, who gave me permission to reprint this story, did so on the condition that Dr. Bruford's transcription of the story, accent-specific spelling and all, be included as is or the whole story be normalized. I chose to normalize the spelling out of deference to my readers who are unused to Dr. Bruford's kind of transcription. However, it was a hard choice because the sound and even the lilt of the original were affected by the normalization. For those interested in the original transcription, I suggest you look up the original book. You might also want to check out *Scottish Traditional Tales*, also edited by Dr. Bruford and Donald Archie MacDonald. There is a Greentrax Scottish Tradition double CD to go with that book. The following story in this volume, "The Inexhaustible Meal-Chest," presents another interesting choice along these same lines. Each story in *Fairy Legends of Donegal* was printed in Gaelic on one page with a normalized English translation on the opposite page. I have included only the English translation in this anthology.

Collections of folktales serve many purposes. They preserve the tales and the ideas and cultures of the people who tell them, thus the literal transcription can be very important. However, folktales are also one of the most effective means of leaping cultural barriers and getting glimpses into cultures not our own. In this case, an editor might have to choose to lose some aspects of the original culture in order to make the story comprehensible and enjoyable to someone in another culture.

129. "The Inexhaustible Meal-Chest": Máire MacNeill, trans., Seán Ó hEochaidh, collector, *Fairy Legends from Donegal* (Dublin: University College, 1977), pp. 336–43. Seán Ó hEochaidh, Máire Ní Néill, and Séamas Ó Catháin, *Síscéalta Ó Thír Chonaill/Fairy Legends from Donegal*, Baile Átha Cliath/Dublin: Comhairle Bhéaloideas Éireann, 1977, pp. 336–43.

An interesting article written about this story is Patricia Lysaght, "Charity Rewarded: A Biblical Theme in Irish Tradition, with Glimpses of Medieval Europe," in Ingo Schneider, ed., *Europäische Ethnologie und Folklore im internationalen Kontext* (Frankfurt am Main: Peter Lang, 1999), pp. 617–45.

130. Eleanor Roosevelt from her speech "The Great Question," given to the United Nations in 1958.

131. George Eliot, *Middlemarch*.

132. "The Long Haired Girl": John Minford, trans., *Favorite Folktales of China* (Beijing: New World Press, 1983), pp. 143–60.

133. "The Good Lie": Arthur Scholey, *The Discontented Dervishes and Other Persian Tales* (London: Andre Deutsch, 1977), pp. 35–36.

134. "Ayak and Her Lost Bridegroom": Francis Mading Deng, *Dinka Folktales: African Stories from the Sudan*, illus. Martha Reisman (New York and London: Africana Publishing, Holmes & Meier Publishers, 1974), pp. 107–10.

The tales in this book were recorded among the Dinka of the Sudan, a Nilotic people who are cattle herders and subsistence cultivators. Dinka settlements and tribes are quite scattered and isolated from one another. Dinka refers to some twenty-five mutually independent groups which have physical appearance in common and cultural uniformity. They are among those in the Sudan less transformed by modernization.

For the Dinka, stories should not be told during the day, but at bedtime, as a prelude to sleep, for both children and adults. Most storytelling groups are made up of women and children, although men may also tell stories in their sleeping-place with older boys. The storyteller often interrupts the story by asking "Are you asleep?" and the storytelling session will continue only as long as there are still people awake. The last storyteller is likely to be the last person awake, so the final story will be left incomplete.

One of the main characteristics of Dinka folktales is their concern with family relationships. In Dinka society, families form lineages and clans, which on the political level form the sections, subtribes, and tribes. The insider/outsider distinction is strong. In the folktales, outsiders are often represented by animals, often a lion.

135. "Bluejay Brings the Chinook Wind": Ella E. Clark, *Indian Legends from the Northern Rockies* (Norman, Okla.: University of Oklahoma Press, 1966), pp. 112–14.

Told by a member of the Flathead-Kalispel tribe.

The Chinook wind is a warm wind of the Northwest. In January or February or March, it may melt overnight the ice-locked rivers and strip the lower lands and slopes of their snow.

The Salishan linguistic family was in the Pacific Northwest.

136. "The Lions of Vancouver": Marion E. Gridley, *Indian Legends of American*

Scenes (Chicago and New York: M. A. Donahue, 1939), pp. 122–23.

137. Ernst Bloch, "Better Castles in the Sky at the Country Fair and Circus, in Fairy Tales and Colportage," in *The Utopian Function of Art and Literature: Selected Essays*, trans. Jack Zipes and Frank Mecklenburg (Cambridge, Mass., and London: MIT Press, 1996), p. 170.

FOR FURTHER READING

Barkow, Jerome H., Leda Cosmides, and John Tooby, eds. *The Adapted Mind: Evolutionary Psychology and the Generation of Culture*. New York and Oxford: Oxford University Press, 1992.

Bettelheim, Bruno. *The Uses of Enchantment: The Meaning and Importance of Fairy Tales*. New York: Random House, Vintage Books, 1977.

Bottigheimer, Ruth, ed. *Fairy Tales and Society: Illusion, Allusion, and Paradigm*. Philadelphia: University of Pennsylvania Press, 1986.

―――. *Grimms' Bad Girls and Bold Boys: The Moral and Social Vision of the Tales*. New Haven and London: Yale University Press, 1987.

Cosmides, Leda, and John Tooby. "Consider the Source: The Evolution of Adaptations for Decoupling and Metarepresentation," at www.psych.ucsb.edu/research/cep/metarep.html.

―――. "Evolutionary Psychology: A Primer," at www.psych.ucsb.edu/research/cep/primer.html.

Larrington, Carolyne. *The Woman's Companion to Mythology*. London: Pandora, HarperCollins Publishers, 1992.

Lieberman, Marcia R. " 'Some Day My Prince Will Come': Female Acculturation Through the Fairy Tale." In *College English*, 34: 3 (1972): 383–95.

Stephens, John, and Robyn McCallum. *Retelling Stories: Framing Culture Traditional Story and Metanarratives in Children's Literature*. New York and London: Garland Publishing, 1998.

Stone, Kay. *Burning Brightly: New Light on Old Tales Told Today*. (Peterborough, Ontario, and Orchard Park, N.Y.: Broadview Press, 1998.

―――. "Fairy Tales for Adults: Walt Disney's Americanization of the *Märchen*." In *Folklore on Two Continents*, ed. Nikolai Burlakoff and Carl Lindhal. Bloomington: University of Indiana Press, 1980.

―――. "The Misuses of Enchantment: Controversies on the Significance of Fairy Tales." In *Women's Folklore, Women's Culture*, ed. Rosan A. Jordan and Susan J. Kalčik. Philadelphia: University of Pennsylvania Press, 1985.

———. "Things Walt Disney Never Told Us." In *Women and Folklore*, ed. Claire R. Farrer. Austin: University of Texas Press, 1975.

Sugiyama, Michelle Scalise. "Food, Foragers, and Folklore: The Role of Narrative in Human Subsistence." *Evolution and Human Behavior* 22 (2001): 221–40.

———. "Narrative Theory and Function: Why Evolution Matters." *Philosophy and Literature* 25:2 (2001): 233–50.

Tatar, Maria. *The Hard Facts of the Grimms' Fairy Tales*. Princeton, N.J.: Princeton University Press, 1987.

———. *Off with Their Heads!* Princeton, N.J.: Princeton University Press, 1992.

Weigle, Marta. *Spiders and Spinsters: Women and Mythology*. Albuquerque: University of New Mexico Press, 1982.

Zipes, Jack. *Breaking the Magic Spell: Radical Theories of Folk and Fairy Tales*. New York: Routledge, 1979.

———. *Fairy Tale as Myth, Myth as Fairy Tale*. Lexington: University Press of Kentucky, 1994.

———. *Fairy Tales and the Art of Subversion*. New York: Routledge, Chapman and Hall, 1991.

———. *Happily Ever After: Fairy Tales, Children, and the Culture Industry*. New York and London: Routledge, 1997.

———, ed. *The Oxford Companion to Fairy Tales: The Western Fairy Tale Tradition from Medieval to Modern*. Oxford: Oxford University Press, 2000.

INDEX